CHINA

Bay
of
Bengal

THAILAND

Bangkok

Pattaya

VIETNAM

South
China
Sea

PHILIPPINES

BRUNEI

Zamboanga

MALAYSIA

Kuantan

Singapore

INDONESIA

OCEAN

IA

# The Heart and the Fist

BOOKS BY ERIC GREITENS

*Strength and Compassion: Photographs and Essays*
*The Heart and the Fist*

# The
# HEART
## and the FIST

The Education of a Humanitarian,
the Making of a Navy SEAL

*Eric Greitens*

HOUGHTON MIFFLIN HARCOURT
BOSTON · NEW YORK

For information about permission to reproduce selections from this book,
write to Permissions, Houghton Mifflin Harcourt Publishing Company,
215 Park Avenue South, New York, New York 10003.

www.hmhbooks.com

Library of Congress Cataloging-in-Publication Data
Greitens, Eric, date.
The heart and the fist : the education of a humanitarian, the making of a
Navy SEAL / Eric Greitens.
p.   cm.
ISBN 978-0-547-42485-9
1. Greitens, Eric, date.  2. United States. Navy. SEALs—Biography.  3. United States.
Navy—Officers—Biography.  4. United States. Navy—Officers—Training of.  5. Humanitarian
assistance, American.  6. United States—Armed Forces—Civic action. I. Title.
V63.G74A3 2011
359.9'84—dc22  [B]  2010026071

Book design by Robert Overholtzer, Boskydell Studio

Maps by Jacques Chazaud

Printed in the United States of America

DOC 10  9  8  7  6  5

TO THE MEMORY OF MY GRANDFATHERS

*August Greitens, Chief Petty Officer, United States Navy*
*Harold Jacobs, Corporal, United States Army*

# Contents

# Preface

This is a book about service on the frontlines. I've been blessed to work with volunteers who taught art to street children in Bolivia and Marines who hunted al Qaeda terrorists in Iraq. I've learned from nuns who fed the destitute in Mother Teresa's homes for the dying in India, aid workers who healed orphaned children in Rwanda, and Navy SEALs who fought in Afghanistan. As warriors, as humanitarians, they've taught me that without courage, compassion falters, and that without compassion, courage has no direction. They've shown me that it is within our power, and that the world requires of us—of every one of us—that we be both good *and* strong. I hope that the stories recounted here will inspire you, as these people have inspired me. They have given me hope, and shown me the incredible possibilities that exist for each of us to live our one life well. For each of us, there is a place on the frontlines.

**The Mission Continues**    A portion of the author's proceeds from the sale of this book will go toward supporting The Mission Continues. The Mission Continues empowers wounded veterans to serve again here at home and brings communities together to honor the fallen through service.

# Part I ★ ★ ★

# MIND AND FIST

# 1 ☆

# Iraq

THE FIRST MORTAR round landed as the sun was rising. Joel and I both had bottom bunks along the western wall of the barracks. As we swung our feet onto the floor, Joel said, "They better know, they wake my ass up like this, it's gonna put me in a pretty uncharitable mood." Mortars were common, and one explosion in the morning amounted to little more than an unpleasant alarm.

As we began to tug on our boots, another round exploded outside, but the dull whomp of its impact meant that it had landed dozens of yards away. The insurgent mortars were usually wild, inaccurate, one-time shots. Then another round landed—closer. The final round shook the walls of the barracks and the sounds of gunfire began to rip.

I have no memory of when the suicide truck bomb detonated. Lights went out. Dust and smoke filled the air. I found myself lying belly-down on the floor, legs crossed, hands over my ears with my mouth wide open. My SEAL instructors had taught me to take this position during incoming artillery fire. They learned it from men who passed down the knowledge from the Underwater Demolition Teams that had cleared the beaches at Normandy.

*SEAL training* . . . One sharp blast of the whistle and we'd drop to the mud with our hands over our ears, our feet crossed. Two whistles and we'd begin to crawl. Three whistles and we'd push to our feet and run. Whistle, drop, whistle, crawl, whistle, up and run; whistle, drop, whistle, crawl, whistle, up and run. By the end of training, the instructors were throwing smoke and flashbang grenades. Crawling through the mud, enveloped in an acrid haze — red smoke, purple smoke, orange smoke — we could just make out the boots and legs of the man in front of us, barbed wire inches above our heads . . .

In the barracks, I heard men coughing around me, the air thick with dust. Then the burning started. It felt as if someone had shoved an open-flame lighter inside my mouth, the flames scorching my throat, my lungs. My eyes burned and I squinted them shut, then fought to keep them open. The insurgents had packed chlorine into the truck bomb: a chemical attack. From a foot or two away I heard Staff Sergeant Big Sexy Francis, who often manned a .50-cal gun in our Humvees, yell, "You all right?"

Mike Marise answered him: "Yeah, I'm good!" Marise had been an F-18 fighter pilot in the Marine Corps who walked away from a comfortable cockpit to pick up a rifle and fight on the ground in Fallujah.

"Joel, you there?" I shouted. My throat was on fire, and though I knew that Joel was only two feet away, my burning eyes and blurred vision made it impossible to see him in the dust-filled room.

He coughed. "Yeah, I'm fine," he said.

Then I heard Lieutenant Colonel Fisher shouting from the hallway. "You can make it out this way! Out this way!"

I grabbed Francis's arm and pulled him to standing. We stumbled over gear and debris as shots were fired. My body low, my eyes burning, I felt my way over a fallen locker as we all tried to step toward safety. I later learned that Mike Marise had initially turned the wrong way and gone through one of the holes in the wall created by the bomb. He then stumbled into daylight and could have easily been shot. I stepped out of the east side of the building as gunfire ripped through the air and fell behind an earthen barrier, Lieutenant Colonel Fisher beside me.

On my hands and knees, I began hacking up chlorine gas and spraying spittle. My stomach spasmed in an effort to vomit, but nothing came. Fisher later said he saw puffs of smoke coming from my mouth and nostrils. A thin Iraqi in tan pants and a black shirt, his eyes blood red, was bent over in front of me, throwing up. Cords of yellow vomit dangled from his mouth.

I looked down and saw a dark red stain on my shirt and more blood on my pants. I shoved my right hand down my shirt and pressed at my chest, my stomach. I felt no pain, but I had been trained to know that a surge of adrenaline can sometimes mask the pain of an injury.

I patted myself again. Chest, armpits, crotch, thighs. No injuries. I put my fingers to the back of my neck, felt the back of my head, and then pulled my fingers away. They were sticky with sweat and blood, but I couldn't find an injury.

*It's not my blood.*

My breathing was shallow; every time I tried to inhale, my throat gagged and my lungs burned. But we had to join the fight. Mike Marise and I ran back into the building. One of our Iraqi comrades was standing in the bombed-out stairwell, firing his AK-47 as the sound of bullets ricocheted around the building.

Fisher and another Marine found Joel sitting on the floor in the chlorine cloud, trying to get his boots on. Shrapnel from the truck bomb had hit Joel in the head. He had said, "I'm fine," and he had stayed conscious, but instead of standing up and moving, his brain had been telling him *boots . . . boots . . . boots* as he bled out the back of his head.

Fisher, Big Sexy, and I charged up the twisted bombed-out staircase to find higher ground. The truck bomb had blown off the entire western wall of the barracks, and as we raced up the staircase over massive chunks of concrete and debris, we were exposed to gunfire from the west. Iraqi soldiers from the barracks—this was their army, their barracks, and we were their visiting allies at this stage of the war—were letting bullets fly, but as I ran up the stairs, I couldn't see any targets. At the top of the stairs, I paused to wait for a break in the gunfire, sucked in a pained, shallow breath, then ran onto the rooftop. A lone Iraqi soldier who had been on guard duty was already there, armed with an M60 and ripping bullets to the west. I ran to cover the north-west, and Francis ran out behind me to cover the southwest. As I ran, a burst of gunfire rang out, and I dove onto the rough brown concrete and crawled through a mess of empty plastic drink bottles, musty milk cartons, cigarette butts, dip cans, and spit bottles—trash left behind by Iraqi soldiers on guard duty.

As I reached the northern edge of the roof, I peered over the eight-een-inch ledge to check for targets and caught sight of a tall minaret on a mosque to the northeast. It was not uncommon for snipers to take positions inside minarets and shoot at Americans. It would have been a far shot for even the best sniper, but as I scanned the streets, I kept my head moving, just in case.

Women and children were scattered and running below us, but no one had a weapon. Far off to the north, I saw armed men running. I steadied my rifle and aimed. I took a slow breath, focused my sights, laid the pad of my finger on the trigger . . . *no*. Those were Iraqi police from our base.

I called to Francis, "You see anything? You have any targets?"

"Nothing."

*Nothing.* The sun rose. We felt the heat of the day begin to sink into the roof. We waited. We watched. My breathing was still shallow, and I felt as if someone had tightened a belt around my lungs and was pull-ing hard to kill me. I glanced over the ledge of the roof again. *Nothing.* I assessed. We had plenty of bullets, and my med kit was intact. We had the high ground, good cover, and a clear view of every avenue of ap-proach. We'd need some water eventually, but we could stay here for hours if necessary. Sitting there in a nasty pile of trash on the rooftop of a bombed-out Iraqi building in Fallujah, I thought to myself: *Man, I'm lucky.*

Travis Manion and two other Marines then ran up onto the roof. Travis was a recent graduate of the Naval Academy, where he'd been an outstanding wrestler. I came to know him while we patrolled the streets of Fallujah together. Travis was tough, yet he walked with a smile on his face. He was respected by his men and respected by the Iraqis. A pirated copy of a movie about the last stand of three hundred Spartan warriors had made its way to Fallujah, and Travis was drawn to the ideal of the Spartan citizen-warrior who sacrificed everything in defense of his community. He likened his mission to that of the warriors who left their families to defend their home.

I glanced at the minaret again. The sky was blue and clear. A beautiful day. The radio crackled with traffic informing us that a Quick Reaction Force of tanks was on its way. After the explosion and the gunfire and the rush of adrenaline, the day was quiet and getting hot. Tanks arrived, and a few Humvees rolled in for a casualty evacuation of the injured. Because we'd been in the blast, Francis and I were ordered to leave with the casevac for the hospital. I called over to Travis: "You got it?"

"Yeah, I got your back, sir."

All the armored Humvees were full, and so a young Marine and I climbed into the back of a Humvee made for moving gear. The Humvee had an open bed. For armor, two big green steel plates had been welded to its sides. Lying flat on the bed of the Humvee, we had about as much cover as two kids in the back of a pickup truck during a water-gun fight. As we drove for the base, we'd be exposed to fire from windows and rooftops. We readied our rifles, prepared to shoot from our backs as the Humvee raced through Fallujah, bumping and bouncing over the uneven dirt roads.

When we'd made it out of the city, I asked the young Marine beside me if he was OK. "You know what, sir?" he said. "I think I'm ready to head home after this one." Somehow that seemed hilarious to us and we both laughed our heads off, exhausted, relieved.

At Fallujah Surgical, I was treated among a motley crew of Americans and Iraqis, many half-dressed, bedraggled, bloody. I asked about Joel and was told that his head injury had been severe enough that they'd flown him straight to Baghdad.

When I got back to the barracks, I pulled off my boots, peeled off my clothes, and threw my armor in a corner. Everything reeked of chlorine. I stepped into a shower. As the water ran over me, I rubbed my scalp. Down fell tiny bits of concrete from the explosion. I watched as the pieces fell to the shower floor and washed down the drain. *That was close.*

For the next few weeks I spent every night hacking and coughing in bed. When I woke in the morning and tried to run, my lungs hurt. I felt like they had been zipped half-shut. Still, I ran every day, and eventually I could take a deep, full breath. I lost a bit of my hearing for a few weeks, but it could have been far worse. Not everyone I served with that day would be so lucky.

One month later, Lieutenant Travis Manion would be dead.

When Joel Poudrier arrived at my apartment in D.C., it was the first time I had seen him since the truck bomb. On that day, he was kneeling on one knee outside the barracks as a corpsman tended to his bleeding head wound. Joel was an intel officer. He had worked closely with the Iraqi troops in Fallujah, and he knew the names, stories, and falafel preferences of the Iraqis as well as he knew his own men. Jovial and levelheaded, he smoked a good-luck cigarette before every patrol. His wife sent him gourmet coffee, and in Fallujah he had packed his office with boxes of candy bars and tubs of cashews on offer to anyone who walked in to see him.

We talked about his son's baseball, his golf game. He told me that a psychologist had been sent to evaluate him after his injury and had asked Joel if he had any issues with irritability. Joel said, "I'm always irritable before my morning coffee, but what the hell does that have to do with a suicide truck bomb?"

He was recovering well, and he told me that he wanted to go back to Iraq to rejoin his unit. He bent his neck and showed me the scar where they'd stapled his head back together. I dug my body armor out of a black duffle bag and showed him where the blood—his blood—still stained my armor.

"Can I have that back?"

"You should have ducked," I said. "Do the Manions know we're on our way?"

"Yeah, I called 'em just as I was pulling up here."

We drove together to the Manion home in Doylestown, Pennsylvania, where we met Colonel Tom Manion, Travis's father; Janet Manion, his mom; Ryan, Travis's sister; and Dave, Travis's brother-in-law.

Tom Manion told us how Travis had been welcomed home. The roads were lined with people saluting or holding their hands over their hearts. The American flag flew from the extended ladders of fire trucks, while police, neighbors, and friends formed a three-hundred-car procession to escort Travis's body from the church to the gravesite. Tom told us that he had talked regularly with his son on the phone while Travis was deployed, and that they had made plans to run the Marine Corps Marathon together that fall. Now he couldn't run with Travis. "I was glad, though," he said, "that all of those people had come out to say, 'Welcome home, warrior, welcome home.'"

Later we pulled out a map of Fallujah and spread it flat on Colonel Manion's desk. Joel was able to explain the details of Travis's death in Fallujah and the patrol Travis had been on that day.

*"This is the industrial sector, here . . ."*

We tried to give his dad as much information as we could about the work Travis had done in Iraq and the life he had lived there. Travis's teammates had sent pictures of a ceremony they had performed to honor him in Iraq. In the photographs, U.S. Marines and Iraqi troops gathered around a rifle pointed into the ground with boots on either side; Travis's helmet hung on the butt of the rifle. Joel went through the pictures one at a time. He explained who all the men were—Iraqis and Americans—who had been there to honor Travis in Iraq.

*"Sometimes their snipers set up here . . ."*

As we sat for dinner on the porch with the entire family, Joel and I were both thinking, *This is Travis's seat; he should be here.* Janet Manion brought food out and we passed it around the table.

*"Travis had a group of Marines . . ."*

Yet for all their suffering, Travis's family was not consumed by bitterness, or rage, or despair. The Manions had lost their only son, yet they impressed me with their desire to honor Travis's life.

The phone rang. Someone on the other end asked about the correct letter and number display of Travis's rank: "First Lieutenant." The caller was engraving something for the family.

Travis died four weeks after we'd been on the roof together in Fallujah. The citation for his Silver Star read:

> As First Lieutenant Manion's patrol concluded a search of a suspected insurgent house, it came under precision small arms fire attack. With the Corpsman grievously wounded by enemy fire and the attack developing into a full-scale ambush, First Lieutenant Manion and a fellow Marine exposed themselves to the increasing fire to pull the Corpsman out of the kill zone. After recovering the Corpsman and administering first aid, First Lieutenant Manion led his patrol in a counter attack personally eliminating an enemy position with his M4 carbine and M203 grenade launcher. As he continued to direct the patrol another Marine was wounded by the enemy's accurate fire. He again moved across the kill zone, under fire by five insurgents, to recover the wounded Marine. Iraqi Army reinforcements, halted by an improvised explosive device, were unable to advance on the flank of the insurgents, and First Lieutenant Manion and his patrol found themselves taking fire from three sides. While fearlessly exposing himself to gain a more advantageous firing position and drawing enemy fire away from wounded Marines, First Lieutenant Manion was fatally wounded by an enemy sniper. His courageous and deliberate actions inspired the eventual counter attack and ultimately saved the lives of every member of his patrol.[1]

When Travis said, "I got your back," he meant it.

Travis had been a student of Greek history, and I thought of Pericles' speech to the families of the Athenian war dead, in which he said, "What you leave behind is not what is engraved in stone monuments, but what is woven into the lives of others."

As Joel and I drove home, I thought about the connection between hot, brutal warfare in distant lands and the kind of community spirit we had seen both at the Manions' home and among many Iraqis in

Fallujah. I had seen it before in Bosnia, Rwanda, Cambodia, and other places where courageous people found ways to live with compassion in the midst of tremendous hardship. Across the globe, even in the world's "worst places," people found ways to turn pain into wisdom and suffering into strength. They made their own actions, their very lives, into a memorial that honored the people they had lost.

On the frontlines—in humanitarian crises, in wars overseas, and around some kitchen tables here at home—I'd seen that peace is more than the absence of war, and that a good life entails more than the absence of suffering. A good peace, a solid peace, a peace in which communities can flourish, can only be built when we ask ourselves and each other to be more than just good, and better than just strong. And a good life, a meaningful life, a life in which we can enjoy the world and live with purpose, can only be built if we do more than live for ourselves.

On the drive, Joel and I decided that we'd do something for the Manion family. We would find a way to ensure that Travis's legacy—and the legacy of all those who served and sacrificed—would live on.

Joel pulled his car up to the curb in front of my building. We both stepped out, and I shook his hand and pulled him into a hug.

"Thanks, brother."

# 2 ☆

# China

Men wanted: For hazardous journey. Small wages, bitter cold, long months of complete darkness. Constant danger, safe return doubtful. Honour and recognition in case of success.[1]

I N 1914 ERNEST SHACKLETON planned to set sail from England on his ship—the *Endurance*—bound for Antarctica. Once there, he would lead the first expedition to cross the frozen continent on foot. It is alleged that when Shackleton placed this advertisement, he received five hundred responses. It was to be a great adventure.

As a kid growing up in Missouri, I'd been addicted to the Choose Your Own Adventure series of books, in which I could create my own story. *Journey Under the Sea* began, "Beware and Warning! This book is different from other books. You and YOU ALONE are in charge of what happens in this story. There are dangers, choices, adventures, and consequences . . . You are a deep sea explorer searching for the famed lost city of Atlantis. This is your most challenging and dangerous mission. Fear and excitement are now your companions." Goose bumps rose as I read by flashlight until two in the morning.

Like many American kids, I grew up in a world populated by heroes. I read about Pericles, who built democracy in Athens, the Spartans, who fought for Greece at Thermopylae, the Romans, who gave us law. I read about King Arthur and the Knights of the Round Table, who fought sorcerers, trolls, and giants, and protected the weak. I read about the Israelites, who escaped slavery and journeyed through the desert. And I read about great American heroes: George Washington, who crossed a frozen Delaware River and led America to victory; the colonial forces at Bunker Hill, who held their fire until they could see the whites of the British troops' eyes; Abraham Lincoln, whose words at Gettysburg laid the dead to rest and called a nation to its duty; Martin Luther King Jr., who announced to the world, "I have a dream."

I loved history, but this rich view of the world also left me afraid. My big fear was that God and my parents had made a terrible mistake and that I'd been born at the wrong time. I sat in the library and read stories of people discovering ancient cities and settling wild frontiers. I read about warriors and explorers and activists and statesmen, but I'd look up from the book and stare out the window of the public library onto the green, freshly mowed grass outside, and the world looked very safe to me. It seemed that all the corners of the earth had been explored, all the great battles fought. The famous people I saw on TV as a kid were athletes and actresses and singers; what did they stand for? Had the time for heroes passed?

My second, related, fear was that I'd miss my ticket to a meaningful life. I had been told—perhaps since kindergarten—that if I wanted to live a successful life, I had to go to a place called college. College, they said, was "the ticket." I understood that they gave out tickets after high school, and if you wanted one, you had to have good grades. When I came home with my report card from third grade, it read: Eric Greitens, HANDWRITING: B-. When I told my mom that I got a B minus in handwriting, she said, "That's OK."

"But will they still let me go to college?"

My parents cared a lot that I was a good person. They wanted me to treat others with kindness. They wanted me to be respectful. They wanted me to try hard. They wanted me to be a team player. But while they cared about these "character" things, they weren't particularly concerned about whether I got great grades.

This was always made clear at science fair time. I was left to my own devices to imagine, create, and construct a science fair project. I had little help. So, in third grade, I set up an experiment to determine whether or not cut tulips lasted longer in water, soda, or beer (my dad's Budweisers). Every day for a few weeks I recorded data on tulips as they wilted sitting in beer. I cut out my cardboard display in the basement, scavenged some spray paint from the garage, and in uneven passes of the can, I painted my display and then wrote on it in black marker my hypothesis: "Cut tulips will last longer in water than in soda or beer." My plan for science fair day was to set up a glass of water, a glass of soda, and a glass of beer, with a tulip placed in each. I would display my results, written in pencil on notebook paper, next to the tulips.

The day of the fair, I was astounded to see that my classmates had well-constructed and perfectly painted wood displays made to the exact specifications of the science fair regulations. What's more, their displays showcased robots and gardens and springs and typewritten analyses of data, some with tables.

Undeterred, I set down my spray-painted display, laid down my pencil-and-notebook-paper results, and cracked open my beer. I poured a full glass, then dropped the tulip in. As I was arranging the tulip in the soda glass, however, I knocked over the beer tulip, and Budweiser spilled all over my display and began to run down the table and onto the floor. The horrified parents whose children had built steam locomotives from scratch looked on as my mom—ever resourceful—used the bottom of the sweatshirt she was wearing to mop up the beer. We had a quarter can of Bud left, so I poured the remaining beer into the glass, dropped the tulip in, and left my science project to the fate of the judges and posterity.

The judges frowned on my experiment, and when I received their judgment—a white ribbon for "participation"—again I asked, "Will they still let me go to college?"

This theme continued for a while.

When I lit a pile of leaves on fire to keep myself warm while waiting for the school bus, and then accidentally set the whole bus stop on fire: "Will they still let me go to college?"

I had been told, over and over again, that college was the place where I could pursue big dreams. College was the place where life began. College was the first step into the "real world," where every great purpose could be pursued.

So I went to college. And after just a few weeks, I felt that I'd been lied to. I remember the moment. I had decided to study public policy, because public policy was concerned with—I believed—the great affairs of the world. It was the study of all we had in common and how we could improve the world together. Yet in my first class, Introduction to Public Policy Studies, the professor droned, "First, we calculate the values of the proposed outcomes." He scratched a graph on the chalkboard. "Then we assess the probability of achieving those outcomes." He scratched again. "And then we multiply." He scratched a final time. "Now we know what decision to make."

*This was public policy?* Great decisions about the fate of the world made by multiplication? Where was the romance, the energy, the great causes? When were we going to talk about how to live well, how to lead, what to fight for? They had promised me that in college we would dive into the deep pools of the world's wisdom about how to live, but instead I was being taught how to plot decision trees. They had promised me that in college we would learn how to shape the world, but they wanted me to do it with math.

I struggled. I took up a new sport. I considered a new major. I talked with everyone who would meet with me, and soon I realized that my journey wasn't going to be handed to me: *I had to choose my own adventure.*

And then one day I saw my advertisement. It wasn't as dramatic as Shackleton's, but in the student newspaper I discovered a chance to win a grant to conduct an independent-study project overseas during the summer. Applicants like me who had never been abroad before would be given preference. I tucked the newspaper under my arm and walked to class.

The grant offered a chance to see the world, but where should I go?

My uncle was in the broom business, and he had once made a trip to China to visit a broom factory. That was all the background I had, but I put together a grant application to study in China.

When I left for the airport, I did not know any Chinese language. I did not know anything about Chinese culture. And I knew almost nothing about Chinese history. I did, however, own a new hat. Inspired by Indiana Jones, I went to the mall and purchased one. Mine happened to be of the Australian Outback variety. Walking through the airport with a brand-new pack on my back and the Australian Outback hat on my head, I was ready for adventure.

I flew from St. Louis to Dallas to San Francisco to Beijing. On the final leg of the flight, I asked an elderly Chinese woman sitting next to me to give me a crash course in Chinese. She asked me my family name, and I told her, "It's Greitens, pronounced like 'brightens,' but instead of a B, it's a G." She told me that in China, I'd be better off as "Mr. Eric," and then she taught me a few key phrases. By the time we landed, I was able to say, "I am hungry. Feed me."

Han Lin was a friend of a friend of my uncle's. She picked me up at the airport and drove me to a Beijing hotel, and I woke the next morning jet-lagged and thirsty. Everyone in America had warned me over and over again that even touching the water in China would lead to dysentery, diarrhea, diphtheria, and a host of other maladies. I had purchased a water heater, but after five minutes of unsuccessfully trying to boil a cup of water in the hotel bathroom, I threw caution to the wind, opened the faucet, filled a glass of water, and drank.

I went to the window and opened the curtains on a bright, beautiful Beijing day. I looked down on a street teeming with commuters pedaling bicycles. I was really here. I was abroad. I was traveling. Before leaving for my trip, I had put my finger on a globe at the position of

St. Louis, Missouri, and another finger on Beijing. I was now standing on the other side of the world, and a wide smile broke across my face.

This was 1993, and China seemed much more foreign then than it does now. The China of 1993 was, in my mind—and the minds of most Americans—much closer to the China of 1989's Tiananmen Square massacre than to the China of the 2008 Beijing Olympics. China was becoming increasingly open to the West, but was still associated primarily with Communism and oppression, not business and growth.

My plan was to go to Changchun, a city in the northeast of the country that was often referred to as China's Detroit. I would study China's emerging business sector, and I would have some time to get to know the country.

Changchun was not a popular destination for tourists. With the exception of a few Germans at a Volkswagen plant, I didn't see any other foreigners in the city. My trips to the factories were interesting, but I also wanted to learn about Chinese culture, so when the receptionist at my hotel invited me to join her kung fu class, I accepted.

We arrived at a school gymnasium at four thirty the next morning. The shifu—translated literally as "teacher-father"—was about five feet five inches of packed muscle under a gray crewcut. I guessed that he was around sixty years old. He wore a light blue cotton shirt with embroidered ties for buttons, the cuffs folded back against the sleeves. He spoke in a slow, steady voice that exuded self-possession. When he walked between the lines of students doing their *taolu*—a fight dance of choreographed punches, kicks, and blocks—he reminded me of a predator on the prowl. On my first day, he demonstrated a move by placing his fist against my chest. With a sudden shout, he opened his fist and knocked me backward into the wall. The other students nodded dutifully. The shifu helped me up only to knock me backward again.

My friend the hotel receptionist explained, "Shifu punch you to show how to destroy enemy."

Ready to learn the secrets of destroying the enemy, I returned the next morning. After some stretching, I joined the lines of students. The shifu faced the class and bowed. With the palms of their hands flat against the sides of their legs, all the students bowed, and they began the taolu in unison.

The assistant shifu was a police officer in his mid-thirties. Each day he wore what looked to me like a pair of loose black pajamas. He was about five foot six. If I met him on the street, I would have thought: *short, tubby guy.* When he stood on one leg to demonstrate a strike, however, or when he kicked with ease at a target six and a half feet off the ground, he moved with incredible power. He spent a lot of time with me. My friend translated: "The assistant shifu says you must learn kung fu. If you go back to America and are bad, he will be shamed." Once, when I was practicing a set of strikes, he came up behind me, grabbed my chin with his right hand, and put his left hand on the base of my neck. His hands turned quickly and I heard every vertebra in my neck crack like a thunderclap of cracked knuckles.

I toiled for a few weeks until the class graduation. The graduation was a series of tests of skill. In the first test, a student centered his chi—his inner power—and grounded himself. He stood with his legs spread as if riding an invisible horse, hands together in front of his chest as if in prayer, and eyes focused straight ahead. The assistant shifu set a rolled rag on top of the student's head. Then the assistant shifu set one red brick on the student's head. Then he set another brick atop that one, and then another. It looked to me like a balancing exercise to test how still the student could remain while each heavy brick was stacked on his head. Nine, ten bricks were set on the student's head. I thought, *I can do that.*

Then a folding chair was placed next to the student, and the shifu stood on its seat. The shifu gave a command and the assistant shifu ran to the corner of the room. The assistant shifu returned holding a sledgehammer.

When I saw the sledgehammer, I said a small prayer. The prayer was in English, and I thought it had been quiet, yet somehow everyone in the room—who had understood the test from the beginning—sensed that until that moment, I had had no idea what was happening, and they all smiled.

The shifu swung the sledgehammer in a wide arc through the air and brought it down on the top brick. The bricks cracked clean down the middle, straight to the final brick, and the broken halves fell to the side of the student. Standing in this pile of debris, the student turned and bowed dutifully to the shifu, apparently thanking him for the experience. The student turned back to his classmates with a smile. I was standing next in line.

I held up my hands and protested in English—"No, I'm sorry, that's not . . ." Very well, they said, I could take the tests in any order. The assistant shifu drew a sword. I watched again as one of the students centered his chi and grounded himself. The student looked straight ahead and focused his chi in his suprasternal notch (the flesh just under the Adam's apple and between the clavicles). The shifu placed the pointy edge of the sword against the student's neck and started to push. I thought the sword would go straight through the man's neck, but as the shifu pulled the sword away, I saw that he'd left only a small red scratch. When the assistant shifu approached me, I stepped backward, thinking to pass on this test also, but the assistant shifu spoke forcefully to my friend, who turned to me and said, "The shifu says that it would be very bad for Chinese kung fu if you die. It would also be bad if you do not test. The test is important for their honor and for you. He says that you can pass the test if you try."

I was sure that my family would take little consolation knowing that I had given my life "in honor of Chinese kung fu," but I stepped forward. I set my hands in prayer in front of my chest, and as the shifu put the point of the sword against my neck, I focused all of my energy on my throat. He pushed forward, and I felt the steel point of the blade against my neck, and then suddenly I was bowing. I had apparently passed the test.

It was the first time in my life I had been overtly tested for martial honor. I was nineteen years old. I left the class that day with an appreciation for kung fu. I also left with a pair of steel railroad-spike nunchucks and a sword. I never thought I would need these or any other weapons—the world's violence happened offstage for me. I wanted to make a contribution somehow, somewhere, but I didn't think that my fight would involve armed violence.

Later in the summer I returned to Beijing, and Han Lin helped me to get a job at her company, where I could teach English in the afternoons. I expected only a few students for the first English class, so when three or four students walked in, I said hello and tried to make small talk. A few more students arrived, then a few more. Soon, I had a classroom packed with fifteen students eager to learn English. As I greeted each student, I heard an incredible range of abilities. Some of the students were almost fluent; others struggled with "How are you?"

I stood in front of the class. I had no idea how to teach English, and I had no idea how to teach students at so many levels of ability, so I decided to open the class for free discussion. I would take and answer questions. Maybe a few people would get something out of the dialogue.

I introduced myself, then said, "I'd like to learn together."

A hand shot up. "Mr. Erica, what is freedom of speech in America?"

It seemed an odd first question, but every pair of eyes was glued to me, waiting for an answer.

"Well, in America, we have one document that forms the basis for our government. That document is the Constitution, and the Constitution includes a Bill of Rights that gives rights to every citizen. One of those rights is the right to say almost anything you like." I was going to explain more, but it was clear that I'd already lost some of the class.

Another hand shot up. "Mr. Erica, what is freedom of assembly mean for you?"

A student to my right glanced nervously at the door, then got up from his chair and shut it. I assumed that he was concerned our voices might be disturbing others in the building and I continued on. The third question was also about the Bill of Rights.

Many of the students in the class were in their early to mid-twenties, and I soon found that they had been student activists at Tiananmen Square in 1989. For many of them, I was the first American or Westerner they had spoken with since then. The room came alive with dozens of eager hands, and I did my best for over an hour to explain what Americans thought about what had happened at Tiananmen. They were not looking to me as a guide on democracy; most were just curious to understand what Americans thought about what they had lived through.

After class, a group of us rode bicycles to dinner and continued our discussion over dumplings and vegetables. We spoke in hushed voices. The student who had closed the door in the classroom explained to me, "Mr. Erica, the government does not like us to talk about June 4 [Tiananmen]." This pattern of discretion and secrecy continued throughout my stay. Every time a political subject came up, someone would shut their office or dormitory door. No one spoke about politics in public. One night, I saw a man arguing with a soldier in Tiananmen Square. I stopped my bike to see what was happening and one of my friends pulled on my shirtsleeve and said, "Mr. Erica, I am sorry, we must go."

Still, the students who sat around the dinner table were eager to tell me about their experiences. One described the days she had spent with her friends at the demonstrations. She felt that they were going to change history. She had not been there the violent evening of June 3 and early morning of the fourth, but a friend of hers had helped to carry another bleeding friend out of the square and to an apartment for medical care.

I had watched the TV coverage of June 4, 1989, and I remember footage of tanks, trucks full of soldiers, and crowds of students. The government crushed the protest. Chaos and confusion reigned as reporters announced that shots were being fired at unarmed protesters. Students on bicycles and rickshaws carted away the injured. Other people pushed rickshaws through the streets, running injured friends to the hospital. I remembered watching TV several days later and seeing pictures of a now-famous man who stood in the path of a line of rolling tanks. As the tank pivoted to drive around him, the protester moved and blocked the tank's path. He stood his ground.

As I was talking with the students over dinner, I realized that this was the first time I had ever spoken with people who had been part of shaping history. I had watched them on TV. Now I saw that those courageous activists were very real people. Some of them liked soy sauce on their dumplings; others drank more than they ate. Some of them were unshaven, some of them joked constantly, and some had big dreams of going to America. History was alive today. It was made by people: courageous, determined, thoughtful—it was made by people my age.

We rode back to the workers dormitory. I stayed with two men in a cramped room with a concrete floor and concrete walls covered with posters of movie stars, cars, and singing girls. We stayed up talking about San Francisco, the Cultural Revolution, Harley-Davidsons, Mao Zedong, World War II, the Year of the Tiger, and American women.

For the first time, I felt that I was representing and speaking for a group of people: Americans. When the Chinese asked me questions about the American media and democracy, they weren't asking me because they were interested in what I had to say. They were interested in what Americans thought. I felt unqualified to represent all of the United States, but I had a glorious time riding bicycles to and from work, teaching in the afternoons, going out for dinner with my new friends. Many had dreams of traveling to the U.S., and they had questions such as, "How much does an apartment cost in Los Angeles?" and "Do they have rock 'n' roll clubs in Boston, or only in Memphis?" They wanted to know how hard it would be for them to get a job in America, how hard it would be to get a scholarship.

One night in the dormitory, when only two other people were in the room, one of my new friends placed a small canister of film in my hand. He said, "These are photos I took of June 4 protests, but I cannot develop them. Please take these home and develop them. Know what really happened here."

I took the film canister and shook his hand. I felt like I'd joined an underground resistance movement.

One Friday night, a group of us were playing darts in the workers dormitory when there was a knock at the door. Two police officers stepped into the room and spoke to my friends. My friends turned to me with pale faces and said, "Mr. Erica, the policeman wants you go to police station."

"Why?"

"To make paperwork."

I looked at my watch: nine o'clock. I said to my friends, "Please explain to the officers that I would be very happy to assist them with their paperwork, and that I would be pleased to work with them. I would be more than happy to come to the police station on Saturday morning or on Monday morning, but I cannot go with them at nine o'clock on a Friday night." This was translated to the police officers. The officers spoke again to my friends, and then my friends turned to me.

"Mr. Erica, you are going to the police station, now."

Han Lin and I were driven to the police station in the back seat of a police car, accompanied by another man from the dormitory, who whispered to me, "They can't do anything to us. China is different now."

When we arrived at the police station, we were directed to a waiting area, where we sat on green couches and whispered to each other. At about ten o'clock, they called us down a hallway. I followed Han Lin. She was directed to a room on the left; I to a room on the right. As I stepped into the room, I saw two police officers sitting behind a gray metal table. One of them was dressed in civilian clothes and the other wore his police uniform. A single bare light bulb dangled from a wire, and I saw that they had set out a single cigarette for me next to a pack of Marlboros. (I knew from my Chinese friends that American cigarettes were in high demand. The cigarette was clearly intended as a friendly gesture.) They shut the door.

The walls were concrete, and the room contained nothing but the metal table, a filing cabinet, two officers, me, an empty chair, and the cigarette. I sat in the empty chair, and one of the officers pulled out a lighter. He politely urged the cigarette on me. I declined. Then the questions began.

"What brings you to China?"

"I came to study and to learn," I said.

"You like it here?"

"I like it very much. The Chinese people have been very friendly, and I have learned a lot."

"Who got you job here in Beijing?"

"My friends and my colleagues at the company," I said. "I help during the day, and teach a class in the afternoons."

"Do you have work permit?"

"No."

"What you teach them?"

"English."

"Teach anything else?"

"Grammar."

"Who in the class ask questions about American government?"

"Hmmm." I thought about how to respond.

"Who in the class ask questions about freedom of speech?"

I explained that there were different students on different days, many discussions about many subjects, and it would be hard for me to say with certainty what any particular student had asked about any particular subject. The room grew hot. I could hear Han Lin crying across the hall. The officer in civilian clothes looked hard at me as Han Lin's crying grew louder. I figured that I was in no danger. I was a nineteen-year-old kid in their eyes. I knew that I wasn't worth an international incident. My friends, however, had jobs they needed and dreams of going to America, and I didn't want to put their jobs or their dreams in jeopardy.

"Why you teach English in this company?"

"What you do during day at company?"

"You have friend at company?"

At about midnight, I said to the man dressed in civilian clothes, "I am very happy. It has been a pleasure speaking to you for two hours. I have done the best that I can in answering your questions. Now, I think it would be best if we called the American embassy."

The officer pulled out a yellow softbound book with red writing on the cover. He opened it. The text was in Chinese. He ran his finger across several lines of text and then pointed his finger at me. "You have broken the Chinese law. You *must* punish." I put my hands in the air in a gesture of no bad intentions. Again, he stabbed the page with his finger and then pointed at me. "You have broken the Chinese law. You *MUST* punish."

"I understand what you are saying, and we can continue to talk, but I would like to call the American embassy if possible." In his broken English, the interrogator said to me, "You know, if we must, but only to hit the Americans." I looked at him and tried to smile. I had no idea what he was saying. Was this a threat? I put a confused look on my face. "I am so sorry, my friend. I don't understand exactly what you are saying."

"We can call American embassy, but only if you are hit." This sounded like a bad deal.

The officer was getting flustered. He was sweating and smoking and struggling with his English. Eventually it became clear to me that he was saying that he would only call the embassy if an American had been hit or injured in Beijing. They had no obligation to call the embassy otherwise. I had broken the Chinese law, not the American law. I was in China. They were free to question me as long as they liked.

I asked for water. They brought a glass and we continued to talk, but shortly after, the questioning came to an end. They took my passport and explained to me that they were going to keep it until Monday, when I could come back and pick it up.

That Monday, I returned to the police station and paid a fine of roughly nine dollars. They asked me to sign a number of papers—all in Chinese—before I received my passport. I didn't know if I was declaring myself an enemy of the Chinese state, signing a receipt for the fine, or pleading guilty to a minor infraction of the law. But I signed, I got my passport, and with the passport, I could get home.

Several days later, I boarded a plane back to the United States. Security was different then, and inside my backpack I had the railroad-spike nunchucks, the kung fu sword, and—wrapped inside a pair of socks—the film canister from Tiananmen Square. As I went through security, the sword and the nunchucks were pulled from my pack. The weapons were handed to airline staff, and a kind stewardess said, "I cannot allow you to bring these with you to your seat, but you can pick them up from me at the end of the trip." No one mentioned the film. Also tucked deep into my pack was the Australian Outback adventure hat.

I left a lot of my naivety in China. I also left a lot of my fear. I learned that history was very much alive, and I'd met solid ordinary people who moved it forward. As I sat down in my seat to fly home, I was thinking less about choosing an adventure and more about choosing a path with purpose. But the adventure continued, and I'd soon come to think that maybe I'd been born at the right time after all.

# 3 ☆

# Boxing

WHEN I RETURNED from China, I resumed the cushy life of a college student. It felt even emptier than before. At Duke, professors invited and encouraged comments from all of us—nineteen and twenty years old. We would talk about what we thought of American foreign policy, Aristotle, and medical ethics. By virtue of being at Duke, and being students, we were entitled to participate, entitled to have an opinion, even though we had zero experience to guide any of the comments we offered. I wanted to earn something, to test myself. I might not have been able to change the world as a student, but I knew that I needed to live through something hard and real to become better.

My grandfather had grown up in Chicago during the Great Depression, and he used to tell me about his experiences boxing there—the rough gyms, the hard poverty, the harder discipline. His stories were full of all kinds of characters, yet the boxers he spoke of—those who were righties and those who were southpaws, those who talked a lot and those who were quiet, those who boxed and those who brawled—all seemed to have a sure sense of how to walk in the world. That was something I wanted—the steady confidence that comes from passing through tough tests. I figured, why not test myself in the ring?

•   •   •

I pulled into the E. D. Mickle parking lot on a September evening of my sophomore year. Stepping out of my car, I walked through shards of brown beer bottles littering the ground. The gym stood on a rough section of Alston Avenue. Housing projects hung along the street, and men lingered at a gas station on the corner. As I walked up the steps, I heard the sound of punch bags bouncing on their chains. When I pushed open the door to the gym, the men inside barely looked up. No one spoke to me. I saw that I was the only white guy there and that this was very clearly a different set of characters from the Duke classroom crowd.

The gym was one long room. A boxing ring sat at one end, and a speed bag hung on the wall behind the ring. There were mirrors on the wall for shadowboxing. Three heavy bags hung from the ceiling. In the middle of the gym, fighters skipped rope and trainers worked their boxers with punch mitts.

I walked to a corner and set my bag down on a blue tumbling mat. I had no idea how to train as a boxer. I did a set of pushups until I got tired, then I turned over and did a set of sit-ups. I had bought a set of hand wraps from a local sporting goods store, and I stood up and started to wrap my hands.

A man walked up to me—about five foot five, muscled shoulders under a tank top, stubble on his chin, gloves slung over his shoulder.

"Hey man, you wanna spar?"

I didn't have to think about this for long. "No," I said.

He looked at me. "Man, how you gonna learn to box if you don't spar?"

I had no answer for him, so I walked to the equipment closet and pulled on headgear. I chose a pair of red gloves and yanked them on.

I climbed into the ring, unsure of what to do. *Do I just stand here? Shadowbox?* My opponent stepped up the ring stairs and ducked between the ropes.

He shuffled toward me and I put my hands up. He threw out a jab that tapped my forehead. I swung back at him and missed. He moved left and right. He jabbed me high and then hit me in the gut low. He danced around the ring. He smiled. He hit me again and chuckled. I ran at him to throw a fist and he cracked me in the mouth. I threw and missed and he dropped a right hand against my forehead. He smiled when he threw punches, and I could sense other men in the gym watching. He could have knocked me out, but I wasn't worthy of that. The beating was comic. I was pathetic. Once he'd had his fun and made his point, he turned without a word and walked out of the ring.

When I went back to the gym the next day, men chuckled, but they left me alone. I walked to the same corner and set my stuff down. I did pushups and sit-ups until I was covered in sweat. I thought about skipping rope, but I didn't know how, so rather than do something that guaranteed that I would look like a fool, I decided to punch a heavy bag, which only gave me a very good chance of looking like a fool.

For several days, I talked with no one, beyond "Hey" and "You done with that?" and "Yeah."

One day Bob Pugh—a weathered former fighter and the gym's manager—walked up to me as I punched at a heavy bag. "You're telegraphing your right." I knew that there were many things I was doing wrong, but I appreciated his gesture of conversation.

"How do I fix that?" I asked.

"You gotta get a trainer."

"Who's the best trainer?"

"Earl. Earl and Derrick."

"Are they here?" I asked.

"No, they're training outside the gym now, but I think I got Derrick's phone number."

Bob walked into his office and came back with a torn corner of a piece of white paper—the back side of a carryout menu—and on it he had scratched in blue ink a phone number.

Derrick Humphrey was twenty-six years old. He stood six foot two, and he had the powerful build of a tall, fast fighter. He worked construction. He had a few marks on his record from an ill-disciplined youth, and a scar across the bridge of his nose. I assumed then that the scar was from boxing; he later told me that his mother had cracked him across the face with a wooden stick for acting up as a kid.

He lived in an apartment with a near-empty living room. Gray carpet lined the floor. A small table sat against the wall and on it was a lone framed photograph of Derrick's mother. A phone sat on the floor. When we met, Derrick was training for a fight just a few weeks away.

Months later Derrick told me that when I called him, he thought I was likely crazy. He said that at least once a week he had people tell him they wanted to box. They'd be full of questions and interest for two or three days and then they disappeared. Derrick told me that he could tell on the phone that I was white. Then, when I told him that I went to Duke University and that I'd been spending my time at the gym, he said, "I didn't *think* you were crazy, I was *sure* you were a crazy white man. But I like to keep my life interesting, so I told you to come on down."

Derrick introduced me to Earl Blair, his trainer. When Earl was in the Army, he used to be called Bebop, because he walked with a bounce and a smile.

"How are you, how you doin'? So you're ready to fight?"

"Yes, sir," I said.

"Well all right then, all right."

Earl shook my hand hard. He was five foot six, sixty-six years old, and farm-boy strong. His smile filled his face, and he beamed with the joy of a man who was truly grateful for every day of his life.

We walked into the parking lot outside Derrick's apartment. Kids were home from school, and they weaved through the parking lot on their bicycles. Teenagers sat on the concrete sidewalk and talked. Mothers occasionally stuck their heads out the doors of their apartments and yelled for their children. I stood next to Derrick. *This* is the gym?

"OK, now, here we go. Derrick, and, and both of you all, gonna get those knees high. Ready. Time." Derrick and I started running in place in the parking lot, lifting our knees high and punching our fists every step. Earl watched his stopwatch. "Time," he said, and then Derrick walked a short circle around the parking lot and I did the same.

"Got a beautiful day for training here. A beautiful day," Earl said. We rested for what seemed to me about thirty seconds, and then we did the running in place and punching again. It seemed pretty easy to me. I started to wonder about Earl being a great trainer, and I wondered how in the world Derrick could train for a professional boxing match by jogging in place in his parking lot.

We did a few more rounds, then Earl said, "OK, warm-up's over, let's do it for real."

"Time," Earl said, and Derrick started pumping his knees and throwing his punches so fast that the kids on bicycles stopped riding and stood watching him with their mouths open. One boy got so excited watching Derrick that he started to imitate him there in the parking lot, throwing his fists as fast as he could. I tried to match Derrick's speed, and just as I started to feel the burn in my legs, Earl said, "Time." We paused. Then we started again. Knees pumping, fists flying. Earl said, "Time." We paused. Then we started again, and again, and again, and again, and again. Kids were bicycling around us, and when I leaned over during one pause and grabbed my knees, one of the kids said, "That white man 'bout to pass out."

We switched exercises and lay backs-down on the parking lot. We brought our heads off the ground and our feet six inches into the air. Earl said, "Hold it there," and while I held my feet in the air he walked over and punched me in the stomach. My feet collapsed to the ground, and I reached for my gut where he'd punched me.

"Get your feet back up. You can take it. Watch Derrick." Earl walked over to Derrick, who still had his feet six inches off the ground, and he started punching him in the stomach: bam with the right, bam with the left, bam, bam, bam, and with each blow I could hear Derrick exhale and then take another quick breath in through his nose. "Time," Earl said.

We worked through a whole series of exercises that day in the parking lot. We didn't touch a single piece of equipment, and when I scraped my body off the pavement and walked back to my car, I felt more beaten than I ever had after any practice, any race, any workout.

It would be wrong to say that Earl taught life lessons along with boxing, because for Earl, there was no distinction to be made between life and boxing. Every action was invested with significance. How we hung the heavy bag, God's mercy, the way a man should wrap his hands, the virtue of humility, the proper way to lace gloves, being on time, the way a teacher should love his students, the proper way to care for your equipment—these were all part of one solid and unbroken piece.

Earl refused to call himself a coach. As he put it, "A coach makes you more skilled, shows you how to be better at a certain activity—maybe it's running, maybe it's throwing, maybe it's boxing. But what's the point? The point is, after a coach coaches you, you can go and do whatever you want with your new skill. You learn to run, you can go rob a store. You learn to fight, you can go fight in the street. But that's not what I'm about. I am not a coach with players, but a teacher with students. I teach my boxers not just a set of skills, but a way of living."

I paid Earl $25 a week, and I paid him regardless of circumstance. Thanksgiving. Christmas. Still I paid. Earl had told me, "Twenty-five dollars a week. Paid on Monday. We talk money up front. Then there's no misunderstandings. No excuses. Twenty-five a week, whether you train five days or none at all. Twenty-five a week," Earl said.

Earl explained that paying for something made a man appreciate it more. He'd learned that lesson before. "Trained kids for free. But then the kids didn't have nothin' invested in it. Walk right on by the gym if they didn't feel like trainin'. I couldn't count on anythin'. I know it might seem like a lot. When I first told Derrick, Derrick didn't think he could pay. But have you missed one week, Derrick, in five years? No sir. Prays on it. Works hard, and he gets what he needs. I always say, you might not always get what you want, but you always get what you need. I know it's not a lot. I know my time is worth more than that. I'll get paid later. But it's important all the same."

Earl made us say a prayer before we started every practice. He would say, "Just go on and say whatever is right for you to say," and we would shut our eyes and say a silent prayer. I had—before boxing—never been someone who prayed on a daily basis, and it felt uncomfortable at first. But boxing is a violent discipline, and after a few days of getting cracked in the ribs, praying seemed like a sensible way to begin.

For Earl, the gym, or the parking lot, or the patch of mud behind North Carolina Central University where we would sometimes train—any location where men came to make themselves better—was his place of worship, and the tasks of boxing were his rituals. We wrapped our hands and tied our gloves with solemnity. When Derrick sat down to tape his fists before a fight, he held his right hand out for Earl, fingers spread as wide as he could. Earl poked a hole in the gauze with a scissors. He shoved his thumb through to open up the hole. He then took the gauze off his thumb and slipped it over and down Derrick's thumb. Earl rolled the gauze across the top of Derrick's wrist and around the bottom. Derrick watched his hand. Earl rolled the gauze around Derrick's wrist six times, tightly. He rolled a strip diagonally across Derrick's hand to the knuckles. He laid twelve lengths of gauze across Derrick's knuckles. He wrapped around and down, making four loops around Derrick's thumb. "Keep 'em spread," Earl said. Derrick spread his fingers wide. Earl didn't want Derrick's fingers wrapped too tightly—cutting off the flow of blood to Derrick's hand. Earl crisscrossed the gauze around Derrick's hand and wrist, then finished by wrapping the wrist three times. "Tape," Earl said, and I gave him a piece of tape. "Tape," and I gave him a piece of tape. "Tape," and I gave him a piece of tape. Earl pushed Derrick's fingers into a fist. "How's that feel, Derrick?"

It wasn't until years later—when I watched some men sharpen knives and clean rifles and pack their gear for a military operation—that I saw this same sanctified attention to preparation.

Learning at Duke and learning to box were very different endeavors. Duke was all about reading and talking. In the gym, we *did* everything and talked about almost nothing. "Earl, how do I throw a jab?"

"Watch Derrick. *Do* as he does." End of discussion.

And that's what I did. I watched as Derrick found an open spot and started to skip rope. The rope moved, faster to warm up, then slower, tick-tick, tick-tick, sliding under feet that seemed barely to leave the ground. A minute of work and then, knees high, higher, the rope tick-ticking faster, Derrick threw his hands across his body and back again—the rope crossing, dancing, ticking, gliding—working sharp and powerful. Then he slowed, watching the other fighters, the rope calm, his mind running. The rope flew furious again—over, under, left, right, flying, cutting, the gym in motion, the rope tick-ticking, enclosing the fighter in a clear cloud of movement—flying, ticking, sweeping, moving, bearing all the weight of a man now at work.

After two weeks, Earl put me on the heavy bag. For two weeks, I did nothing on the bag but learn to jab.

"Time," Earl said, and I stepped away from the bag as Derrick stepped to it. "There's your picture, Eric. Watch how Derrick works the bag."

It was Friday night, and I was sitting in the back seat of Earl's Oldsmobile. Earl and Derrick rode in the front. Earl always had a heavy foot—"I like to be able to get out the way"—and we were flying down the highway. Derrick had a fight at the Ritz in Raleigh that night, and I was on my way to help work the corner. My mind drifted to my friends at Duke who were out partying. I wondered if I was missing out.

Earl and Derrick were talking about how to make sure they got paid. Out of curiosity I asked from the back seat, "How much can a guy usually make in one of these fights?"

"Well," Earl said, "I imagine you could probably get four hundred dollars for a four-rounder. Don't you think, Derrick?"

And before I could say anything: "Shoot yeah, Earl. Bein' white an' all. Eric'd get four hundred easy."

"And plus, Derrick, you know, they might put in a little extra because it would be his debut and all. You know, fightin' for the first time after three weeks a trainin'."

"That's exactly right, Earl. Eric might walk out there with five hundred dollars in his pocket."

"Yeah, baby, you could probably make about five hundred for a four-rounder. Now that's just for starters. You get a few more fights under your belt, then you'll be in the *big* money."

When they had finished laughing at the prospect of my debut after three weeks of training, they told me that most boxers could get about forty or fifty dollars a round.

After a few more weeks of training—when Earl knew that I was there to stay—he told me it was time to buy my own equipment. Earl wasn't going to let me use the equipment in the gym closet anymore. "We all work on this bag here. And when it finally break down, we each gonna put in to get a new one. Everything else, each one a my boxers has they own equipment. Own gloves, own rope, own hand wraps, own cup, own mouthpiece, own Vaseline. Why? Because I want to teach my babies to take care of what is theirs. Learn to 'preciate something. They take good care of those gloves, put Vaseline on 'em, put 'em out to dry when they get home, wash the strings. Compare that with them gloves and headgear they got in the closet there. Nobody pays that equipment no respect, none. But look here, go on, look around, every piece of equipment we got we keep it like brand-new. Brand-new. We're separate, and we're gonna keep it separate."

Just after I said my prayer, he handed me a copy of a Ringside catalog. As I flipped through the pages of gloves, headgear, punching bags, and groin protectors, Earl pointed out each item he thought I should buy. "Those gloves are the best ones you can get. And that headgear, that's the same one Derrick uses and it takes care of him." Earl pulled an old calculator from his pocket and I wrote him a check for the order.

A few days later, Earl walked in carrying a cardboard box that read RINGSIDE BOXING in black letters. He wore a big smile on his face, and he seemed to have even more pep in his step than usual. He pulled out all of my gear—headgear, gloves, mouthpiece, boxing boots—and as he handed me each piece, I felt like I had arrived. I wasn't a boxer yet, but I was now at least a real student. Because it was a big order, Ringside threw in a few free items, and when Earl pulled out a black ball cap that said RINGSIDE across the front, he took off his REAL MEN PRAY hat and pulled on the Ringside hat for himself. "Oh yeah," he said, grinning wide. "We got everything we need."

When we finished our day's work, I went into the locker room and took off my new gloves and my new hand wraps. I held my hands splayed in front of me and looked at my knuckles. The skin was torn from punching on the heavy bag. Scar tissue would start to grow soon. But for now, I savored blood on my hands, the small cut in my lip, the soreness in my jaw. I had begun to earn the strength that comes from working through pain and it felt good. I filled the sink with hot water and sank my hands. When I pulled my dripping hands from the water, hints of fresh blood came to the surface of each knuckle. I looked in the mirror. I squeezed my jaw and my cheeks and my nose, checking for soreness. I stood there awhile looking at my face. I realize now that I had only taken the barest first step on a years-long journey. I was not particularly tough. I certainly was not any good. But I was becoming stronger and I liked it.

For Earl, every action, even something as simple as washing the strings of your gloves, had a moral component. If you didn't wash the strings of your gloves every week, it meant you didn't care about your equipment. If you didn't care about your equipment, you didn't care enough to train properly. If you didn't care enough to train properly, you shouldn't be here. If you shouldn't be here, you should leave right now. It was a vicious train of logic. But in the gym, it worked.

For many of the men, the boxing gym was their refuge from an outside world that was chaotic and unpredictable. The boxing gym was beautiful in that it provided order and discipline and silenced braggarts. There was no show, no trash talk, no puffed chests. "You got something to say? Say it in the ring."

Earl tried, but even with his strict discipline, he could not protect all of his boxers. He carried memories of casualties like ghosts in his mind. The most painful memory for Earl was of his first student, Beaver. Earl told me the story one day after practice as I stood leaning against the ring.

"Beaver had an older friend named Ernest. They grew up together, lived in the same neighborhood 'round Clark Street. When I first started training him, Beaver was in seventh grade and Ernest was in ninth. Beaver always felt he could never beat Ernest, because Ernest was bigger. But after several years of training Beaver, I told Ernest, 'I've trained Beaver. You can't beat him anymore.'

"But Ernest wouldn't take my word. He was gonna try Beaver anyway. Well, you know what happened. Beaver beat him up on the street. When I heard about it, I told Beaver, 'Why don't you leave Ernest alone? Stay away from him. You know he ain't no good. And why don't you stay off Clark Street.'"

"What was Clark Street?" I asked.

"Clark Street had all kinds of mess on it, kids makin' trouble, and I told Beaver to stay away from there. Well, Ernest was the type of young man for whom it was impossible for him to live down a beating. So the next day, Ernest went after him.

"Late in the afternoon, I was looking for Beaver to pick him up for practice. I saw a young man laying in the street, and I thought it was some random man who got drunk and was laying out. Then I looked closer. I looked at his feet. *Those are Beaver's tennis shoes.* I jumped out my car. Ernest had shot him, and my baby's laying in the street dying. I heard one of the kids say, 'Here come Earl,' but just then I saw Ernest was spinnin' tires, gettin' away, and my mind was taken off my baby and I hopped in my car and I'm after Ernest, driving all over Henderson. He ran to the police station, but I think that I should have stayed there and held my baby. I sometimes think that when Beaver heard somebody say, 'Here come Earl,' he probably thought everything was going to be all right. But I ran off after Ernest, and Beaver died alone there in the street."

Tears collected in the corners of Earl's eyes.

"That's my regret. I was hurt because Beaver was so disobedient. I just told him the day before, stay off of Clark Street. I just told him the day before, 'You know Ernest no damn good. Leave Ernest alone.' He was only eighteen. I had 'im hardly five years. My first student, my first baby."

Earl's life had taught him hard lessons, and his focus on virtue admitted no exceptions: if you did not wash the strings on your boxing gloves, you were—so went the logic train—an unworthy man. Earl was incredibly demanding of us, and of everyone around him. A man who didn't take proper care of what was his was not a man.

And it was also true that a boxer who used his strength to inflict pain on the weak was less than a dog. "I wouldn't even call 'im a dog, 'cause I have known some good, beautiful dogs in my life, and any man that goes 'round and beats up on women, beats up on children, he ain't even as good as a dog, no sir." God, in Earl's view, had invested every person with strength, and it was our duty to develop that strength. "What did my Father give you muscles for? What did he give you brains for? Now look here, I may not be the strongest man on the block, not the smartest man on the street, but I know that my Father didn't give me what I have for me to waste it." The logic train went like this: every person had strength. Therefore, every person had a duty to develop their strength. Therefore, every person had a duty to use their strength in the service of God. Sometimes that meant skipping rope properly. Sometimes that meant helping a young kid lost in the world who'd been blown into the gym. Sometimes that meant calling me at five o'clock in the morning—I was a college student—and telling me to come over to his house to help him move a refrigerator.

Earl rarely used the word, but his whole system of teaching and his whole way of living was built around the concept of honor. You honored God by using your time wisely, and you honored your fellow man by treating him with respect. You honored your teacher by calling him "sir," and he honored his students by challenging them to face pain and become stronger. Earl had come to associate charity with pain, and he believed that love did its deepest work when applied to a wound.

When our gym was shut by the city, Derrick and I trained on the track at North Carolina Central University instead. Often it rained, and when it rained we couldn't spar or work the bag because our equipment, much of it leather, would be ruined. The rain made our runs fresh-feeling and clean and difficult, but it also turned the dirt patch to mud, and so working the heavy bag became impossible for a day or two. We sparred, but without a ring it was harder to cut a man off and fewer punches were thrown. When it snowed we ran circles around the track, clearing away two paths of red track hidden under a blanket of white.

Usually, as Derrick and I ran in circles around the track, Earl would sprint back and forth across the football field, cheering us on. We were his focus—unless, of course, there were women walking the track. Earl would put a huge smile on his face. "Well hello, ladies, how you doin'?" Earl was sixty-six years old and the women often made the mistake of thinking he was harmless. He would say, "Yeah, these my babies, my boxers." By my junior year, Earl was dating a woman in her early thirties.

Derrick and I ran side by side around the track. We wore our gloves and we threw jabs and uppercuts and hooks and short shoulder punches as we ran. We bobbed our heads behind our hands.

A fence circled the track and guys from Central walked by, outside the fence, and yelled, "Adriaaaaaaane," doing a bad Rocky imitation.

Or, "When you all gonna be ready for Tyson?" Or, to me, "Hey, white boy, I'll box witchya. You all need somebody to spar wit your white boy?"

Derrick said, "Don't worry 'bout them, Eric. We got work to do." We kept running.

We passed Earl and Earl said, "There they go. What a team." We ran past and he yelled, "One professional world champion and one amateur about to make his mark." Then, as he sat down in the chair that the football coach often left out by the track, Earl said, "Yes sir, gonna get there. This is what we need."

For three years I trained with Derrick and Earl. I had wanted to box in the Golden Gloves tournament my junior year, but I fractured my leg playing football over Christmas break, and the tournament in February of my senior year offered a final chance to compete before graduation.

For weeks I ran in the early darkness of every morning, thought of boxing during the day, and slept hard at night. Before the drive to the tournament, I stepped on the scale and smiled to see that I had cut my weight to 156 pounds. As Earl and I drove through a storm to Charlotte, North Carolina, my stomach was empty and my eyes were clear.

Three years I'd spent sweating at the heavy bag, often until my knuckles bled. The fruit of all that labor was now to be realized in a few fights that—by the rules of amateur boxing—could not last longer than six minutes.

We entered the weigh-in room and saw a fat sweating man sitting behind a table piled with USA Boxing amateur fight booklets and scattered pieces of paper. The top of a pen poked out of his thick hand.

I walked to the man and introduced myself.

"Oh yeah, yeah, from up in Durham. You called me a few times, didn't you? Well, let's get you weighed in."

"One fifty-six." I had hit my weight exactly; 156 was the upper limit for light middleweight.

"Beautiful," Earl said.

"Oh, good. You're a novice." The Novice division of Golden Gloves is for fighters who have competed in no more than ten fights. "Well, we need somebody at Novice Light Middle. With this storm, we've had all kinds of guys cancel on us. We'll be lucky to have twelve fights. Half the card's going to be unopposed. Can't remember last time we had weather like this."

Earl said, "Who's our opponent?"

"Well, we don't have one right now in Novice."

"We want to fight," Earl said.

"Well, we want you to fight, too. But you need an opponent."

We were told to wait until registration closed. I went upstairs and later Earl came up holding a piece of white paper. On it, my name was listed in the "Blue Corner" column next to "156 NOVICE." I was fighting "Vs. UNOPPOSED."

I looked down at my gym bag and the small cooler at my feet. I felt ridiculous for having made such careful preparations.

Earl and I watched a few fights. We waited until I was called in the ring and given my trophy for showing up to scattershot applause.

As we walked out through the lobby, Earl spoke to my back. "Hold that trophy right." I held the trophy limply, upside down, in my left hand. "Hold on," Earl said. We stopped in the lobby and Earl turned me to face him. "Now look here, Eric. You are the Golden Gloves Novice Champion. You earned that trophy. Now go on and hold it right. You been workin' hard three years now. Real hard. And you can box. You did everythin' you needed to do and more. You did everything you could. You earned that. That there trophy is goin' up on the mantel. Right for everybody to see. Baby, all we can do is do right. That's all we can do. And you've done that. Everything else is up to my Father. You know how to fight. Look at all the guys you beat in the gym. You been workin' hard. Almost three years."

"Yeah, but I would have liked to have fought for it," I said.

"I know you would have, baby. Don't you think I know that?" Earl put his hand on my shoulder.

· · ·

Earl did know I wanted a fight. One evening a pro fighter named Mo "Too Sweet" came down to the track where Derrick and I were sparring. Maurice was a professional fighter whom Earl had trained off and on. Mo did his road work on the track at Central, and sometimes he'd come down to work the bag with us.

"Earl! How you doin'?"

"Beautiful, beautiful. How are you?"

"All right. I got a match coming up in a few weeks and I've been looking for someone good to spar with. Can I work with Derrick?"

"How about Eric?"

"Eric?" Mo looked at me.

Earl said, "Eric's no joke. Plus he's closer to your weight."

Derrick fought at 168 pounds, and I fought at 156. Maurice fought around 147.

"Eric, huh? All right." Mo smiled. "I'll be sure to take it easy on him."

I had watched Maurice fight and win at the Ritz in Raleigh. He was a talented professional fighter. I thought to myself, *Earl might have lost his mind.* But after the Golden Gloves disappointment, I wanted a fight.

I stood in front of Earl as he held my glove open for me, its hollow fist aimed at the ground. I slid my hand down and into the cool glove until the tips of my fingers touched the end and I curled my fingers back into a fist. I set my gloved fist firmly against Earl's stomach and Earl bent slightly, his powerful fingers tightening and drawing and tightening at the crisscross of the laces.

Earl doubled the knot and tucked a loose end of lace into the glove. He tied my other glove and I turned to face Maurice.

Earl set down orange cones to carve out a ring on the track. Maurice and I touched gloves. I was used to fighting Derrick, who, at six foot two, had a much longer reach. Maurice was shorter than I was, and so I was able to close with him easily. I jabbed and felt the full force of my punch crack on his face. I watched as his head snapped back. It was probably the best punch I'd ever thrown. I followed Mo around our makeshift ring, and I kept jabbing and the jabs kept cracking.

As Maurice slid around the ring, I realized, *He's running from me.* I hit Mo and he cracked me back hard, and our sparring grew in intensity. I threw a right that knocked Maurice in the side of the head and he stumbled. I pursued him. He turned and unloaded a right hand full of malice that flew past my head. We weren't sparring anymore. We were fighting.

Earl had been working with me on throwing a right hook to the body followed by a right hook to the head. I jabbed first, then I shot my fist into Mo's ribs, and then with a twist through the hips I turned the punch over and brought my fist barreling over Mo's low left hand and smashed his temple. Mo stumbled again, then turned his back on me and walked out of the boundary of the ring.

"I told you Eric could fight," Earl said.

Derrick said later that night, "Eric, I thought you were 'bout to kill Mo in there. You got yourself a little fight in you now."

That night Earl called me. "Need you to come over the house. Come when you can." And he hung up.

"Hey, Earl," I said when I walked in.

"Well, all right."

"How you feeling?" I asked.

"Oh, I feel good," he said.

On his dining room table lay a little piece of gold-colored metal next to my Golden Gloves trophy. Earl picked up the piece of metal and handed it to me. My name was engraved across it. I held the piece of metal and felt oddly formal knowing that Earl had used my last name.

"Now," Earl said—he wasn't going to give me a chance to say any-thing—"turn that over. See that piece a tape, that backing there? Take it off."

"OK."

"Now, press it right into that marble part. Right below the man."

I pressed my name into the trophy, right below the golden figurine of a man jabbing.

"It looks like you, the way you fought Mo. How's it sticking?" Earl asked.

"It's good."

"All right, well, you take that on home with you. See you tomorrow night if the Lord spares me."

"Thank you, Earl."

# Part II ★ ★ ★

# HEART AND MIND

# 4 ☆

# Bosnia

M Y MATERNAL GRANDFATHER, Harold Jacobs, was born in Chicago in 1916 and grew up during the Great Depression. His father, Samuel Jacobs, was a bookbinder from Warsaw, Poland, and his mother, Rebecca Newman Jacobs, was from New York. We always called my grandfather "Shah." He thought it was a reference to the former kings of Persia. My mother and my aunt have a different interpretation. When my grandfather was talking one day, I ran up to him (I was about two years old at the time) and yelled, "Shah!" My mom and aunt think that what I meant was "shush." "Shah," it turns out, is also a word for "quiet" or "shush," and my grandmother used to say it a lot to my grandfather. My grandfather could talk.

One time I pulled a frozen pizza out of the oven, and Shah began, "What's that you got there? You know, that's not really a pizza. The only real pizza they make is in Chicago. The stuff people have in St. Louis, that's not pizza. Chicago pizza, that's real pizza. Some people think that if you put a little bit of sausage on a pizza, you got sausage pizza. That's not real sausage pizza. You want a sausage pizza? You put on sausage and there's sausage on the whole thing. See how there are some pieces there that don't have sausage on it? What is that? What's a sausage pizza without sausage? What did I tell you? The only real

pizza is made in Chicago. You know, when I grew up in Chicago . . ."
And so it would go, with Shah talking about everything from the Harlem Globetrotters to forklifts to the stock exchange to baseball—"The problem today is that they rush these kids. No time in the minors. Used to be every ballplayer was trained. Take Rod Carew. Incredible hitter, sure, but he still knows how to bunt if he has to. These kids today, they don't know how to bunt 'cause they get rushed."

As a kid, I loved to hear him talk. His stories about fighting during the Depression—"We carried our clothes wrapped in newspaper to the boxing gym"—first fired my interest in boxing.

For the last eight years of his life, after my grandmother died, my grandfather was on his own. He filled his time with travel and study, and told me wonderful stories about his experiences. Shah went to Mexico to take a class on art, and he walked the museums of Mexico City. He visited with us in St. Louis, and he took classes at the local community college.

One afternoon when Shah was living in Cleveland, my aunt Audrey came home and pressed the play button on her answering machine. She heard my grandfather's slurred speech and called for an ambulance. Shah had suffered a stroke.

When I first saw him after the stroke, Shah was seated on a stationary bicycle, wearing a white shirt, gray sweatpants, and new sneakers. The wisps of gray hair that normally lay flat over the top of his head were waving in the air as he pedaled with great effort—push the right foot down, left foot down, right foot—and despite the effect of the stroke on his speech, he told me about his plans to get to Mexico again.

He never did make that trip. By the summer of 1994, he had suffered a second stroke. I visited him a few times that summer. At one point, he had to be fed through a tube connected to his stomach because he couldn't swallow. By then he was unable to speak. I remember him holding a pencil and scratching a note to my mom and aunt that read, "Don't let them starve me."

I was preparing to make a trip of my own, and he was excited for me. I was going to fly into Vienna and then take a train to Zagreb in Croatia, to work with children who were orphaned by the war in the former Yugoslavia. He communicated to my mother that Vienna had great coffee; Eric should have a cup in Vienna. If he had been able to talk, I can only imagine the soliloquy I would have received about coffeehouses in Vienna. Shah even gave my mom a few dollars so that I could enjoy a coffee.

On my last visit to see Shah before my trip, I went to the nursing home alone. I had stopped to buy him a tube of chapstick, knowing that his lips were often dry and cracked. When I arrived he was lying in his bed. I put a hand on his shoulder, and he took my other hand in his and gave it a good squeeze. I handed him the chapstick and he grasped it lightly. He focused his eyes and pursed his lips. He lifted the chapstick to his face and tried to apply it, but the tube wavered an inch away and the balm never touched his lips. I stood there and watched. The effort tired him, and he set his hand back down. I should have reached across, taken the chapstick from him, and helped him. Instead, I only watched as he struggled. Since that moment, I've looked back many times, disappointed with myself. I was motivated to fly across an ocean for adventure and a good deed, but there I was incapable of a simple helping hand with my own flesh and blood. It was the last time I would see my grandfather alive.

Shah's life had been full of real, hard experience—struggling through the Depression, fighting in World War II, raising a family in a poor neighborhood—and I know that he would have understood my desire to box, and he would have also appreciated my desire to serve.

In the summer of 1994 the war in the former Yugoslavia was raging, and campaigns of ethnic cleansing were ravaging Bosnia. After Shah's war, World War II, and the horror of the Holocaust, the world had said, "Never again." Yet every day people fled burning homes, women were assaulted, and children were orphaned by vicious acts of violence. I volunteered to work with the Project for Unaccompanied Children in Exile. Together with several other students, I raised money to cover our expenses. We intended to fly to Europe and live and work in refugee camps in Croatia.

I took a semester of Bosnian, but I found the language difficult. When I was on the train from Vienna, I was very proud that I was able to use the one complete sentence I knew in the language: *Ja sam u vlaku za Zagreb*—"I am on the train to Zagreb." How that sentence was supposed to carry me through weeks of work in refugee camps, I had no idea, but if I were ever again on a train to Zagreb, I could let people know.

On the train, a middle-aged Bosnian woman wearing jeans, a rumpled jacket, and thick-framed brown glasses heard my accent and stopped me in the passageway.

"Are you an American?"

"Yes."

She asked me where I was going and where in America I was from. Then she said, "Why isn't America doing anything?"

"Doing what?"

"Why isn't America doing anything to stop the ethnic cleansing, to stop the rapes, to stop the murders? Do you know what is happening to the people of Bosnia? You know what's happening. Now why don't you do anything about it?"

I had no answer. I tried to explain that I was here to help.

"If you're going to help, why don't you *do* anything?" Her hands were shaking. She added, "You'd help us if we had oil."

I walked past her and stood at the window of the train. We had crossed into Croatia, and I took my first look at the hills of the Croatian countryside. A red compact car was driving on the road parallel to the train tracks. I raised my hand to the open window and waved. The man riding in the passenger side of the car stuck his hand out his window and flicked me off.

I was dropped off with another volunteer next to a gravel path that led to the Puntizela refugee camp. As the car drove off, kids from the camp came running toward us. They looked like any group of American schoolchildren. Most wore clothes that had been donated by Americans or Europeans and they smiled and they were clean and they seemed well fed and healthy and happy. The only refugees I'd ever seen were on the news, and they were always portrayed as dirty and distraught and lost in misery.

The kids swamped us. They asked, "Have bonbons?" or "Have chocolate?" Those who could not speak English simply opened their hands or scrunched the tips of their fingers together and touched their lips to signal for treats. The more inquisitive began asking, "You're volunteering here?" Two boys grabbed my hand. I thought that they wanted to hold it, but they turned my wrist—they wanted to look at my watch. Another boy was running circles around us as we walked. One of the boys looking at my watch glanced up at me and then at the running-in-circles boy and then back at me and frowned and shook his head and rolled his eyes, the international signal for "that one's a bit crazy."

Behind the kids followed Dario and Jasna. A married couple, they were refugees themselves and ran the volunteer projects in the camp. Dario was about five foot seven, a barrel-chested guy with black hair and a face covered in stubble. Beneath the stubble his smile was full of joy, but twisted just enough at the corner of his mouth to make you think he was about to fire a sarcastic bullet. I reached to shake his hand.

"Hey, how are you doing? Welcome to paradise," he said with a chuckle. He spoke to the kids in Bosnian, then told us, "The kids love you already, and they'll keep loving you as long as they think you've got candy." He laughed again.

Jasna was a little shorter and much quieter. With dirty-blond hair and a meek but warm smile, she walked slightly behind Dario and barely said a word in our first meeting. Later I'd learn that Jasna's English wasn't great, but she managed a wicked sense of humor. She was the more practical of the pair. She made sure that as volunteers we had a place to stay and that we knew the work schedule. She told us when lunch would be served. It was a good team: Dario kept everyone's spirits up and Jasna kept the camp running.

The Puntizela camp was outside Pula, Croatia, a beautiful city that was home to Roman ruins, including the Arena, one of the largest amphitheaters in the world. The stone walls of the ancient structure still towered 106 feet in the air, providing shade for the ice-cream vendors who set up shop on the stone streets. The refugee camp was set in a park on the edge of the Adriatic Sea. Bright blue water glistened off a rocky beach, and the area was surrounded by tall cypress trees. The refugee families lived in trailers. The trailers were cramped, but given my expectations about how miserable refugee life was going to be, I was surprised when I saw families living in trailers at a seaside resort.

I started a soccer team with one of the refugee boys, helped in the kindergarten, played chess with the teenagers, and talked with the adults. I sat in trailers with families and drank endless cups of coffee. Beyond my one complete sentence in the language, I knew enough Bosnian phrases and could say them with enough conviction to give the false impression that I actually knew what I was talking about. I'd often sit for long periods not understanding a word as my hosts took long drags on their cigarettes, paused, and then exhaled a flurry of words and smoke, animatedly chopped the air with their hands, and kicked away from the table in disgust. I tried to nod my head at appropriate moments. At times a refugee who spoke good English — often a teenager who would roll his eyes because the old men were repeating themselves — would translate their conversation for me in dollops.

"Then the Serbs came to his house. He told them to go away, but . . ."

"And now he is talking more about his cousin . . ."

"Still more about his cousin. He was, like, twenty-eight year old."

The beautiful setting of Puntizela couldn't mask the underlying reality of what had happened to the people who had come here. I heard stories of horrific violence. Although I knew that Dario and Jasna were refugees, I didn't connect the word "refugee" to direct violence until Dario and Jasna said they were from Banja Luka.

Banja Luka was strategically important to the Serbs because it was where the old Yugoslav Army had built major military complexes and stored munitions. When the war broke out, the Serbian Army took control of the city, hanging white rags on door frames to mark Bosnian homes. Soldiers stormed these homes to take dishes, televisions, furniture, jewelry—whatever they wanted. Serbian soldiers beat old men with the butts of their rifles, smashed fingers with crowbars, and dismembered bodies with their knives. Serbian soldiers repeatedly raped women and girls. They shot or slit the throats of anyone who resisted.[1]

Mosques in Banja Luka that had stood hundreds of years were riddled with bullets; others were shelled. For some mosques stubborn enough to outlast the shelling, explosives were laid at the foundations and detonated. The fresh rubble was cleared and the land designated for use as parking lots and garbage dumps.[2]

Men, women, and children were rounded up and taken to concentration camps like Manjaca. Community leaders were singled out and taken to other locations where they were severely beaten and tortured. They often "disappeared," never to be seen again.[3] Bosnians were forced to give up the houses that they had lived in for generations, and they were made to pay for the "privilege" of leaving for refugee camps.[4] Many of the families that I met, victims of the ethnic cleansing, had been forced to grab what they could and walk away from their homes. Often, the buses packed with refugees were diverted to killing fields.

Torture and deprivation were, however, not limited to Banja Luka. In cities and towns across Bosnia, the Serbian Army forced men, women, and children into mosques and held them there for days. Occasionally they threw the Bosnians a snatch of bread or gave them a few ounces of water. The prisoners were forced to defecate on the floor of the sacred mosque where many of them had prayed and worshiped nearly every day of their lives. After starving them for days, the Serbians "offered" pork to the Bosnian Muslims and asked them to denounce the teachings of the Qur'an.[5]

The details I heard were often so sickening, I found it hard to believe that the people sitting in the trailers telling me these stories were in fact the same people who had lived them; the stories seemed to come from another world entirely.

A Bosnian man in one of the camp shelters told me that his wife had been dragged from their house and later raped. Both of his brothers had been killed. He had heard from a neighbor that one of his brothers had been tortured before he had been shot. His sister and parents lived in a different city, and he was not sure if they were alive. He lifted his shirt and showed me the scar on his stomach and chest left by a grenade that had been thrown into his house. He considered himself lucky that his children and wife were alive. He started to cry. His children—a boy and a girl—sat listening in the corner of the shelter.[6]

One night all of the refugees in Puntizela gathered for a party in a common room that sometimes served as a classroom for the school. Music played, and everyone was drinking beer. After a while some of the teenagers started to throw the empty beer bottles on the concrete floor, and shards of brown glass soon littered the room. One drunken teenager hung on my shoulder and said, "This is Bosnian tradition. Don't be scared. We drink this shit beer and party in this shit place." But many of the older refugees left and walked back to their trailers. One boy cranked the music painfully loud and yelled something I didn't understand, and then two boys jumped into each other as if in a mosh pit and started to wrestle standing on the glass-covered floor. More bottles smashed on the concrete.

I was twenty at the time, and it seemed to me that the older teenagers struggled more than anyone else in the camp. Those who were parents and grandparents in the camp were actively involved in taking care of their children, and they found purpose in that love and that work. The younger children were generally resilient, as kids are. But the war had hit the young adults just as they felt their real lives should have begun. They were trapped in the refugee camp with no prospects for a job, no prospects for further education. They had limited opportunities for fun, few chances at marriage. In their situation, I might have been smashing bottles myself.

On many nights, I sat in the common room as a radio played and the refugees talked and played chess. Denis, fifteen years old, was one of my frequent chess opponents. He wore jeans and a donated T-shirt, and often had a cigarette hanging from his lips. As we played, he would ask me questions about America, questions about where I had traveled, questions about my education.

The conversations were one-way. Every time I asked him a question, he laughed and shook his head. He didn't want to talk about his life, and what was I going to ask him? I couldn't ask him the kinds of questions I'd have asked the average American kid: What do you want to do when you graduate? What subjects do you like in school? What do you want to study? Do you have a girlfriend? What do you like to do on the weekend? Denis had no school, no job, no girlfriend, no way to think about a future beyond the camp.

Denis always used the word "shit" to describe his current life. "Shit trailers, shit food, shit clothes, shit TV." He didn't want to talk about the past. He'd smoke while we played, and most of the time he angled away from me, talking to other people while I studied the board. I would move my chess piece, he would turn his head to look at the board, move quickly, and then return to his conversation.

I'd often play chess for hours. I was a weak player, and even the eleven-year-olds sought me out. One young boy always sat and stared at me while we played. He played on the soccer team that I had started, and chess was his chance to turn the tables and coach me. After each one of his moves he would watch as I analyzed the board. When I took too long to move, he would roll a short circle in the air with his hand: "OK, OK." A moment came in every game when, after one of my moves, he would begin to shake his head, as if he had hoped that just maybe this time I might have provided some real competition. Disappointed, he would proceed to put me into checkmate. The only way I could maintain my pride was to remind the eleven-year-old, "Well, I'll see you on the soccer field tomorrow."

"OK, OK."

We gave vitamins to the kids in the kindergarten, and one day I brought a bottle of vitamins to soccer practice. With all the boys standing in a line, I handed out a "vitamin for athletes." I used a combination of English and Bosnian and charades to tell them that this would make their muscles grow. But one of the kids—nine or ten years old—yelled, "Those are the vitamins from the kindergarten." I said, "Yes, but the kindergartners can't do the exercises to make their muscles strong. If you take the vitamin *and* do pull-ups, you'll grow strong."

One of my happiest moments in the camp came when an older man in a wheelchair rolled himself out to watch our soccer game. Soon others came out with blankets. They smoked and talked and clapped as they watched the kids play. The game became an afternoon ritual. One afternoon, however, almost all of our fans were gone. Had I done something to offend them? I asked the man in the wheelchair, but my Bosnian and his English couldn't connect. I asked one of the kids where our fans were and he said, "They are watching *Dallas*."

"The TV show?"

"Yes." Every day, I learned, the women of the camp crowded around a tiny black-and-white television to watch episodes of the American show, broadcast—I believe—from Italy.

Because everything was new to me—the language, the location, the Bosnian coffee, the chess—I was learning and having a great time, and I lost sight of how hard this life was on the people around me. At some level, this trip was for me another adventure, a diversion away from the comforts of home. I could leave at any time.

Walking back to my trailer with another volunteer after lunch one day, I complained about the food: the same hot mush again. She gently suggested that my problems paled next to the refugees', and I snapped out of my selfish concern.

After several weeks I moved on to work in a second Croatian refugee camp. Gasinci camp, outside the city of Osijek, was what I had imagined a refugee camp to look like. Hundreds of prefabricated shelters had been set up, laid out in straight lines like a military encampment. In Puntizela, everyone knew each other. Gasinci, by contrast, was crowded with refugees, many of whom were strangers to one another. This was no seaside resort. Volunteers from Croatian nonprofits, as well as International Committee of the Red Cross, United Nations High Commissioner for Refugees, and UNICEF personnel were also packed into the camp.

My first morning in Gasinci, I woke suddenly to the sound of exploding artillery. I shot straight up in bed and hit my head against the upper bunk. The Croatian Army regularly conducted maneuvers on a hill near the camp, and eventually I got used to the sound. In the early years of the war, there was intense fighting between Croats and Bosnians, and despite the alliance they now shared against the Serbs, the tensions of the past still lingered in the camp. A few days into my stay, Croatian soldiers shot two puppies that the kids in the kindergarten adored. None of the kids were injured, but the refugees were supposed to be protected by the UN, and the aid workers felt that the incident had to be addressed. I watched as outraged workers for the High Commissioner for Refugees debated what to do. In the end they decided to write a letter.

Before I'd left for Bosnia, people had been debating the role of the UN in responding to the ethnic cleansing. What should the UN Protection Force be allowed to do? What role should international aid organizations play? How can the UN use its power to shape events? As I watched the outraged workers type their letter—not fifty yards from where the puppies had been shot in front of the kindergarten—I realized that the UN High Commissioner for Refugees had no real power. The United Nations only brought in aid when the people with guns allowed them to. The UN, it turned out, couldn't take a stand to protect anyone. Not the kids in the camp, and later, tragically, not the people of Srebrenica.

In July 1995 the Serbian Army began shelling Srebrenica, a town that the UN had deemed a "safe zone" for Bosnian refugees escaping the terror of the war. Days later, the Serbian Army entered the Srebrenica camp. Serbian general Ratko Mladic requested a meeting with General Thom Karremans of the Dutch United Nations peacekeeping force and demanded access to the refugees. The Dutch battalion had only four hundred or so men to protect thirty thousand refugees. Faced with the

Serbian Army's superior numbers and firepower, the peacekeepers allowed the Serbian forces to advance.

As word that they had been abandoned spread through the camps, thousands of Bosnian men fled through the woods. Those that remained were packed onto buses and driven by Serbian soldiers to soccer fields and old warehouses. Some of the men and boys were lined up and shot. At other killing fields, men and boys were mowed down by machine guns. Before they were shot, some had their eyes gouged out, their ears and noses cut off. Some were taken to warehouses, stripped down, and packed tightly inside before hand grenades were lobbed into the buildings.[7]

In all, more than eight thousand men and boys, ranging in age from fourteen to seventy-eight, were slaughtered, and nearly thirty thousand refugees were deported to Serbian-controlled territories over a period of five days. Srebrenica remains the most heinous massacre to take place on European soil since World War II.

Later, when I thought about the UN workers in Gasinci writing their letter, when I read about what had happened at Srebrenica, I realized that there was a great dividing line between all of the speeches, protests, feelings, empathy, good wishes, and words in the world, and the one thing that mattered most: protecting people through the use of force or threat of force. In situations like this, good intentions and heartfelt wishes were not enough. The great dividing line between words and results was courageous action.

Sitting in Gasinci, I understood the anger of the woman who had approached me on the train: "Why don't you *do* anything?"

I tried in my own small way to be protective. In Gasinci, a director of one of the nonprofits asked if we could bring all of the kids outside to meet a donor that afternoon.

"Why?"

"The donor wants to throw out gum to the kids and I would like you to make photographs."

I could imagine the scene: a donor standing with a bag of candy, surrounded by children, and tossing out gum like he was throwing feed to animals in a zoo. I said to the director, "Why doesn't the donor sit down with the kids and talk with them? The kids can show him what they've been working on. I can take photos of that."

"Yes, but they want photos of the donor handing out gum."

"I won't take those photographs."

"But you must."

Many of the aid-organization advertisements for refugee children made the kids look as pitiful as possible—dirty, hungry, begging. The children I worked with in the Gasinci camp did need help, but they were also entitled to their dignity. You wouldn't walk into an elementary-school recess in America and start tossing out gum and taking photos of "desperate children." So why here? These kids were smart and creative. They were survivors; they deserved more than to be showcased like animals in a zoo.

"Actually, no." In an effort to be sure that I was understood, I added, "I don't must," and I walked away.

One night, as buses filled with refugees drove into Gasinci, a Red Cross worker told me that some of the families had been forced from their homes and then made to watch as their houses were burned to the ground. In the shelters, I listened as old men smoked and argued about the future. Occasionally someone would translate, but I couldn't follow the conversation very well. The smoke was always heavy. Once I cracked the window an inch and stuck my nose near the window to get a breath. The men laughed at me. But the conversation was serious. One man was shouting and gesturing at the camp. He believed that all the young Bosnian men living there should be out fighting.

I remember a man in the camp telling me—as he gestured at his hut—that he appreciated the shelter. He appreciated the bread. He pointed to where his children could play, and, he said, he appreciated the volunteers and the crayons and the schoolwork. But, he said, "we need the Serbs to stop burning villages and raping women and killing brothers."

• • •

It was in Gasinci that I got my first lesson in international diplomacy. There was a woman in the camp who worked with the Project for Unaccompanied Children in Exile. She was married to a Croat, and her sister was married to a Serb. This was not uncommon. Lots of Croats and Serbians intermarried in the former Yugoslavia. Yet with in-laws on different sides, the war had strained the family. She told me, however, that her entire family was gathering for a dinner and she invited me to take a break from the refugee camp. She was very insistent. "You must come to my house. I will give you good meal." And so I went.

"Welcome, welcome. Eric is from America. He is working with Project for Unaccompanied Children." I made my way around the living room of a very comfortable home in the city of Osijek, filled with the smells of warm food and the tension of relatives who didn't much like each other. I said hello and learned names, and then we were seated.

The two sisters sat at opposite ends of a long wooden table lined with children and friends and family. During dinner, I was asked about my work, my studies. Some of the conversation was in Serbo-Croatian, and though I couldn't understand the words, I could sense the strain between the two sisters: short words, tight smiles, narrowed eyes. They passed around seasoned chicken, potatoes, vegetables. After we finished the main course, the hostess disappeared into the kitchen and then reemerged. "Eric, you must eat my dessert. Everything is of my produce, this cherry, this cake, this icing, all of my produce. Please, you must have some."

Then her sister followed quickly out from the kitchen. "And this dessert is of my produce. Please. This is of my produce."

The other sister said, "Choose what you like." Both sides of the family looked on.

It was my first exercise in international negotiation. *Should I side with the Croatian host cake or partake of the Serbian pie? Should I be objective and pick the dessert I really wanted? How could I ease tensions and create peace?* The sisters watched at either end of the table. I reached for one metal cake server, and then I grabbed another. With a server in each hand, I dug in and plopped a piece of each dessert on my plate at the same time. "These both look so good. I hate to take so much but you have to excuse me. There is no way I could pass up one of these." I felt like King Solomon.

Then my host said, "Please, you can eat them now. Tell us what one is your favorite."

Checkmate.

At the end of my work in Gasinci, I returned to Zagreb and met up with the other American volunteers. We had a few days to finish the report we were writing about unaccompanied children, and one night we took a trolley into the center of the city for a night out. It was late when we walked back to our trolley stop for the ride back to the hotel, and we realized that the trolleys had stopped running. The square was empty of people, and there were no taxis. Our hotel was several miles outside Zagreb, and we didn't even know which direction to start walking.

As we discussed what to do next, the sound of laughter came from around the corner of a building. Out stepped a gangly Croatian, maybe six foot four, who was flirting with his tipsy girlfriend. He pinched her and she playfully slapped him. With the rest of the city deserted, I had no other options. I walked up to them and used my best Croatian.

"Gdje je, Hotel Park?"—Where is Hotel Park?

He whipped his head around when he heard me speak. "You are America! Ohhhhhhh my sweet home Alabama! OK 'merica, OK 'merica. Follow me." So we followed him as he staggered along, pointing to me and singing, "America, America, Sweet Home Alabama!" He tugged at his girlfriend as he skipped through an underground pedestrian tunnel, his voice reverberating. "Sweet Home, Alabama!" I didn't know if he was taking us to Hotel Park, Alabama, or to his house for a drink.

"OK 'merica," he said. He stood at drunken attention and pointed. "Odel Park." I might be the only person in the world for whom this is true, but still today every time I hear "Sweet Home Alabama," I think of Zagreb.

• • •

I was in Zagreb when I called home. My aunt answered and I talked with her quickly before she handed the phone to my mom. "Hello," she said, and I knew from her voice that my grandfather was dead. When she actually got the words out, she started to cry. "I thought he was waiting for you to come home."

I finished the call and set the phone down. I thought of my last moments with Shah. An inch lower to touch his lips. That's all it would have taken. Here I was in a foreign country, out to save the world from genocide, and I didn't even have the courage to reach over the bedside to help my grandfather.

When I returned to Duke at the end of the summer, a friend invited me to speak at a local church. The congregation, she said, wanted to learn more about the ethnic cleansing in Bosnia.

On a Sunday afternoon, I stood at the front of a room before some twenty people seated in metal folding chairs. The man who introduced me said, "We've all read in the newspaper about what's happening in Bosnia, but you're the first person any of us have heard from who's actually been there."

I pressed the forward button on a slide projector and proceeded to show my photographs. A picture appeared on the screen of a girl drawing a house on the ground with a chalky rock.

The photos were mostly of individual children and families living in the two refugee camps where I had worked. I pressed the forward button, click-clack, click-clack, and showed a picture of refugees stepping off the bus into Gasinci, and commented on how many of them had lost friends and family members.

Click-clack, click-clack.

"This woman is knitting as part of a project set up by the Red Cross."

Click-clack, click-clack.

"This boy's mother was killed in Bosnia . . ."

Click-clack, click-clack.

"This is where all the kids went for classes . . ."

Click-clack, click-clack.

"These are the shelters where refugees lived in the camp."

With each turn of the carousel, I could see that this was the first time that the members of this church had connected on a human level to what they saw and heard about in the news. When they read about thousands of people driven from their homes, it was abstract. When they saw one family dragging a bag across a field in search of shelter, they understood.

When I finished showing the photographs, the lights flickered back on and I offered to take questions.

A white-haired gentleman raised his hand just above his head, and in a dignified Carolina accent said, "This may seem like a silly question, but where did they get their food when they were in the refugee camps?"

The questions continued like this.

"Where did they get their clothes? How did they wash their clothes?"

"Did any of them get to return to their homes?"

"What happened to the rest of the girl's family?"

The folks in the church wanted to know not about an issue, but about another human being's life.

The photographs and video footage that people saw on TV were often of moments of incredible tragedy: women wailing, children bleeding. The photographs I showed were of people who were very much alive, some of them smiling, and the folks in the church didn't just see a little Bosnian girl drawing a picture of a home. They saw a little girl who could have been their daughter, one of their friend's daughters, or their own granddaughter.

The pictures I shared from Croatia contrasted with the typical international aid photographs that showed desperate people, desperate babies, in faraway places. My pictures didn't fit that story. When looking at photographs of ordinary people doing ordinary things—albeit in a situation that was anything but ordinary—it was hard to dismiss the war in the former Yugoslavia as simply "ethnic violence" or "ancient hatred."

One of the church members asked, "Why did they want to kill the Bosnians?"

Before I'd left for Croatia, I would have had at least a partial answer to the question. I would have described the rise of nationalist politics and ethnic tensions, the weak response of the U.S. and the United Nations. After having lived in the refugee camps, I was, I think, a bit wiser, and I said, "I don't really know *why,* any more than I know why any human being ever abuses or tortures or kills any other human being."

The final question came from an elderly lady sitting in the back row. She asked, "What can we do?" It was a simple question, and one that I should have anticipated, but it caught me off-guard. I could have told her to send used clothing and toys overseas, or to donate money to organizations that helped refugees. But the anger of the woman I had met on the train from Vienna—*Why isn't America doing anything?*— and the words of the refugee in Gasinci—*We need the Serbs to stop burning villages and raping women and killing brothers*—echoed in my head.

The pause extended longer than I had intended and the audience looked expectantly at me for an answer.

"We can certainly donate money and clothing, and we can volunteer in the refugee camps. But in the end these acts of kindness are done after the fact. They are done after people have been killed, their homes burned, their lives destroyed. Yes, the clothing, the bread, the school; they are all good and they are all much appreciated. But I suppose we have to behave the same way we would if any person—our kids, our sisters, brothers, parents—were threatened. If we really care about these people, we have to be willing to protect them from harm."

# 5 ☆

# Rwanda

MY SUMMER WORKING with Bosnian refugees had been organized by one of my professors, Neil Boothby. It had left me hungry to do more: to document the lives of people living with courage through tragedy and find a way to help them. Before I graduated, I accompanied Neil, who had left Duke to join the United Nations High Commissioner for Refugees, to Rwanda. There, I would witness suffering on a scale not seen since the Holocaust and the purges of Stalin and Mao.

On the drive to Kigali, I bounced in my seat as we bumped along the rutted dirt road in a white Land Rover, a bold, black "UN" painted on its door. Attached to the vehicle's front bumper was the tallest radio antenna I'd ever seen. A reed of thin metal, it shot twelve full feet into the air and jerked and danced as we rocked along the roads. I patted my lucky shirt—a pale safari-style shirt that I'd worn into China and Croatia—to check—probably for the seventh time—that my passport, my money, my ticket home, were all still hidden and safe.

The name "Rwanda"—virtually unknown and unspoken in the West only a year earlier—had become synonymous with death, cruelty, madness, rivers choked with the bloated bodies of the dead, and piles of human corpses so numerous that bulldozers had to be used to ingloriously corral them into open-pit graves. It was May 1995.

I watched through the window of the car and studied every detail of the streets. Two boys in tattered shirts ran barefoot along the road beside us—the bigger boy chasing the smaller with a stick. A wooden roadside stand offered cigarettes, phone cards, and cookies and crackers. Its owner—a willow of a man standing barefoot in oversized black pants, a pinched black belt, and a red button-down shirt—raised his hand in a halfhearted gesture to slow us, as though we might make a purchase. A boy soldier with an AK-47 strapped over his right shoulder fixed unfriendly eyes on the UN vehicle, and then on Neil.

Neil had moved his family here. He served as the senior director of programs for the orphaned and abandoned and lost children of the genocide. As in Bosnia, these children were referred to as "unaccompanied," a word that belied the horrific violence by which they had often been deprived of their parents.

Neil spoke to the driver: "Tournez à gauche."

After French-speaking Belgians had colonized Rwanda in the 1920s, many Rwandans became fluent in French, in addition to speaking the native language of Kinyarwanda. Many Rwandans blamed the Belgians for exacerbating—or, some argued, inventing—differences between the country's Tutsi and Hutu ethnic groups in order to facilitate colonial rule. By claiming that the Tutsis had Caucasian ancestry, the Belgians "justified" their superiority. Tutsis held many dominant positions in society, and to hold a Tutsi identity card conferred privileges. But identities were not fixed. There were wide friendships and extensive intermarriage among Hutus and Tutsis, and for the right price it was possible to purchase a Tutsi identity card and "become" a Tutsi.

We turned down a side street and pulled into the United Nations compound. The compound stood on the grounds of an old elementary school that had been converted into offices for aid workers. It was guarded by UN soldiers from India. Dressed in sloppy fatigues, the soldiers on duty listlessly opened the gate.

Neil showed me his office: a wood table and metal chair in an old classroom that he shared with a UN worker from Canada. The various international aid workers were all dressed in hiking boots, hiking pants, and safari shirts. Books written in a dozen different languages were tucked into their cargo pockets. The entire world, it seemed, had sent men and women to help—but only after more than eight hundred thousand Tutsis had been slaughtered by Hutus over the course of one hundred days.

In 1959 the Hutus overthrew the ruling Tutsi authority and shortly thereafter gained independence from the Belgians. The Hutu leadership ran the country for three decades, marked by outbreaks of violence in 1959, 1961, 1963, 1967, and 1973.[1] Thousands of Hutus and Tutsis were killed, and thousands of Tutsis fled to neighboring countries. In 1973, Hutu president Juvenal Habyarimana successfully executed a coup d'état, and instituted one-party rule two years later. For a while the killings were stanched, but Tutsis continued to be excluded from positions of power. By the late 1980s, Tutsi military forces that had been part of the exodus threatened to sweep back into Rwanda and retake power, and in 1990 the Hutu elite used government-owned media to begin a propaganda campaign proclaiming that Hutus were the "pure" and "true" Rwandan race. On leaflets handed out in run-down bars, in newspapers sold by street vendors, and on radios strapped to bicycles, messages of hate and racial superiority were carried everywhere. At the same time, the government and allied groups began to stockpile machetes and build the Interahamwe—groups of militiamen organized to kill at a moment's notice. Intermittent violence plagued Rwanda during the early 1990s, and the rhetoric of bloodshed grew increasingly strident. Ethnic tensions ratcheted higher when the first democratically elected president of Burundi, on the southern border of Rwanda, was assassinated by his Tutsi military in 1993. Some propagandists encouraged the killing of Tutsi children. As one Hutu broadcaster said, "To kill the big rats, you have to kill the little rats."[2]

On April 6, 1994, a rocket hit Hutu president Habyarimana's plane, and Habyarimana, along with the Hutu president of Burundi, Cyprien Ntaryimira, was killed in the crash. Habyarimana's extremist military advisors blamed the tragedy on Tutsi forces. Within hours, the Interahamwe flooded the streets, carrying machetes, grenades, and AK-47s.[3]

One hundred days later, the most heinous genocide since the Holocaust was over. Between eight hundred thousand and one million Tutsis and moderate Hutus had been slaughtered.

Driving through Kigali, Neil and I had passed the gates of the Hôtel des Mille Collines. "During the genocide, that hotel was a haven for refugees," Neil told me. The manager of the hotel, Paul Rusesabagina, saved 1,268 lives during the genocide, a story later made famous by the movie *Hotel Rwanda*. Paul was destined to become a friend, but at the time, I didn't even know his name.

Neil and some of his colleagues from the United Nations Children's Fund were using humanitarian aid funds to pay for programs to aid war-affected children across Rwanda and in the bordering nations of Tanzania, Uganda, Burundi, and Zaire. The UN often made grants to nonprofit organizations working on the ground, yet many of the reports that these nonprofits sent back from the field—"73 women and children attended a health clinic and were treated," or "24 adults were counseled"—were vague. Neil and his team needed to know more. It was difficult to tell which programs were having an impact and which were inefficient, and while Neil and his team frequently went into the field, they couldn't see everything with their own eyes. Neil had given me a simple mission: accompany UN aid workers and other humanitarian personnel to visit the sites of aid projects throughout Rwanda. Look. Listen. Ask questions. Take photographs. Take notes. Then report back.

I was not—as many were in Rwanda—an academic researcher bedecked with degrees. I was not an anthropologist. I was not a social worker. I was not a nurse or a doctor. With only one summer of experience with Bosnian refugees under my twenty-one-year-old belt, I was an expert in nothing.

My inexperience, however, had a double edge. Although I was unaware of some of the basic facts of the relief effort in Rwanda—I didn't know, for example, that the Red Cross missions from different countries could be antagonistic to each other—I was also unencumbered by prejudice and expectations, so I could ask simple questions.

"If the aid workers have access to two four-by-four trucks, shouldn't they be bringing health services out to the villagers rather than having sick families, sick kids, walk miles to get to the health clinic? Why don't we drive from village to village and bring the equipment and doctors directly to the people who need them? Wouldn't that allow us to serve more people, especially the ones who are too sick to get here on their own?" Often, there were good reasons why things were run a certain way, but my questions sometimes pointed to flaws in the system, as well as human flaws: corruption, vice, laziness.

Another advantage was that I was a volunteer. I had paid for my plane ticket and my few expenses with documentary-photography grants, so no one owned my time. I was, moreover, willing to travel long distances in cramped trucks to visit remote projects. Whatever I lacked in knowledge, I tried to make up for with energy.

One day I jumped into a truck with another UN aid worker and off we drove for the border between Rwanda and Tanzania. "We're going to monitor a repatriation," the aid worker, Jill, told me. "These are refugees who fled and are now crossing back from Tanzania into Rwanda."

Jill was a small-boned American who spoke fast, one word following the next in an intelligent, intense train of thoughts as she recounted her time in Rwanda. Born Jewish, she had converted to Christianity. She had a degree in library science from the University of Hawaii, short brown hair, and a laugh that spilled out fast and stopped short.

"How many are coming across?" I asked.

"Maybe a hundred, maybe two hundred. We never really know until we get there."

When we arrived at the border, I watched as a stream of refugees walked into Rwanda across the no man's land between the two nations. Under their fists men carried blue and white plastic containers filled with water. Over their shoulders they carried burlap sacks and plastic bags filled with their possessions. They sweated under their loads, many of them dressed in jackets. These were the only clothes they owned, and they wore them back into the country they had fled.

The women carried children in their arms or wrapped tightly against their backs. They wore cloth headwraps, on top of which they balanced misshapen bags full of clothes and pans and jugs and keepsakes and other objects that constituted all their belongings. Any child who could walk could help, and so young girls carried their small brothers and sisters bundled and sleeping across their backs, and dragged jugs for water and bags full of food. I saw a black piece of Samsonite luggage being dragged on its last stubborn wheel across the stony dirt as the refugees made their way to a UN water truck.

The water truck sat on the Rwandan side of the border, and I began photographing the children as they went to fill their jugs. Intrigued by my camera, the kids posed and played in front of it, striking poses with their fists in the air and their arms draped about each other. I laughed with them as they clowned. A girl smiled under a wide-brimmed umbrella, its yellow and red panels faded by the sun.

I was just about to take the girl's picture when I felt a hand grip my shoulder from behind. A man with an AK-47 slung over his shoulder spun me around, grabbing my camera with his other hand. I yanked it away from him. He was two inches shorter than I was, and I could tell from his effort to take my camera that he was weak. I could also tell from his eyes that he was scared. He pointed at my camera and shook his head, saying, "No. No," as he reached for it again. I turned my shoulder toward him and pulled the camera back. "No," he said.

"OK, OK," I said. "OK." I put my hand lightly on his shoulder. "OK."

"No photo."

"OK," I repeated.

"No." He waggled his finger at the unmarked border just past the water truck and once again grabbed for my camera. When I again pivoted away from him, he turned his palm up and curled his fingers toward himself, the universal symbol for "Give it to me."

"OK," I said. "I will give you my film. OK." I hit the rewind button on the camera and as the film started to rewind, his eyes shot from me to the camera and back again — was I playing some trick on him? — and I kept my hand on his shoulder. He stood there under his black beret,

sweating through his fatigues. I popped the film out of the camera
and handed the roll to him. He took the film, and suddenly a wave
of relief broke over him and he smiled at me—sweat gathered on his
brow—and he said, "Yes."

I walked back to Jill and we stood and watched as dozens of families
straggled across the border. They filled their jugs at the water truck and
boarded a bus that the UN had chartered to take them into Rwanda.
They packed into the bus, four and five people per bench, bags of belongings piled in their laps and in the aisles, off to see what remained
of the places they had abandoned months ago. Would their homes still
be standing? Would other families be living there? If their homes were
gone or occupied, where would they sleep tonight?

Men climbed atop the bus. Boys handed up bags and jugs and boxes
to be lashed to the roof. Teenage girls with baby brothers and sisters
strapped to their backs stopped at the entrance to the bus and shifted
the younger children into their arms. I admired these families, if only
for their stubborn will to keep going. Back at college I'd been reading
about courage in my philosophy classes. There were a number of defi-
nitions of courage, but now I was seeing it in its simplest form: you do
what has to be done day after day, and you never quit.

During another trip into the field, we wound over the hills of Rwanda
on our way to a health care clinic. As our tires splattered mud, we
passed small houses nestled into the lush hills. Alongside the road,
a boy wrapped his arms around the trunk of a tree. He pressed the
side of his face against the rippled bark as if he were resting his cheek
against the belly of his grandfather. Then he set his legs to push, and he
scooted up the trunk and knocked ripe avocados to the ground. Our
windows were rolled halfway down, and as we passed the fruit fields,
I could smell tea leaves and the sweetness of newly ripened bananas.
Coffee bushes were bursting with ruby-red coffee fruit. Thin farmers
swung hoes to claw at the brown earth of the terraced hillside.

I saw only a small ribbon of a vibrant country. To the north of
Kigali, silverback gorillas roamed the jungles of Volcanoes National

Park. Many Tutsi rebels resided in this area, and one of the many concerns about the violence in Rwanda and Zaire was that it would destroy the habitat or increase the poaching of these endangered species. In the northeastern grasslands of Rwanda, giraffe, waterbuck, sable and roan antelope, aardvark, zebra, buffalo, black rhinoceros, elephant, hippopotamus, and crocodile called the plains their home.[4] On early mornings, the place took on a mystical quality as fog clung to the mountains. To the southeast, the forests supported thirteen species of primates and hundreds of species of birds that rose every morning with the sun.[5] It was a tragedy that such a beautiful country, so vibrantly full of life, had become synonymous with mass killing.

Yet the images of refugee camps and border crossings that flooded the international broadcast media did not tell the whole story. They left an impression of desperate, downtrodden, despairing people. I quickly learned that the media traffics in tragedy, but often misses stories of strength.

At the clinic, I saw dozens of women and children sitting in the grass talking under the high sun. Many of these women had walked with their children for miles in hopes of getting bandages and antibiotics at the clinic, and now they waited. They had carried children with earaches and children with blurry vision. There were other families, however, whose children seemed healthy and playful, and when I asked one woman why she had come to the clinic, she said, "So my son can play and also to talk to the doctor." Some of them had come for conversation. They waved me over. The spokeswoman for a cluster of curious women asked, "You have children?"

"No," I said, "I do not have any children." She translated this to her friends. Then I said, "Your children are beautiful." They all smiled.

I sat down in the grass. It was a wide-open day, and for a few moments there under the high sun as children ran and played, I felt as though I might have been at a kid's birthday party in a park. At any minute, someone might bring out a cake.

A Rwandan aid worker, a middle-aged woman with her hair wound atop her head, sat down next to me. She had an air of gravity, and the other women turned their eyes toward her. The aid worker's dress was a single sheet of blue cloth wrapped crisply about her. She smiled. I later found out that she had raised five children, that she was a former schoolteacher and a survivor of the genocide. Her husband had not survived. She had a particular way of pulling her hands through the air to illustrate points as she spoke, almost like she was conducting a symphony. She knew some of the women seated here, and she seemed to have taken on the role of counselor or assessor of needs at the clinic. Women started to tell the stories of their survival. The aid worker translated for me snatches of detail and dialogue.

I heard stories of families fleeing for their lives, parents running with their children into the forest to escape machete-wielding packs of thugs. A woman whose arm had been injured in a machete attack told the aid worker that she had been mistaken for dead and thrown in a pile of corpses by the side of the road. There she waited all night until the Interahamwe—exhausted by the hard labor of raping and hacking human beings to death—fell into a drunken sleep in the early morning. Only then did she run away.[6] Another woman explained that her neighbor—a woman she had played with as a child—had a son who joined the Interahamwe and became a murderer. The stories they told were straightforward: "Then she ran out of her house, but her sister was behind, and they caught her and they raped and killed her that afternoon."

I struggled with taking photographs that day. I wanted to capture their portraits, to share what I saw with others. Few Americans had seen this: Strong people. Survivors. Solid. Steadfast. I knew that these women weren't perfect, and that it was foolish to cast someone as saintly simply because she had suffered. These women might also have been trivial and jealous and mean and small. But the enormity of their achievement outweighed their human faults. These women had suffered more than I could have ever imagined, and they still were willing to welcome me, to talk with me. After all the betrayal they had lived through, all the hardship, they were still willing to trust a stranger.[7] If people can live through genocide and retain compassion, if they can take strength from pain, if they are able, still, to laugh, then certainly we can learn something from them.

And yet I hesitated to lift my camera. Photography is an art that—perhaps like no other—has an element of capture and possession, and because of that it can have an element of aggression. In some cultures people believe that if you take their photograph you are literally carrying away a layer of their souls. If I raised my camera, I would be asking to take a piece of each person who had suffered and then to share their story with others. As I sat debating about whether I should take pictures here, one woman stood before me, propping up her young child on his two wobbly legs, encouraging me to take his photograph.

She smiled at me and laughed, and when I lifted my camera, I looked through the viewfinder and saw a whole group of women smiling back at me.

Driving back to Kigali, I thought about what I was trying to do. Some people had spent years serving in Rwanda. I was going to be here for six weeks. How was I supposed to contribute? I decided I could at least take photographs like the ones I had just snapped, and show Americans a glimpse of Rwandan lives, with their many facets: joy, loss, displacement, strength, hardship, compassion.

I had learned as a teenager the importance of understanding how others lived. When I was sixteen years old, Bruce Carl, my Sunday school teacher, took me—a kid from the suburbs—to spend the night in a homeless shelter in downtown St. Louis.

Bruce was a former basketball player, probably about six foot two, and he bounded through life with the happy energy of a man with good news to share. He directed a youth leadership program, and he encouraged those of us in the group to question authority and also to serve. When he took us to the homeless shelter, he said, "I want you to listen. Learn."

And so on a winter night in an urban church, I sipped chicken soup from a Styrofoam cup, pale crackers floating and softening and breaking as I talked with homeless men. When one of the men mentioned his job, my face betrayed my surprise, and he said, "You thought none of us had a job?"

"Yes, I did think that." I said, "I'm sorry."

"Don't apologize, young man; how about you just work my shift tomorrow?" He burst out laughing, and the rest of the night he kept telling everyone, "Young man here gonna work my shift tomorrow, he gonna work my shift."

Later, I stood with two other men at a window looking out on a freezing St. Louis night. As the shelter doors were locked, I saw a man walking hunched over on the other side of the street. He leaned into the icy wind. "Tonight's a bad night to be out," said one of the men.

Later that night, Bruce sat down next to me. I was surprised when he said, "This is terrible."

"What's wrong?" I asked.

He lowered his voice. "They're giving food and shelter, but they don't have any job-training or substance-abuse programs. They keep running things this way, these people will stay homeless forever." Just as Bruce was challenging the participants in his leadership program by bringing us to the shelter, he wanted to see the men in the shelter challenged as well. Just as Bruce respected us, he respected the homeless men, and he believed that if you respected someone, then you had to ask something of them. These men, he believed, should be involved in their own recovery.

Bruce was both compassionate and demanding. Compassion was primary. He thought it criminal that people could grow up oblivious and unresponsive to the suffering of others. These are your *neighbors,* he would say. But he was hardheaded enough to know that having a loving, wide-open heart was only a start.

In Rwanda, I photographed some unforgettable scenes. Hundreds of orphaned young children on a playing field, dressed in donated clothes, packed together and bouncing up and down on their toes in some game, following the chants of a man yelling through a bullhorn. A church full of the skeletal remains of dozens of people who had sought shelter from the genocide, only to be attacked with grenades and machetes.

America had turned its back when we knew that the genocide was happening. Two days after the assassination of Habyarimana, major U.S. newspapers reported massive killings of the Tutsi population. On April 11, 1994, the undersecretary of defense, the key advisor to the secretary of defense, read a memo that stated that "hundreds of thousands of deaths" would ensue. Another memo stated that the Rwandan government wanted to eliminate the entire Tutsi population.[8] We knew.

Roméo Dallaire, the UN commander in Rwanda, estimated that with just five thousand well-equipped troops, we could have saved eight hundred thousand people. But instead of acting, the global community dragged its feet. U.S. secretary of state Madeleine Albright delayed the vote in the United Nations to send troops. Even after the UN finally agreed to a resolution authorizing the sending of troops, months passed before the soldiers actually landed. With every day that ticked by, another ten thousand Tutsis died. After two and a half months of UN inactivity, eight African nations volunteered to send their own men, provided they could get armored personnel carriers. Instead of providing the equipment to these willing nations, the United States leased it to the UN.[9] Nothing arrived in time to save a single life.

Almost four years after the genocide, President Bill Clinton visited Rwanda and spoke to the Rwandan people. He said, "We did not act quickly enough after the killing began . . . We did not immediately call these crimes by their rightful name: genocide."[10] His words did nothing to bring back the dead or to erase the memories of brutality.

One afternoon in Kigali, as I sat outside a restaurant waiting for a ride, I struck up a conversation with a Rwandan man who sat beside me. He had studied English in Kigali and hid with his sister and two young neighbor girls during the violence. He told me that during the genocide he thought of Elie Wiesel—the Holocaust survivor—and he asked me if I'd read Wiesel's memoir *Night*.

"Yes, I have," I said. "It's a wonderful book."

"Yes. It is a powerful story."

The world is full of stories of courage, too infrequently told. Many people risked their lives to care for others in Rwanda. I found that those courageous people often drew upon stories from their faith and their family. There were people, for example, who offered shelter to neighbors and friends who were in danger. Some felt alone at the time, the only person in the village providing secret shelter. Yet there were many such people across the country. I heard many stories of courage, many versions of Paul Rusesabagina and *Hotel Rwanda*.[11]

At one point during my stay, Neil dropped me off on the Rwandan side of the border with Zaire. In Zaire, I'd learn a lesson in diplomacy and political corruption, and I'd get a taste of the complexities of international charity.

In front of me in the customs-inspection line was a man dressed as a priest—gray suit, white clerical collar. As the priest approached the customs desk, he lifted a brown satchel onto the table. I watched as the young customs agent unsnapped a silver buckle and pulled the sides of the satchel open, his eyes growing wide. Gingerly putting his hand in the bag, he pulled out a short pile of American hundred-dollar bills. I'd never seen before, and have never seen since, such piles of money—stacks of hundreds bound together crisply and tied with rubber bands. The priest was carrying, it seemed, some forty thousand dollars.

After the satchel had been emptied and the money repacked, the priest rebuckled the bag and walked into Zaire. Zaire was a dangerous place. Some of the Hutu refugees in the camps in Zaire had killed and incited others to kill during the genocide. Rumors swirled that these genocidaires were using the camps to regroup and rearm. Some of the rumors involved possible French government financing of weapons for the largely Francophone Hutus. Other rumors implicated priests in the Catholic Church. I had no idea if any of these rumors were true, but as I watched the man dressed as a priest walk into Zaire, I was reminded of how much more I still had to learn.

My hiking backpack held a few shirts, film, pens, and notebooks. I passed quickly through customs and walked toward Zaire. Twenty yards of dusty road separated the Rwandan point of exit from the Zairian point of entry. As I stepped into Zaire, I bent slightly to duck under the arm of a traffic gate. A man sitting on a rickety chair next to a card table stuck his hand out, and I handed him my passport.

"Do you have a visa?"

"No, I'm sorry, I don't have a visa."

"You must go back to Rwanda to get a visa."

"Where in Rwanda?"

"In Kigali."

I had been told that fifty bucks would get me across the border. I didn't know if the fee was legitimate or an established bribe.

"I thought I could get my paperwork taken care of here."

"Well, it is difficult to do, but it is possible."

"I understand that the fee is fifty dollars, or perhaps you could accept this from me as a thank-you for your help and an apology for the inconvenience I've caused."

"Yes, no problem, sir."

Using a mangled ink pen, I scratched my name on a sheet of white "entry point" paper. The official took the paper, spun in his seat, and lifted a rock that sat on a tall stack of stained forms. He put the sheet of paper I had just signed on top and replaced the rock. I was officially in Zaire.

As I stepped toward the customs hut in Zaire, a military jeep came barreling toward me, dust rising. The jeep stopped five feet from me. A soldier wearing a black T-shirt and a black beret stood in the back of the jeep, and he aimed a mounted machine gun at my chest. With his left hand, the soldier pointed to a flag being raised behind the customs hut. A scratchy recording of music played in the background. Now I understood. There was a ceremony. An anthem was being played. I needed to pay my respects. I stood straight and looked at the flag. A bead of sweat trickled down the right side of the soldier's face. He narrowed his eyes at me. The gun was still pointed at my chest, his right index finger an inch from the trigger. Once the flag was raised, the soldier shouted at the driver, the vehicle barreled away, and I stepped with shaking legs into the customs hut.

The soldier inside pointed to the floor, and I dropped my bag there. As he stumbled toward my bag I could smell that he had been drinking. He unzipped my backpack and pushed my clothes back and forth. He then stood and looked at me with glazed, bloodshot eyes and lifted his hand in front of my face, rubbing his thumb against the four fingers of his right hand—he wanted money. With his left hand, he made a fist, thumb out, and tilted his head back—he wanted alcohol. I played dumb. "No, I don't have any alcohol." He made the money and drinking motions again. Again I played dumb.

Three other soldiers carrying AK-47s walked into the hut. I studied every detail of their hands, their weapons. I had been warned by Neil that aid workers had been shot and killed in Zaire. I imagined myself having to wrestle a rifle from one of them. Who would I grab? How? They mumbled to each other, and one of them bent over the bag and pushed again at my clothes. Another soldier blocked the entrance. I knew that they intended to rob me of something, and I thought about bolting through the door, but where would I run? Back to Rwanda? My mind was racing through the possibilities of escape and the paying of bribes when a Land Rover four-by-four pulled up outside the customs hut.

Out stepped a white woman with blond hair that stood three inches higher than the top of her head. She wore a big smile. Before I'd heard her say a word, I knew: *American.* She carried a bag of cookies in one hand and a carton of apple juice in the other. As soon as she said "Howdy, y'all" to the Zairian soldiers, I knew that I was safe. She handed out the juice and cookies—"Y'all be good now"—and the soldiers smiled back. I grabbed my bag and jumped in the truck, and we were on our way.

My savior was a born-again Christian from Texas who had come to work in Zaire with the nonprofit Food for the Hungry. Karen was the first woman I had ever met who talked about Satan as if he were a ubiquitous and decidedly unpleasant neighbor who was hard to shake.

"Oh yeah, well Satan's just busy as can be here, busy as can be. You know, talkin' with people, corruptin' their minds, turnin' their hearts to evil. Just yesterday, we had a woman never did read her Bible, just get up and start a fight with another refugee over a cooking ladle. Well no wonder, she was just sittin' there all day havin' a little conversation with Satan."

She jerked the wheel and then quickly righted the truck. "Yep, Satan is *everywhere*," and I wondered for a moment if we had just avoided hitting Satan in the street.

Goma, Zaire, was home to the largest of the refugee camps surrounding Rwanda. Some 1.2 million survivors were packed together on an arid, rocky volcanic plain. The majority of the refugees had walked dozens of miles carrying their youngest children and everything they hoped to keep. In a train of refugees miles long on a road packed with the distraught, many spent the journey desperately afraid that they would become separated from their children.

They arrived in a camp that festered with unhygienic latrines and muddy water, a scarcity of food, and disease. When the refugees first settled in Goma, a cholera epidemic swept through the camp and carried thousands to their deaths. Refugees hiked for miles to chop down trees for cooking wood, so the area around Goma was quickly deforested. Refugees built shelters of rocks and sticks that they covered with the blue tarps provided by the United Nations. They filled these rocky hovel homes with donated blankets on which lay their often-sick children, while the parents waited in long lines for food distributed by international aid organizations.

The United Nations High Commissioner for Refugees, United Nations Children's Fund, Save the Children, World Vision, and a legion of workers from other small nonprofit organizations buzzed about the camp. I was there months after the first refugees had arrived, but the camp still had no central organization. The Red Cross put up a large wooden board nailed to two wooden poles dug in the ground. On the board families and aid workers posted pictures of missing children and pictures of children found living alone in the camp. The UNHCR was nominally in charge, but it lacked the personnel to effectively organize the camp, and the Rwandans had little interest in being controlled by the UN. By night the camp often turned violent as old scores were settled, and as the sun fell most of the aid workers drove out of the camp to houses nearby, where they slept behind security walls protected by armed guards.

The UN workers came from around the world. Many of them were highly qualified professionals: an engineer from Guatemala, a logistician from New Zealand, a doctor from Bangladesh. Some of them were motivated by the UN mission, but many also came for the attractive Western salaries, the generous per diems, the schools for their children, the homes in Nairobi. The most intensely motivated volunteers—those who worked twelve to fourteen hours per day for no or very low pay at small nonprofit organizations—were often religious, and those that I came to know were mostly American evangelical Christians.

They began every day, every meeting, and every meal in prayer. They were absolutely committed to saving souls and to saving lives, and they worked with a feverish intensity, as if the day of reckoning might come at the end of the week. While some of them fit the stereotype of the clueless Christian missionary—one once asked, "Why doesn't the president of Africa send more food?"—many were both deeply committed and deeply knowledgeable. They had attempted to learn the language, they understood the culture, and they made real friends among the refugees.

At their worst, the evangelicals seemed indifferent to the feelings or experiences of the men and women around them. One day I was photographing an outdoor church service in Goma. Karen stood up to preach, and a refugee translated as she spoke. Karen explained to the crowd of genocide survivors sitting on the rocks under the high sun, "If you do not make Jesus Christ your personal savior, you will go to hell." She pulled a book from her chair to demonstrate. "It is a law, like the law of gravity." She held the book out with a straight arm and then let it fall. It thudded on the platform.

"It is like the law of gravity. It is a law. Accept Jesus, or spend an eternity in hell."

After Karen spoke, I asked a man what he thought of her sermon. His answer came back to me through a friendly translator: "She had a beautiful message."

I said, "Tell me what she said."

"She said that we cannot always carry everything on our own," the man explained through the interpreter. "If we try, we will drop things. We must ask for God's help to carry our burdens." Apparently Karen's translator had taken some liberties with her sermon.

But if Karen and some of her friends were sometimes out of touch, they also rose every day with the sun and spent hours tending to the needs of sick children, ordering supplies, distributing food, tracing children, and reuniting families. They may have been culturally clumsy, but every day I came to admire them more for one simple reason: they were here in Rwanda. They were working. I was visiting for weeks. They were working for months.

I thought of the many well-intentioned discussions I'd had in university classrooms about cultural sensitivity and cultural awareness, and I could imagine some of my classmates rolling their eyes if they heard aid workers pray, "Lord, please help these Africans." But the fact was that none of those classroom conversations ever saved a life, while some of these committed volunteers were weighing infants in slings every day and providing food to lactating mothers. A lot of the international aid that I saw was not always as helpful as it could be, and some of it was even harmful. The world, however, would be a darker and colder place without it. Whatever her flaws, Karen was feeding hungry families every day.

A young Rwandan man who volunteered with Food for the Hungry asked me to walk with him into the camp. He led me to a group of boys. Their "home" was a collection of long sticks tied together and covered with pieces of black plastic and blue tarp. Their floor was the earth, which in Goma was black, jagged volcanic rock so hard, so barren, that weeds could hardly grow there. When I arrived, a boy lay curled in a dark, tight space where the back wall of the shelter angled to meet the ground. I motioned for him to come out. He crawled out of the shadow of his shelter, dragging one foot behind him. I saw the open wound on his ankle, and as I bent down I could smell the white pus-filled flesh. It was badly infected.

"Where is the nearest medical tent?" I asked.

The volunteer pointed. "It's over there, but it is a long way."

One of the boys spoke to the volunteer. "The boys say that they went to the tent before but they were told to leave."

"They won't tell me to leave," I said.

I picked the boy up and started to walk over the rocky ground. Two of his companions followed behind us. They spoke again to the volunteer, who told me, "The boys say that they were told not to come back."

"That's OK," I said. "No one told me."

The white tent stood on four poles on the rocky ground, and the bright Red Cross symbol announced it as a place of aid. I walked inside with the boy and saw three nurses sitting and talking on plastic chairs. One cot held an old man whose open, lifeless eyes suggested that he might have come here to die. I watched his stomach rise and fall against a brown T-shirt pocked with holes. I set the boy down and he hopped on one foot toward the nurse. I was ready for a fight if they told him to leave, but the nurse—a refugee who had been hired by the Red Cross—sucked air through her teeth as she looked at the wound. She showed the infected ankle to the other nurses, they conferred, and she reached for a bag of cotton balls and bottles of alcohol and iodine. The boy sat and lifted his ankle toward the nurse. She held his leg, her hands sheathed in blue latex gloves, and as she dabbed around the wound I could see the boy's skin shine as layers of dirt washed away. The nurse spoke to the boy—he was no more than eight years old—and he closed his eyes as what I think was alcohol was rubbed into the infected gash. She wrapped his ankle in a clean white bandage. I thought to ask why the boy had been previously turned away, but all of the nurses had been incredibly kind, and I didn't want my words to be mistranslated. I thanked them all and we walked out of the tent.

The boy hobbled back to his friends, and by the time we had reached his shelter, his friends were gathered outside and singing. They were bouncing on bare feet, wide smiles, elated. Some of them thought he would surely die, like so many others whose wounds became infected and went untreated. They began dancing around me and singing a joyful song. The Rwandan aid worker I was with turned to me and whispered, "They are singing 'thank you' for what you did."

I was barely able to force a smile. I was glad to help, but this was absurd. These boys had survived the unendurable to reach here, but could not get the most basic help once they arrived. As an American, I had paid an insignificant bribe at the border, was bailed out with apple juice and cookies, and could walk unchallenged into any part of the camp I wished. I told the aid worker to tell the boys thank you for their song, and I asked if I could talk with them. They gathered closer, and he said, "Yes, yes, they wish to know who you are."

I asked if I could give them a gift from my hometown, and I pulled from the pocket of my cargo pants a stack of St. Louis Cardinals baseball stickers. "Please tell them that this is from my home in America." I handed out the stickers showing the team logo, a red cardinal perched on a baseball bat, and then I sat down and the boys sat with me.

The oldest boy was sixteen, and he was the clear leader of this group of fifteen boys who lived together in the refugee camp. All of the boys were "unaccompanied," and their eyes were far wiser than the eyes of most American children. They could be playful, but they sat with a gravity and held their shoulders back with an air of self-possession that was rare among children. It was like sitting with young soldiers. When I smiled at them, all fifteen faces smiled back. The leader was wearing a T-shirt—holes throughout—and a pair of donated shorts. I asked him to tell me about the other boys in his group. One by one he pointed to his companions, describing them for me as the aid worker interpreted. "This one is very powerful with making fire and cooking. This one is very powerful with the soldiers from Zaire; they like him. This one is very powerful with singing." It may have been some quirk of the translation, but as he went around the group, the leader described each boy as powerful in some way.[12]

One of my favorite photographs from Goma was of a refugee who came every day to the center for unaccompanied children. When he walked into the aid tent, dozens of children would stand and run toward him. He would play games with the children—running, tagging, jumping, singing. He had no toys, no supplies. He simply brought himself and happiness. In the photograph, the man's arms are raised and the children are shouting, some jumping, their faces full of joy.

The international community had watched the genocide in Rwanda without lifting a finger. Ultimately, it had taken a military victory—that of the Rwandan Patriotic Front, a Tutsi army that swept down from Uganda—to bring an end to the killing. We should have sent military assistance, maybe even U.S. Marines. Instead, too late, we sent money and food.

I thought of the survivor who stood her child up for me to photograph, and as I left Rwanda I thought of the way that parents love their children. They hug them when they need love, they care for them when they are sick, heal them when they are injured. But parents also protect their children when they are threatened. Wouldn't it be strange to find parents who would hug their children, would tend to their wounds, but wouldn't protect them from getting hurt in the first place? Nations are not parents to the world's people. Yet the basic fact remains: we live in a world marked by violence, and if we want to protect others, we sometimes have to be willing to fight. We all understand at the most basic level that caring requires strength as well as compassion.

One day I stood outside a health care clinic in Rwanda as a volunteer pointed to a young girl with a deep machete scar that ran from behind her right ear across the back of her neck. We look at a scar like that—we reflect on the evil that human beings are capable of—and we are tempted to walk away from humanity altogether. But when that same child smiles at us, when that same child lets us know that she has survived and she has grown, then we have no choice. We have no choice but to go forward in the knowledge that it is within our power, and that the world requires of us—of every one of us—that we be both good *and* strong in order to love and protect. I felt that I had done some good in Rwanda, but I knew that I had far more to learn, far more to do.

# 6 ☆

# Bolivia

I RETURNED FROM Rwanda grateful for the opportunity to once
again immerse myself in university life. After my despair freshman
year, when my first class on my first day of my first semester at college did not meet my grand expectations, I'd grown to appreciate the
incredible education I had received.

I read Milton and Shakespeare and Plato and Locke, learned something of the world's major religions, studied economics and philosophy
and science and ethics, read the classics and history and contemporary
literature, learned an art and a foreign language. I was fortunate, both
in and out of class, to read many of the major works in the Western
canon, and to read them under the guidance of insightful, patient, and
demanding teachers, the majority of whom were not infected by the
need to "deconstruct" texts based on their own "neo-something" bias
or a "something-ist" school of thought. Instead, they taught them, as
the American classicist Edith Hamilton once described the great works
of literature, "the strong fortresses of the spirit which men have built
through the ages."[1] By entering these fortresses, I became stronger, so
that by the time I stood under the sun with a group of friends at graduation in May 1996, I had been given the greatest gift an education
could provide: I had a better idea of what it meant to live a good life,
and what it meant to be a good man.

Socrates taught the importance of living an examined life, and at Duke I was able not only to examine my life but also, by reading deeply, see all of the rich possibilities that life offered. My discoveries were almost embarrassingly simple, but for me they were profound. The Greeks, for example, had a word, *eudaimonia,* that meant something close to "human flourishing," or living a good and complete life. How strange, I thought, that we don't have such a word in English. The Greek word that we often translated as virtue, *arête,* actually meant "excellence," and another word, *phronesis,* was translated roughly as "practical wisdom." It was fascinating to see that the people who invented the world's first democracy and laid the foundations for the science, literature, and art that we continue to build on today actually had a way of thinking about the world, a way of speaking about the world, that I had never considered.

I was awed when I read Lincoln's Gettysburg Address and heard the echoes of a speech that Lincoln had studied—one made by Pericles at Athens nearly twenty-five hundred years ago. When I read Martin Luther King's "Letter from Birmingham Jail," I could see the imprint of the philosophy King had studied: the works of Saint Thomas Aquinas, written in the thirteenth century. When I studied the Constitution, I understood why America's Founding Fathers—schooled in classical literature and history—had divided power among three branches of government. Understanding these historical and intellectual influences added a new depth to my thinking. I was humbled to see that conversations across the centuries had addressed fundamental human questions, and that by sitting down with the right book, I could learn from a Roman legionnaire, a fifth-century bishop, or an early American farmer his insights about what it means to live well.

Of course, the university had its share of blowhards who were underworked and overcritical, but they were a minority. Whether by luck or a fortunate set of choices, I came in contact with professors who rejoiced in living a full life, and whether they would have articulated it this way or not, they believed in the need for citizens in a democracy to be able to think independently.

I was fortunate also that I had professors who, while appreciating the value of contemplation, understood the importance of doing, of translating thoughts into deeds. In this regard they followed the American essayist Ralph Waldo Emerson, who believed that action was essential: "Without it," Emerson wrote, "thought can never ripen into truth."[2]

During my last semester at Duke, I met a woman who had just returned from a trip to Bolivia, where she had worked in a home for children of the street. The home, Mano Amiga, was run by two of her friends. She described it as an oasis of joy in the desert of poverty, abuse, crime, and destitution where most street children lived, and she described her friends as the closest thing she knew to living saints.

Duke's parting gift to me took the form of a photography grant that paid for a plane ticket to Santa Cruz, Bolivia, and as I packed my backpack with film, camera, notebooks, and some well-worn travel clothes, I was beginning to feel like an old pro. This was my fourth trip overseas. In Croatia and Rwanda, I had photographed the remains of the dead and listened to the stories of survivors. I had seen how people—even amid incredible tragedy—continued to care for their children and love each other. I saw people rebuild their lives in small steps, one arm wrapped around their neighbors for support. Despite all the suffering I had seen, I left these places feeling hopeful. I found that volunteers could save lives, bring joy. Bolivia would prove to be a different kind of test.

Hundreds of children live on the streets of Santa Cruz. Commonly referred to as *niños de la calle*—children of the street—these children spend their days shining shoes, begging, selling gum and cigarettes. Some of them return to small cardboard or corrugated metal shelters where they sleep at night, usually in groups and often surrounded by dogs for warmth and protection. The children live in alleys, their shelters in shadow. Drugs, sickness, abuse, injury, dirt, theft, unwashed clothes, pain.

Some children end up on the street after being abandoned. Others flee abusive homes. Yet the street is no escape from violence. Young women, in particular, are often the victims of sexual abuse. Self-mutilation in the form of cutting is common among street children. I would see a young girl—pretty, round brown eyes—stand before a volunteer, wearing a dirty sweatshirt and jeans, holding out her left arm to reveal three black, unclean wounds caked with dried blood.

Sniffing glue is also common among Bolivia's street children. For some children lifting a small white bottle to their nose is a reflex, like blinking. Sniffing this cheap drug eases pain. It also causes permanent brain damage. Seizures, spasms, memory loss, hearing loss: all are common. I would watch one girl—maybe seventeen years old—lift a white bottle, tilt it to her nose, and breathe in deep. Her eyes were wet and glassy as she brought the bottle down from her nose and set it on her pregnant belly.

The Mano Amiga home is located just outside Santa Cruz; for a barefoot child it's about an hour's walk from the center of the city to the gate. My first night in the home, I gathered with the volunteers and all of the children in a large room that also served as the dining hall. Here I'd eat simple breakfasts, lunches, and dinners of bread and stew and steamed vegetables served from steaming black pots.

A tall man, thick boned, with black hair, olive skin, and small glasses that gave him a professorial air, stepped into the room. In the States, I would have described him as a guy who could have played linebacker on his college football team. A big man, he moved slowly. A deep, soft voice gave his words a feeling of pastoral reverence.

He began in Spanish. "Welcome, everyone. My name is Don Thomas. I have been working in and overseeing these homes for years and with great pride and happiness." As Don Thomas spoke, I realized that I had not used my Spanish, the language I'd studied in high school and college, outside of a classroom for more than an afternoon. I strained to understand every word. I listened as he said, "Every time I introduce new volunteers . . ."—and then he turned his head and I lost what he was saying. But then he turned back. "I feel truly blessed that you are here." He smiled broadly. "The work that you do here is not only a

great contribution to the children of Bolivia, but is also a great contribution to all the children of God. On behalf of everyone here"—and
he opened his arms to take in all of the children—"thank you for coming. Now, let us all introduce ourselves."

Jason and Caroline were a young American couple who ran the
home. Jason was a Wisconsin native who approached every task—at-
tending to wounds, refereeing fights, disciplining children—with the
steady gait of a midwesterner walking out to the barn. Caroline, his
wife, was an intelligent, compassionate woman, who in the space of
one minute could gently discipline a child, give instructions in Spanish
about how lunch should be served, tell a volunteer in English where to
find art supplies, and pick up a crying kid from the floor. "I talked to
my sister on the phone," Caroline told me once, "and for her birthday,
her boyfriend got her a diamond necklace. For my birthday, Jason gave
me a back rub." She smiled. Jason and Caroline's work at the home afforded them no material luxuries, but it was evident that it did afford
them the best kind of happiness: simple, deep. I remember thinking,
*What a beautiful way to start a marriage.*

Then the children introduced themselves: Rodrigo, Carlos, Adolpho,
Maribella. They stood up one after another, just as hide-behind-their-
hands shy, crazy-face clowning, and good-student earnest as any group
of American kids. I leaned forward in my chair. I strained to understand them. Some of them swallowed their words and others squealed,
and some of them barely spoke Spanish. Many of the children came
from rural villages surrounding the city, and their native language was
Quechua. I had to reconsider whether I was an "old pro": I had come
to volunteer in a home for kids without even knowing what language
many of them spoke.

One boy—he was maybe six years old—stood and shouted, "I am
Eddie!" and flung his arms to the side as if he were a rocket shooting
through space. Eddie then sat with a smile and bounced in his chair.
The introductions moved on to two more children, after which Eddie
again jumped to his feet and circled the room, curling his arms like a
monkey, scratching his armpits and grunting.

"Eddie," Caroline said simply, and Eddie returned to his seat with a smile.

Then it was my turn. I had decided to introduce myself using the Spanish name I'd been given in my high school Spanish class, thinking it might be easier for the kids to pronounce than "Eric." But when I stood and said, "Hola, me llamo Quí Qué," the children burst out laughing. Even Don Thomas laughed. *Was my Spanish that bad?*

Two of the kids chanted, "Quí Qué, Chiclé, Quí Qué, Chiclé!" I turned to Caroline. She explained to me that Quí Qué is a popular brand of gum in Bolivia. What I'd just said was the equivalent of a Bolivian volunteer announcing in an American home, "Hello, my name is Bazooka Joe!" Later the kids walked up to me, puffing out their cheeks like chipmunks, pretending they were chewing impossibly large wads of gum.

My first day at Mano Amiga began with a lesson in the Bolivian national religion: soccer. Jason and I walked out to a dirt field beside the home, where a pack of boys, some barefoot, kicked around a ragged brown ball scarred with Mano Amiga history. Some of the boys wore donated shoes; some had outgrown their shoes and cut holes in them, playing soccer with their big toes hanging out.

When I was in third grade—the age of many of the boys here—my parents had debated whether or not to buy me a pair of Tony Glavin KangaROOs. Tony Glavin was the star of the St. Louis Steamers indoor soccer team, and the ROOs were special soccer shoes. The ROOs cost thirty-something dollars in 1982. I remember the debate in my house.

"He doesn't need them."

"All of the other kids on the team are getting them."

"They're thirty dollars—and he doesn't need them."

Here in Bolivia most of the kids played in bare feet, and they had as much fun as we ever had. Alone, human beings can feel hunger. Alone, we can feel cold. Alone, we can feel pain. To feel poor, however, is something we do only in comparison to others. I took off my shoes.

In the home, these kids weren't poor. Their recreation consisted of soccer, tag, a dozen other run-and-chase games, marbles in the dirt, bottle caps. In their imaginations, they turned old tires into fighter planes and cardboard boxes into candy stores.

The boys wrestled every afternoon, and José—one of the volunteers—would often roll in the grass, play-fighting with five or six boys. Many of these kids had experienced the physical strength of adult men only in the form of abuse. José taught them to control their strength. He never hurt them and he didn't allow them to hurt others.

Although the refugee children I'd worked with in Rwanda and Croatia had lived through incredible, sometimes vicious trauma, most had an otherwise whole life; loving parents, caring adults. These children of the street were different. While the refugee children suffered greatly, there was a "normal" they would return to one day. Many of Bolivia's street children had abuse and violence sewn into the fabric of their days from the moment they were born.

Every night we had to round up the boys and get them into the shower. Like kids everywhere, many of the boys in the home didn't care about being clean. Jason made a game of it. He'd announce, "Shower time—vamos, vamos, vamos!" We'd raise our arms above our heads like boogie monsters and chase the kids into the shower.

One night, Adolpho was covered in dirt from soccer and had crumbs of food on his face and crushed into his hair. He didn't want to shower. Jason had tried the boogie-monster chase. He tried making it a challenge—"Adolpho, let's see how fast you can shower and get to bed." He tried to reason with him—"Adolpho, I'd feel really happy if you got clean and into bed." Adolpho would not go. It was getting late.

"Adolpho, please, you need to shower and go to bed," I said, gently grasping his wrist. The moment Adolpho felt the lightest pull, he kicked his feet out from under him and fell to the floor. He screamed full-throated, the sound of his open-mouthed terror filling the hall. He flailed his arms back and forth as he kicked at the air. I had two younger brothers and three younger cousins. I'd worked as a camp counselor all through high school, and I'd seen plenty of kids throw tantrums. But this was different. This was the wild fear of a child who'd known abuse.

"Adolpho, Adolpho, relax, relax, you're OK, relax, you're OK."

Slowly he calmed. Adolpho had to build a new normal.

One day I went to walk and photograph in the poor neighborhoods of Santa Cruz. As I turned off the wide paved main streets onto constricted paths of dirt and mud, I caught the smell of rotting trash and urine. I walked through a warren of hovels pressed together like animals in a storm. Lines of laundry hung out to dry. Brown runoff trickled between the houses. Plastic bottles floated on the rivulets of water past discarded rags. If every plastic bag that littered the ground had been a vegetable, it would have been a bountiful garden.

The mud-caked walls and red-rusted corrugated steel roofs formed homes no bigger than a one-car garage. Waved inside by an elderly woman, I walked into one of the homes. The floor was immaculate. A sheet hung from the metal roof to divide the space into rooms. On one side of the sheet, well-worn blankets lay on the dirt floor for a bed. Farther back sat a small iron stove for cooking. Tacked to the wall above the stove was a small crucifix and tacked to the door frame was the image of the Virgin Mary. Just outside, kids ran barefoot, splashing through the puddles of standing water.

When the kids turned to me, I saw their bright smiles under lazy eyes. I saw their arms and elbows and knees and legs, some with open sores. I knew that these kids ate what their caretakers could scrounge for them, or what they could buy with a day's earnings working on the street, or what they could steal. I knew that throughout Bolivia, kids without access to clean water and sanitation died needlessly from exposure to malaria, hepatitis A, and toxic chemicals in polluted water. I also knew that these children lacked access to even the most basic health care to right a lazy eye, set a broken bone, or kill intestinal parasites.

Back on the streets, I passed packs of boys shining shoes, and a little girl—maybe eight years old—selling gum from a box that hung from a strap over her shoulders.

"Chiclé?" she asked.

At night, I went into the streets with a group of Americans who gathered in the city, sang songs to embolden their spirits, and then walked down the small dirt paths to where children of the street lived. They brought with them bandages, hot tea, and bread.

We saw children lounging together in packs—their arms draped over each other, glue bottles in their hands. A boy stood next to a dumpster reading a newspaper, lifting a bottle of glue to his nose with his free hand. The children drank the tea and accepted the bread. I had expected them to be voracious, but they chewed slowly and looked left and right as they ate. Most of them were high.

The volunteers bandaged wounds, and when they rubbed alcohol on an arm they cleared away layers of grime. Brown, rotten bandages were replaced with new white ones that stood out against the children's unwashed limbs. The kids smiled when they were handed tea, and some of them smiled at my camera, but never before had I walked among children like these, children who seemed so much like zombies, their brains wrecked by drugs, the light of their spirits barely flickering under years of daily pain and abuse.

As I walked home that night, I found myself breathing shallow in and out of my nose like I was preparing to fight. *What's the matter with me?* At first I thought I was angry about the street children, angry about their lives. But I soon realized that my anger was selfish. I wanted to see—as I had in Croatia, Rwanda—cause for hope. I wanted to believe that the children's situations could be improved, lives saved, wounds healed. But I didn't see any hope on these streets. Many of these kids were too far gone. Drugs had rotted their brains, and they were already buried under a dozen years of bad habits and locked in a cycle of misery and addiction. Miracles were possible, but it would take a miracle.

In the Mano Amiga home, though, it was different. As one lesson began, Caroline explained to me that during school time, "we teach the kids art and music and painting and sculpture and dance." Eddie ran by, holding a paper plate that had been glued with construction-paper arms and legs and head to make a monkey.

I loved the arts, and I loved watching the kids create art, but I considered whether for these kids, a focus on basic reading and writing and maybe some math would be better. I asked Caroline, "Why do you teach so much art?"

"It lets them see that there are beautiful things in the world, and that they can create them."

Kids like Adolpho and Eddie were incredibly intelligent. Some had survived for years on the streets, and I often saw in their narrowed gazes an emotional maturity that far exceeded that of comparable American children. Yet these kids had never had someone who believed in them enough, loved them enough, to teach them that *they* had value, that *they* could create beautiful things in the world. They had never learned what they were capable of.

In the home, they had to learn the most basic habits. We played a game that the volunteers called, in an English-Spanish mix, the Sniffing of the Manos. Before the kids were allowed to enter the dining hall, they had to line up and hold their hands up, palms out. The volunteers would then inspect each pair of hands to see if they'd been washed.

When Carlos, a ten-year-old, bright-eyed kid, held out his hands to me, I sniffed. I scrunched my face as if I had just smelled something rotten. Carlos and the other kids around him giggled.

"Good. You pass." Carlos danced into the dining room.

I sniffed Pablo's hands. I put a pensive look on my face and Pablo giggled. I stroked my chin and began the interrogation in my simple Spanish.

"Tell me, did you wash your hands with soap?"

"Yes, Quí Qué. I did."

"And how long did you wash your hands?"

"Twenty seconds, like you told us."

"Are you sure it wasn't nineteen seconds? Because if it's nineteen seconds, you'll have to go back to wash your hands again."

"Yes, Quí Qué."

"How fast were you counting?"

"Real slow. *Slow . . . like . . . this,*" he said, carefully drawing out each word.

"OK."

Pablo shot a crazy face at the other kids and ran into the dining room.

"Adolpho!" I smiled at him.

Adolpho, who was two places down the line, roared with laughter and pointed at me when he saw that he'd been caught. He'd purposefully covered his hands in mud and had them hidden—he thought—behind his back, ready to hold them up in front of my face when it was his turn for inspection.

Interacting with the kids helped me improve my Spanish. The children always made an extraordinary effort to be understood. One kid, responding to my quizzical look as he told a story, held up two fingers in a V behind his head and started bouncing around the field. *Rabbit.* I got it then.

As I started to communicate better with the kids, I began to appreciate the importance that the routine of the home played in their lives. The volunteers and children led a life whose daily rhythms were shaped by religion. They recited the Lord's Prayer in Spanish before every meal.

> Padre nuestro
> que estás en el cielo,
> santificado sea tu nombre.
> Venga tu reino . . .

I took photographs of a priest in a white robe as he and several of the children—dressed in white to perform their duties as altar boys—prepared for Mass. For the kids, the rituals of the church and the rituals of the home provided steady, true ground in a life that had been racked by wave after wave of false promises and false starts.

My mom is Jewish, my dad Catholic, and as kids we'd had it great: Hanukkah and Christmas, Easter and Passover. We had attended Sunday school largely because my parents cared that we grew up to be religious, moral people, but my parents weren't too bothered about theology. If you loved God with all your heart and all your soul, they figured that God would help you find your way.

Though I didn't have a very structured religious education growing up, I could see why it mattered to the kids. They needed something solid and constant, because the streets were always tugging at them.

One day Jason suggested that I take some of the kids to the soccer stadium in Santa Cruz to watch a game.

It sounded like fun, and when I mentioned the outing to a group of older boys, they started shouting and jumping around the room.

"Yes, Quí Qué, yes!"

"Quí Qué is the best, the best, the best!"

As we left the Mano Amiga home the night of the game, the kids had a bounce to their step. Pablo whistled at a girl. Rodrigo leaned back and let out an open-throated cheer for his team.

"Rodrigo, please, calm down."

"Yes, Quí Qué, OK. Hey, Quí Qué, give me the money for the micro, and I will pay." He looked at me theatrically with pleading eyes. I handed him the money and he stuffed it into the pocket of his red jacket, yelled, "Thanks, Quí Qué!" and took two fast steps as he pretended to run off with the money.

Now that we were out of the home and on the street, the kids felt like they were teaching me. I was on their turf here, and they were full of advice.

"Make sure you put your wallet in your front pocket. You don't want to get it stolen."

"And be careful when stepping into the micro."

"Yeah, and if you stand right at this exact spot, you can jump on and get a good spot. You don't want to get run over. Stand back and watch me, Quí Qué." The micro, a boxy little van teeming with people, pulled up through the dust. A kid hung out the door and shouted, "To the Centro!" Passengers stepped out holding small children and plastic bags filled with groceries. I piled in after the boys and we crowded onto the seats. "Here we go, Quí Qué!" I saw a string of rosary beads and a crucifix hanging from the driver's rearview mirror. Taped to his dashboard was a peaceful picture postcard of the Virgin Mary, and right beside it was a photograph of a leather-clad blonde straddling a motorcycle.

We drove through the heart of the city at high speed past beautiful multibedroom houses encircled by tall concrete walls. The walls were topped with the jagged edges of broken beer bottles to prevent the un-wanted—like the kids traveling with me—from climbing over them. We flew past little stands selling tortillas, past bakeries, past hair salons. We crossed a bridge over a canal that carried away the sewage of the city and we saw a family picking through garbage in the runoff.

"Quí Qué, look"—one of them would say, pointing down an alley —"that's where I used to live."

Laborers walked the streets, and mothers strolled along the thin sidewalks with their children following behind them as straight and careful as ducklings.

The energy of the boys had been building, and when we stepped out of the micro they bolted for the stadium.

"Hey!" I yelled after them.

They turned back.

"Let's be . . ." I wanted a Spanish word for "cool" but I couldn't think of one, so I settled for "calm."

"Hey, Quí Qué, buy us seats, buy us seats!"

We already had tickets, but the boys wanted me to buy them cushions—plastic shopping bags full of cut newspaper.

"Why?"

"Come on, Quí Qué. Quí Qué we need them to sit on."

"We already have tickets."

"But it's good for your——," and they laughed as they used a word for "butt" that I'd never heard before.

"Come on, let's go in."

The boys were punching and wrestling and shoving wildly as we walked into the stadium, a giant concrete oval with concrete steps cut for seats. I understood now why the guy selling the makeshift cushions had customers. The kids thought I was a tightwad for not buying them.

"Nice seats, Quí Qué. Now my butt hurts," Pablo said. But we didn't sit for long.

As soon as the game started, the stadium exploded with energy. The boys were yelling, and around us men were stomping, drumming, singing, shouting. The tickets we'd bought were cheap even by Bolivian standards. We were standing next to shirtless men covered in dust; they had clearly come to the stadium after a day at hard labor. These men shouted at each good pass, punched their fists through the air, and cheered each solid tackle, the workday behind them and the sun now set.

At one point a fire broke out in the stands. Men had torn open the newspaper cushions and lit them on fire, and more and more newspaper was piled on as the fire grew and the crowd moved back. The players kept playing. The ref kept reffing. The fans kept shouting. *This is crazy,* I thought, *this is great,* and I jumped with the kids and shouted, "Vamos!" I didn't even know the name of the team we were rooting for.

Goals were scored against our team, and when our side seemed unable to press back on offense, the crowd grew restless. What looked to me like a bottle rocket was fired from the stands at the opposing goalkeeper and exploded in the grass. I can't remember if beer was sold or alcohol was smuggled in, but as we left the stadium in a chests-pressed-against-backs throng, I was struck by the smell of sweat and cheap alcohol. It was dark, and the air held the electric energy of men looking to fight.

Finally we stepped out of the stadium. I took a head count. *One, two, three, four, five, six* . . . *One, two, three, four, five, six* . . . I had come here with seven. I now had six. Who was missing?

*Rodrigo.*

"Where's Rodrigo?" I asked the kids.

"He was just here," one of the boys said.

"OK. Let's wait for him."

Fans flowed out of the stadium, and I stood there scanning the crowd. Maybe he'd been separated from us in the crush. Eventually the crowds thinned. When a single drunkard stumbled out of the stadium, I realized that I'd lost Rodrigo.

I could not go back to Mano Amiga minus one child. And what would happen to him? Then I remembered something Rodrigo had told me: he'd once collected fares on the micros. He knew the whole city and many of the drivers. He wasn't lost, I realized. He was off on a little adventure. He could be anywhere. The streets, Jason and Caroline told me, had a constant tug on many of the children, especially those who'd experienced the pain and pleasure-filled freedom of sex and drugs and violence and drifting.

"Where is Rodrigo?" I asked the boys again.

"We were just following you. We don't know," they said.

They were unable to suppress their smiles, and it took a measured effort for me to remain calm as they lied to me. They understood our situation perfectly. I wanted to find Rodrigo, and that meant I had to search the streets. Rodrigo running away had created an adventure for them all.

"OK. Follow me," I said.

I started walking, vaguely hoping to head in the direction of the micro stands, but not sure where I was going.

The kids bounced behind me. I was thinking, *Should I talk to the police? Should I wait in one spot?*

*One, two, three, four, five* . . . Five heads. *I lost another kid.* I scanned the street. Carlos had fallen behind, chatting with a girl.

"Carlos, come on."

"Quí Qué, I'll catch up soon."

"Carlos!"

"Yes, Quí Qué," and he jogged to rejoin our pack.

As we wandered down the streets, the kids drifted away just far enough to linger outside shops, to yell to girls. We walked down street after street for hours.

"Quí Qué, let's do this every night!"

I couldn't return to the home one kid short. But I also couldn't stay out all night. I kept turning corners, hoping to spot Rodrigo.

Then I figured out what I should have done from the beginning. I gathered the boys.

"OK, if we find Rodrigo in the next thirty minutes, I'll take each of you out tomorrow night to get ice cream."

"This way, Quí Qué, this way!" The kids ran, and I ran after them down an alley and then into a square and past three policemen who—seeing a white man chasing children of the street—started to run as well until I said, "It's good, it's good. No problem."

"There he is!" one of the boys shouted, and we all stopped running.

I saw Rodrigo's red jacket and the back of his head where he stood in a line at a micro stand.

"OK. Be quiet, all of you."

I walked up behind Rodrigo quietly and then grabbed him by his shoulders and turned him around.

"Where were you? What were you doing?" He started to speak very quickly and to say something I couldn't understand, but a lying fourteen-year-old in Bolivia is the same as a lying fourteen-year-old in America, and I understood him well enough. I held a fistful of his jacket as we walked. The other kids formed a circle around us: close enough to laugh at Rodrigo, but not too close to me. We hopped on a micro and made our way back to Mano Amiga.

"Thanks, Quí Qué!" the boys yelled as they ran into the home.

I couldn't help but wonder which of their number would ultimately succumb to the lure of the streets.

• • •

One day Juan Carlos, a boy from Don Bosco, a neighboring home for children of the street, was taken to the hospital. His injuries were minor—a broken collarbone—and he was expected to recover quickly, but poor medical care caused complications that led to an infection, and then Juan Carlos contracted typhoid, and then he died. His casket was brought to a small chapel near the home.

I walked Eddie and Adolpho in to see Juan Carlos. The open casket rested on a pedestal three or four feet high, and I picked Adolpho up underneath his armpits and held him so that he could see Juan Carlos. Juan Carlos rested at peace. Dark hair. Closed eyes. He was wearing a white shirt (new), blue pants (clean), and a plastic cross like many of the other children. His hair was combed smooth. The boys said a prayer and ran out. I sat in the chapel to watch as the other children came through.

Pablo, fourteen years old, walked in with Carlos, ten. They stood side by side looking at the body of Juan Carlos. Then Pablo laid his arm over Carlos's shoulder, in direct imitation, I thought, of Jason when he comforted the boys.

Eddie came to me at lunch and dove onto my legs. I pulled him up. "Cómo estás, Eddie?"

"Bien."

He was unusually subdued. He lay down and I held him as if he were a baby, his head resting in the crook of my elbow, his eyes shut, his limbs still. For a child normally so energetic, it was odd. No punching, no singing, no monster faces.

In Spanish he said, "I am like Juan Carlos." He folded his hands in prayer over his chest.

"Do you think that Juan Carlos is asleep?" I said, careful in my Spanish.

"No, he's dead."

"Do you think that Juan Carlos is in heaven?"

"No, he's in the chapel."

At the Mass for Juan Carlos, I stood along the wall, my camera in my hands. I wanted to share this; I wanted people to know what had happened here. I could rattle off a boatload of statistics about poverty and health care in the third world and people would feel nothing. Viewing just a single picture of this boy, who died because of a broken bone, people might understand. But this was a Mass and it didn't feel right shooting pictures, so I kept my camera at my side.

Juan Carlos's father was in the chapel that day. Juan Carlos's mother was—I understood—long dead. His father had wet, red eyes and a slight, birdlike body. He was dressed for his son's funeral in a brown jacket, brown pants, Converse sneakers.

*If Juan Carlos had a father, why had he ended up in a home for street children? Was his father abusive? Had he loved his son? Dumped him in the street?*

A priest hurried into the church, almost a half hour late. In view of the congregation, he put a robe on over a nylon sweatsuit wet from the day's rain. He spoke of his experience with funerals of children and the admirable way the community had dealt with this death. He mentioned Juan Carlos's name twice.

The crowd, wanting consolation from the priest, found none. The eulogy offered no clear outlets for their sorrow. A few solid weepers were in the crowd, but mostly they were left to uncoordinated grieving.

I had heard that Juan Carlos's injury had resulted from his slipping in the shower at Don Bosco. I had also heard that this story had been invented to get the hospital to admit the boy, though it was unclear to me why such a lie would have been necessary. The other story was that Juan Carlos—who had been in and out of the home for children of the street—had been brought to Don Bosco, broken bone and all, by his father.

Was it true that Juan Carlos's father had visited him in the hospital only once in three days, and then for only twelve minutes?

A steady rain turned the roads muddy as we drove from the church to the grave. The coffin rode in the back of a pickup truck. The truck bed was not long enough for the coffin, which hung out the back, through the open gate. Older boys from the home sat in the back of the truck, one hand gripping the side of the truck and the other holding the coffin. Each time the truck hit a bump in the road the boys tightened their grip. We listened to the slap of rain on metal and wood and the rev of the engine and the splatter of the mud.

At the paupers' cemetery, I whispered to a woman who seemed to have some blood relation to the boy. "Yes, please," she said. "I want you to share this with people." I moved to the back of the crowd and raised my camera.

The same priest who was late to Mass at the church spoke at the burial site. At the very end of the service, he said, "Adios, hijo"—Goodbye, son—or was it "A Dios, hijo"—To God, son? The dead boy's father, silent up until that moment, leaned his head back and wailed, as if he'd only just then realized that Juan Carlos was truly dead. He touched the casket, and his fingers lingered there, and then he cried out again as he let his fingers slide from his son.

The older boys bent down, picked up the coffin, and lifted it to their shoulders. They slid the casket into its slot. A small, unobtrusive man—a bricklayer dressed in spackled pants—walked over and quickly, cleanly, set the bricks and applied the mortar, sealing Juan Carlos away with the other lost children of the street.

When almost everyone else had left, a young woman wrote, with her index finger, an epitaph in the still-wet mortar:

J.CO.R.

ERES UN ANGELITO

QUE

ESTAS EN CIELO

JUAN CARLOS

YOU ARE A LITTLE ANGEL

WHO

IS IN HEAVEN

Riding with me in a car on the journey home, a college student who had recently arrived to volunteer held my hand as she slept on my shoulder, exhausted by this death. Back at Mano Amiga, Eddie found me to play a game, and he told me, "Juan Carlos is not in the chapel now."

For all of the violence and tragedy and pain that armed conflict brings, I thought that it might be easier for a child to lose a parent or a limb and to live through war than to grow up abused and abandoned. Most of the children on the streets of Bolivia had never known the comforts of family life, were never going to go to college. Few of them, I guessed, would ever know one whole carefree and happy day in their lives.

If we want to change something, we must begin with understanding. But if we want to love something, we must begin with acceptance. The beauty of what Jason and Caroline had done was to begin with acceptance and love. Then, by virtue of their courage, their intelligence, and their compassion, they were able to change the lives of the children in their charge in a profound way. Their love was built on patience, and their faith helped them to know that they couldn't do everything, but they did have to do what they could.

Later, in the military, I'd read briefs of well-intentioned officers who had designed "programs" to "swiftly rebuild civil society" after war, after institutional collapse. I admired their intentions, but if Bolivia taught me anything, it was that there are some things—like civil society, like character, like a child's belief in the future—that cannot be achieved overnight. Humanitarians, warriors, scholars, and diplomats all do best when we recognize the difference between what we can fight for and what we must accept, between change that can be catalyzed and change that must be built over time, from within. I was twenty-two, and I still believed that I could shape the world through service, but I'd learned in Bolivia that patience and acceptance would be part of the journey.

# 7 ☆

# Oxford

IN BOLIVIA, I REREAD Albert Camus's *The Plague*. In the story,
Bernard Rieux, a local doctor, and Jean Tarrou, a visitor unable to
return home, are caught up in a plague epidemic in the Algerian
city of Oran. Taking a break—for a moment—from fighting disease,
Rieux and Tarrou discuss what it means to live well, and Tarrou says,
"Of course a man should fight for victims, but if he ceases caring for
anything outside that, what's the use of his fighting?"[1]

Doing humanitarian work overseas, I had come to realize that it's
not enough to fight for a better world; we also have to live lives worth
fighting *for*. In my senior year of college I applied for a Rhodes scholarship, awarded annually to men and women who are meant to "fight
the world's fight." Scholars are sent to graduate school at Oxford University in England, and it was at Oxford that I really began to appreciate all of life's beauty: joy, delight, rest, love, tranquillity, peace. These
are things worth fighting for, for others and for ourselves.

Oxford offered an almost unimaginable gift of time, and more opportunity for revelry than I'd ever known. Oxford offered, above all, incredible freedom. I took classes, but there were no grades. At the end
of the year, I simply had to show up and pass an exam. The Rhodes of-

fered a modest stipend, and provided that I budgeted well, I could use it to travel widely. The only real guidance I'd been given was: "Make the most of it."

With its manicured grounds, Queen Elizabeth House looked like an English country manor, and after an interview with the director of an academic program in development studies, I was admitted into a diverse class of students from South Africa, Spain, India, Pakistan, Zimbabwe, and Belgium. During my time there, I would learn as much from the other students as I would from my professors.

I soon found that Oxford not only welcomed diversity but embraced the eccentric. One scholar, "Turkish Tom," who was over six and a half feet tall—if you included his mad-scientist hair—walked the halls of the college in a black trench coat, mumbling about his dissertation, then seven years in the making. Oxford academics really did bike through town dressed in tweed.

A dark wooden desk sat in front of the window in my attic room, and in the morning I'd read and write there as the sun rose over the college chapel. The university hosted lectures on a wide range of subjects, which were open to every student, and one morning I sat at my desk reviewing the university lecture list. With a yellow marker I highlighted lectures in British history, contemporary literature, moral philosophy, the history of science, modern art, Greek civilization, parliamentary politics. It was an academic all-you-can-eat buffet. One day I dropped in on a philosophy lecture. In an ancient room lined with wood shelves weighted with leather-bound books, the professor began, "What is truth?"

Dinners lasted all night. At Lady Margaret Hall, my college, I sat down to "Formal Halls" with British historians, Swiss chemists, Chilean anthropologists, and Polish conductors. In a letter to my family I wrote, "I have no idea how people get work done here. At 5 we start with pre-dinner drinks and then go for cocktails and then sit down at 6:30 for dinner and eat one course after another, and then just when you think it's over you go into another room for chocolates and drinks, and then everyone goes to the pub after that. When you add in two tea times per day and lunch with a friend, I feel like I spend all day eating and drinking and talking."

The Rhodes Trust owned a large log cabin in the Alps, and I was invited there for a "Reading Party." We'd read in the mornings and take extraordinary alpine hikes most of the day, and then each night a member of the group would make an informal presentation and lead a discussion. My presentation was not very memorable, but I did introduce a bunch of international scholars to the American s'more.

I spent a week in an English country manor with friends. We read philosophy and took long walks over worn brown paths that wound through a vibrant green countryside dotted with packs of white sheep. Back at Oxford, we all went punting down the river. With sixteen-foot-long sticks we pushed flat-bottomed boats, ate strawberries, drank champagne and juice, and periodically crashed into the bank.

My American classmates and I tried to make our own cultural contributions. We tried, for example, to introduce the international graduate students to a game of American football. My friend Ed aimed to be a professor, and he patiently explained the rules of the game until all of the international students nodded back at him. On the first play, I called hike, and as I brought the ball up, I saw an open receiver—a British chemist—running across the field. I overthrew the chemist, and when the ball flew past him and hit the ground, a German historian on the other team grabbed it and started running. A Polish engineer tried to tackle him. Ed yelled, "No, no, the play is over!" but just then a Greek linguist threw her shoulder into the German, who crumpled to the ground. Then a South African lawyer on my team threw himself on the downed German, wrestled the ball away, and threw it ten yards forward to an Australian biologist, who bobbled the pass, dropped the ball, picked it up again, and ran into the end zone. My team went wild in celebration.

"Yes!" "Ja!" "Nai!" "Tak!"

Ed was doubled over laughing, his hands on his knees, and I said, "I guess that's a touchdown. Do you want to explain the whole kickoff thing?"

Oxford can be magical at night. As the light of the day softens into dark and the bright traces of modern life recede, what is left are the winding cobblestone streets, the colleges built like castles, the gargoyles who have been smiling and frowning and clowning in permanent expressions of mischief and terror for five hundred years. One night before a concert, I stood outside the old Sheldonian Theatre as the river rush of the crowd's energy flowed around me and people pressed into the theater. A beautiful woman rode past on her bicycle and flashed me a smile. We were together for the next five years.

On Saturday mornings we would make a breakfast of chocolate chip pancakes and cheesy eggs, and then pack fruit in a backpack and head out for a walk along the Oxford Canal. We'd take different forks in the path, turning left where last we had turned right, making our way through overgrown fields and along rivers, and eventually—it works like magic in England—we'd come across a pub where we'd stop for a lunch of fish and chips.

We walked to open-air markets on the weekends, pulled fresh fruit from the stalls, and then packed our backpack with French bread and tomatoes and smoked turkey and Brie and avocado. When the days were long, we'd start off early in the morning and bike for miles over hills and past green fields filled with running horses and grazing sheep. We'd roll past farmers striding with tall wooden walking sticks, their sheepdogs behind them. We'd leave with a map and a "let's head for that town" notion of a plan, and at the end of the day we'd find a pub that served as a bed and breakfast and we'd sit down to a dinner that tasted delicious in our near exhaustion, and then we'd shower and scrub the splattered mud of a day's ride from our bodies and we'd fall into a happy, deep sleep. In winter we'd walk over to the Trout Pub, where we'd order hot chocolate and sit near a fire where they actually roasted chestnuts over the open flames.

Other weekends I'd bike to Rent-a-Wreck and rent a cheap car for a few days, and we'd roll out to explore Britain. Once we headed to Hay-on-Wye, a village full of old bookstores, and once we drove to the Lake District, where we walked through heather-filled fields. In northern

Wales we scrambled up a steep hill to the remains of a twelfth-century castle. We sat on the partially collapsed stone walls and talked, and then we walked down the hill across green fields and past a roaring white stream into a Welsh village, where we took shelter from the rain in a teashop.

We went to Malta and spent two weeks snorkeling in the Mediterranean, exploring the famous old city of Knights Hospitallers and driving around the island in a rented open-top jeep. We took the ferry to Northern Ireland and walked through the city of Galway on Good Friday in 1998, the day the peace accords were signed. On several weekends we escaped to Paris, where we'd wake up late and head downstairs to the local boulangerie to buy a bag of croissants and *pains au chocolat* and walk beside the river Seine.

One morning at the Rodin Museum in Paris I was waiting outside for my girlfriend next to Rodin's sculpture *The Thinker*. The sun was high and I sat peeling an orange. As I split a section in half, every fiber of the bursting fruit seemed to glisten silver. The whole world had opened itself to me. Here was all its beauty, right here in my hands.

I joined the Oxford University Amateur Boxing Club (founded 1881). The head coach, Henry Dean, was to Oxford boxing what Bear Bryant was to Alabama football or Mike Krzyzewski is to Duke basketball. The Varsity Match—the annual competition against Cambridge—was the most important event in Oxford sports, and by the time I joined the Oxford team, Henry had won seven Varsity Matches in a row. It was one of the longest winning streaks in any sport in the history of the Varsity Match. In the privileged world of Oxford, Henry Dean was an island of solid British working-class sense and courage, and boxing at Oxford became a central part of my life.

A few practices into the season, when dozens of men were still training, I asked the team captain how boxers were cut from the team, and he said, "Henry doesn't cut anyone. He doesn't have to." Henry simply subjected everyone to his training.

With all its revelry, life tended to start late at Oxford. A 10 A.M. class was early. But the boxing team was different. The team gathered several mornings a week at the base of Headington Hill, the longest, tallest hill in Oxford. Pedaling through the city before sunrise, I flew down Oxford High Street. The High Street was usually choked with traffic and tourist buses and scholars in gowns, but this early in the morning the city lay quiet like a napping child. I biked past Magdalen College—sitting like an old castle in front of the bridge—and over the river Cherwell.

The ride to practice was a pleasant interlude before a vicious morning. When I arrived, Henry Dean would be standing at the bottom of Headington Hill wearing his rough blue coat, his brown work gloves on his hands, his stopwatch ready. Henry was about five foot nine, and though he had grown stouter with age and now walked with a slight limp, when he was teaching a jab—"You just hit him: Bing! Bing! Bing!"—he still moved like the national champion he'd once been. We would gather at the base of the hill, and at exactly 7:30 A.M. Henry would say, "Let's go," and we'd start off like a pack of gazelles that had just smelled a lion as, arms pumping, feet flying, we ran up the steep hill.

We were a motley, unshaven crew most mornings, and when we ran along the park paths we would startle the half-dozing English ladies taking their dogs for a morning stroll. We ran the paths in wild team races, and then Henry broke us into pairs and we raced against each other in hill sprints. Henry had the course rigged so that at the end of each sprint we jogged downhill. As we reached the bottom of the hill, the whistle would blow and we'd sprint again. When we paused for a fleeting moment, sucking down air, our hands behind our heads, Henry would say, "Cambridge is sleeping right now."

Henry did not tolerate whining, and he did not tolerate cowardice. If someone tried to make an excuse about not showing up at Headington Hill, he'd say, "I don't need to hear about it. These boys don't want to do the work, then they don't want to be boxers. They can leave."

When I first sparred against Dave Crellin, who had never boxed before, I gave him a bloody nose. Dave turned away from me, but Henry turned him back to the fight and said, "Welcome to boxing, then."

People feared Henry's wrath, and they also feared his boxing hygiene. When Dave got a bloody nose, Henry walked to the corner, grabbed a yellow sponge from a bucket of water, mashed the sponge into Dave's face, then bent and wiped the spattered blood off the floor before tossing the sponge back in the bucket. When the next man was bloodied, Henry reached into the bucket again, grabbed the same sponge, and mashed it into the next man's face.

Henry beat us exhausted. "More work, need more work out of you," he'd say as he worked me on the pads: "Bing! Bing! Jab—now!" As he floated around the ring, his limp gone, and with the sound of my fists cracking against the pads echoing through the gym, he'd yell, "Come on!" and keep me punching until I could barely hold my hands in front of my face. When the round ended he'd hit me on the head with one of the pads and say, "Good boxing," and in that moment he couldn't hide the fact that he had a golden heart.

With Henry and the Oxford boxing team I fought all over Britain. In the Town vs. Gown boxing match we squared off against local fighters in a small ring surrounded by tables where men dressed in tuxedoes ate steaks and smoked cigars. We went to the British Universities Sports Association National Championships, and my teammates and I brought home gold medals. We traveled to small working-class boxing clubs and to the Royal Military Academy at Sandhurst, where we walked to the ring behind a military bagpiper.

The Varsity Match my second year at Oxford would prove to be our biggest test and one of the most memorable nights of my "Oxford education." The Oxford Town Hall holds hundreds of spectators for boxing matches. Seats are pressed around the ring and people yell from the rafters, and much of the crowd feels close enough to be splattered with the fighters' sweat. Shadowboxing in the locker room before our fights, we could hear the roar of the crowd. When it was time for my fight and they opened the door to the arena, I felt like I was stepping into a riot.

Students in sport jackets, their ties loosened and their sleeves pushed up, held their fists in the air, screaming, "Hit him! Hit him!" The Oxford supporters chanted "OX . . . FORD!" while the Cambridge fans echoed, "CAM . . . BRIDGE!" Old Blues—boxing alums from years past—sat ringside in their blue blazers, yelling, "Shoe! The! Tab! Shoe! The! Tab!" A "tab" was a Cambridge student and to "shoe" meant to beat without mercy—like kicking someone in the face while they were on the ground. All of the eccentric individuals who made up life at Oxford—the scholars, poets, scientists, philosophers from a hundred different countries and a thousand different cultures—were now nothing more than one screaming-for-blood crowd.

At the beginning of a fight, boxers typically engage in a stare-down with their opponents. They look hard at each other's eyes until the referee sends them back to their corners. Earl had taught me differently.

"Why are you gonna stare in another man's eyes?" He had told me, "Walk to the center of the ring like a gentleman and bow your head with respect while the ref talks. It's gonna make the ref like you and, more important, the other man now has to sit there lookin' tough, starin' at the top of your head. He has to ask himself, Does he stare mean at the top of your head? Should he relax? Should he bow his head too? You've got him confused before the fight starts!

"Then you smile at him and you tell him 'Good luck,'" Earl had said. "Then you're in charge. You're the bigger man. It also confuses him again. A guy that smiles before a fight? Now that'll make a man have to think."

When the referee told us to touch gloves, I looked up and smiled and said, "Good luck."

Henry told me as I stepped in the ring, "The jab, Eric. You use your jab on this boy and you'll knock him out. Nice and easy now."

The crowd was mad with screaming and my opponent stared at me from across the ring. My mind could pick up the voices of my teammates in the crowd: "Go get him, Eric!" And then Henry: "Nice and easy. Nice and easy."

The bell rang and I came forward and threw two jabs. My opponent stepped back and I saw his eyes just over the tops of his gloves. We circled each other in the ring. I threw a jab and felt my fist crack against his face. I pressed forward, and as he backed away I shot two jabs and I followed with an Earl-built, Henry-trained right that caught him cleanly on the chin and immediately his legs buckled a crazy dance and his body started to spasm. I walked to the neutral corner as the ref counted, "Four, five, six, seven," and then the referee saw that my opponent couldn't continue and he raised his hands and waved the fight off.

The crowd exploded in an animal frenzy and I fired my fist in the air. After five years of training, the bout lasted a glorious eighty-four seconds.

We went to Vinnie's for dinner. Vinnie's is the club for Oxford Blues, and it was decorated with photographs of Oxford boxers and athletes from past years: 1892, 1904, 1937, 1972. But for the fact that they went from black-and-white to color, they all looked like the same photograph—year after year—young men trained to fight, looking straight ahead at the camera. To this day, some of my best friends are the men from the Oxford University Amateur Boxing Club, 1998. That year we beat Cambridge 5–4. It was Henry's eighth victory. He would go on to win thirteen Varsity Matches in a row. Those wins, combined with the three victories prior to Henry's arrival, gave the Oxford boxing team the longest winning streak in the history of Oxford sports, an honor it continues to hold. Sometimes, when I'm running in the morning, I can still hear Henry's voice.

"Cambridge is sleeping right now."

Amid the pleasures of Oxford life and the draw of the boxing team, I was still determined to find a pathway for humanitarian work. I wrote a dissertation on the subject. My thesis was simple: What matters for the long-term health and vitality of people who have suffered is not what they are given, but what they do. Rather than simply giving aid to children, it made sense to support children, families, and communities that were already engaged in their own recovery.

I studied the history of Save the Children and learned how its founder, who had established the organization to help starving children after World War I, became critical of giving aid to children as a solution and began focusing on helping families find constructive work. I studied the starvation crisis in Biafra (1967–1971)[2] and the emerging literature coming out of Rwanda. I found the repeated appearance, in the literature on humanitarian crises from World War I to the present, of sets of "recommendations" and "suggestions" that were all strikingly similar. "Lessons," it seemed, had been written down repeatedly, but never learned or put into practice well enough the keep the same mistakes from happening again and again.

I focused on understanding *why* it seemed so difficult for traditional charities to draw on strengths rather than just dole out relief, and as I read about the history of humanitarian movements, I was inspired by the story of Henri Dunant. In 1859 Dunant was an unsuccessful businessman on an errand of personal profit when he woke one morning to find himself near a battlefield littered with the dead and wounded. Troops of the Franco-Sardinian and Austrian armies were lying desperate in the fields of Solferino in northern Italy. Dunant later wrote, "The poor wounded men . . . were ghostly pale and exhausted. Some, who had been the most badly hurt, had a stupefied look . . . [Others] had gaping wounds already beginning to show infection, [and] were almost crazed with suffering."[3]

Dunant stopped for only two days and did what he could to help. Given the enormity of the suffering, his efforts were tragically inadequate. Dunant pressed passers-by into service and wrote letters to the families of the wounded men.

Later he wrote about his experience. Inspired by the reception his book received, he decided to promote a simple idea: soldiers should not suffer and die alone, volunteers should help, and the wounded and those who aid them should be exempt from attack. From this idea, the International Red Cross was born.

Dunant was on a battlefield for just two days. He was a businessman with no knowledge of medicine or war. Yet, on the basis of his experience, he felt that he should form an organization (the Red Cross) and embed a set of principles in the conscience of humanity (his ideas formed the basis of the Geneva Conventions) that became relevant to all people, everywhere, then, now, and forever.

Dunant walked away from the battlefield inspired to change the way that the world took care of those who suffered in war. He could have just as easily walked away disgusted by men's wastefulness of other men's lives, and he could have left dismayed at the minuscule amount of service that a single pair of hands could provide amid so much suffering. Dunant had been preceded by tens of thousands of military men and professionals in various medical corps before him: yet none of them, with all of the time they had passed with the wounded, were possessed of Dunant's vision.

I knew that whatever I wrote and said, I wouldn't have the influence of an Henri Dunant. But I did believe that if I listened well and worked hard, it would be possible to—like Dunant—both make a contribution with my own hands and give testimony to the fundamental strength of human beings. I hoped to call attention to the immense possibilities that exist if we are willing to tap into that strength. So while I worked in the archives during the academic terms at Oxford, I used my breaks to travel and to research and to photograph.

In December 1996 I went to the Gaza Strip. As my cab driver took me to the border, he said, "I've never been to Gaza, and I am never going to go to Gaza. You want to go to Gaza, you serious? The people there, they're terrorists, all terrorists."

On the streets of Gaza I was offered tea and bread by groups of curious men who seemed to hang out on nearly every corner. We sat on boxes and stools on dusty streets and they would ask me, "What are you doing here in Gaza?" "What do Americans know about Gaza?" We talked about politics and history and unemployment and living conditions and trash pickup and the United Nations and Yasser Arafat, as children dressed in donated sweaters played tag in the streets, ran under laundry lines, and sat at piles of rock and stone that they had fashioned into pretend kitchens. Buildings stood pressed against each other shoulder to shoulder as bands of children ran through alleys.

Every conversation seemed political. Every observation was steeped in history. If I asked a child where she was from, she would likely tell me Haifa or Tel Aviv or Jerusalem, even though neither she nor her parents had ever even seen these cities. The adults referred to Gaza—the place where they had lived every day of their lives—with a wave of the hand as "this place." I had to rethink the word "refugee." In Gaza, families had lived on the same block for fifty years, yet they still had dreams of another "home."

Walking the streets bred humility. In 1996 Gaza had been controlled by Israel for nearly thirty years, by Egypt for twenty years before that, by the British for thirty years before that, by the Ottomans for four hundred years before that, and—over the course of the three thousand previous years—by others, including the Crusaders, the Caliphate, the Byzantines, the Romans, the Macedonians, the Persians, the Babylonians, the Assyrians, and the Israelites. I wore hiking boots that had just a few days of dust on them. How much time would it take to even begin to understand such a place?

In Gaza—perhaps more than anywhere else I'd ever been—young people grew up conscious of their history. Not only did they tell me about homes they had only imagined, but even young children—nine, ten years old—recounted their version of the Arab-Israeli conflict. Prominent graffiti portraits of dead Gazan teenagers testified to the most recent clashes. As I watched kids run in the streets, an elderly man quoted Arafat to me. Arafat had said that the womb of the Palestinian woman was a "biological weapon," which he could use to create a Palestinian state by crowding people into the Gaza Strip and the West Bank.[4] The man smiled at me with the smug confidence of someone who believed that every humiliation he had ever suffered, every feeling of powerlessness, every real and perceived assault on his dignity, would one day be rectified in a violent vindication. Gaza had one of the highest population densities in the world. Fifty-three percent of the population was under the age of eighteen,[5] and the children, he believed, were weapons.

The streets were teeming with young men my age. They were all well fed (in part by United Nations support), they had access to some education, but they had no real prospects to ever leave Gaza, and in Gaza there was little work to be had. I'd learned that the classic view of "the poor" as a breeding ground for terrorists and insurgents was mistaken. Poor people, hungry people, rarely dedicate their lives to violence. They are too focused on their next meal. Revolutionaries are often middle and upper class, comfortable but frustrated people who choose violence.

I took a photograph of a young man standing in front of a graffiti mural that displayed a portrait of another young man who had recently died in political violence. The two of them looked as though they could have been brothers: one of them dead, a reminder of the world as it is and has been; the other living, a testament to the world as it might yet be.

I sat down in a little shop in Gaza and ate a one-shekel falafel loaded with fried chickpeas, lettuce, and tomatoes while I scratched notes in my notebook. I was just passing through, and I knew I could never fully understand Gaza or all of the forces that had determined one kid's fate and would shape another's future. "Certainly, I was a tourist," Dunant had written, describing his experience in a war zone, "but a tourist much concerned with questions about humanity."[6]

In a humble building not far from the river Ganges in Varanasi, India, Mother Teresa's Missionaries of Charity run a home for the destitute and dying. Their mission is simple: help the poorest of the poor die with dignity. Many of the patients are seriously physically ill, while some are severely mentally ill, and together, they live in a small concrete compound that is unadorned and true to the mission of the sisters who have pledged to live just as the poorest of the poor do.

I had expected to see only adults in the home, but one boy lived there also. Mentally and physically disabled, he had been abandoned and for years before coming to the home he had begged on the street. He squatted in the home just as he had squatted on the street as a beggar, and he had squatted for so long that he could no longer straighten his legs. He smiled often, but the only word he could say was "namaste." Each time he said it, he would offer the traditional Hindu greeting and bring his hands together in front of his chest and lower his head. The namaste greeting has a spiritual origin that is usually understood to mean, "I salute the divinity within you."

The other patients were all men. Some of them suffered from tuberculosis and their eyes bulged from gaunt, skeletal faces as they lay in bed. Around me, men wrapped in blankets lay dying of other maladies. Other patients were mentally ill. In a country without effective social services, these ill men would have otherwise been subject to the same nasty, short, brutish existence as the destitute, elderly, sick, and insane left on the streets. Here they were cared for.

I had expected to find an atmosphere of sorrow and penance and heavy burden under the shadow of death in this home. This was a place where people had come to die, and the dying were tended to by sisters of the Missionaries of Charity, who express their faith by living a life of absolute poverty and extraordinary hardship.

These sisters, I knew, washed everything by hand just as the poor did. They owned three saris and a pair of sandals and nothing more. But I saw that the sisters sometimes skipped and ran through the home. They shared jokes with the patients. They laughed out loud. They did work that most of us would consider onerous—cleaning vomit from the face of a dying man—and they did it with a sense of great joy and light. My own work in the home was straightforward: wash blankets, feed patients, clean dishes, serve meals.

The sisters were models of compassion, but I struggled to follow their example. On the streets, I was accosted by beggars who were more aggressive than any I'd ever encountered. I had learned not to give money. Many children are sent into the streets to beg for money, and giving money only ensures that more children will be sent into the streets. Some children had even been disfigured so that they might make more effective beggars. A one-legged boy in Delhi sitting on a piece of cardboard on a dirty street scooted after me to beg for "one rupee." I knew not to give money, but when confronted with a hungry child, it's difficult to turn your back. I'd spent many days saying no on past trips, and at the end of those days I'd come home exhausted after repeatedly refusing hungry children. I had made it a habit to carry a bag of food—rolls, bread, cookies, grapes—so that when a barefoot child walked beside me and tugged at my shirt I could give her something. It seemed like a good solution. The children got something to eat. Those who exploited them did not benefit, and I felt spiritually whole. But in India, my plan failed. There were so many begging on the streets that when I handed a roll to one child I was swarmed by a dozen children grabbing at my bag with sore-ridden hands, and when my bag was empty those same children and a dozen more would follow me down the street, begging for money.

One day I visited a Varanasi bakery that made loaves of bread filled with grapes and nuts, and I bought one for lunch. As I sat down to eat on a stairwell tucked away from the crowd along the bank of the Ganges, two boys poked their heads around the wall and looked at me. I looked back at them. Then they stepped out from behind the wall and stuck their hands out asking for money. I was exhausted and hungry and I waved them away with the back of my hand and turned my head. One of them picked up a stone like he was going to throw it at me. I looked hard at him as if to say that I would stand and beat him in the street if he did that. He turned and threw the stone toward the river and then they both ran away. I'd come to work in a place of compassion, but I found that I had stopped looking at people on the street.

One of the patients at the home was a taxi driver who had been gravely injured in an accident but was now almost fully recovered. He had assisted me in my volunteer duties, showing me where blankets were washed, where pans were stored. A kind man, he spent an hour each day doing the most basic of physical therapy with the namaste boy in the hopes that one day the boy might be able to straighten his legs and walk again. He fed the other patients. One of the more severely mentally ill men spent all day conversing with himself, and my kind friend always made an effort to talk with him. My friend was, however, nearing the end of his stay. The home was for the dying. He had recovered. He was a welcome volunteer, but the sisters had told him that it was time for him to move on.

One day he showed me around the outside of the home, and as we walked he pulled out a cigarette and started to drag on it. We stood and talked. Then one of the sisters came out and started to yell at him and I felt like a busted teenager. I can't remember what language she was yelling in, but the man replied, "It [the cigarette] is only one rupee, sister," but the sister told him that would be one less rupee that he'd have when she kicked him out of the home. The sisters were as tough as they were compassionate.

On another day I walked into the home as one of the sisters was serving lunch to the patients, and she handed a cracker to my friend. Without a thought he set the cracker in his left hand, dropped a quick chop on it with his right hand to split it in two, and then handed me half. The man owned nothing. He did not even own the pants he was wearing, the shirt on his back, the sandals on his feet. Yet when he was given food and he saw that I had none, the first thing he did was to hand half of it to me.

After my time at the home in Varanasi, I traveled to the home for the destitute and dying in Calcutta. My first morning there, I went to a room that served as a chapel where I had been told the volunteers were to gather. I stepped in a few paces and stood. The room was quiet. A few dozen people sat facing an altar. I looked to my left, and there sitting alone in a wheelchair, her eyes forward, was Mother Teresa. I had read her biography and her writings, and I knew how miraculous—I don't think there's a better word for it—her life had been. And here she was, sitting silently just a few feet away. I spent that day volunteering in the home. I washed blankets, and I fed an old man, shrunken on a green cot, his eyes wide, who had come there to die.

Mother Teresa's missionaries were able to embrace people—complete with all sorts of weaknesses, failures, foibles, strengths, and faiths—and work with them wholeheartedly. The sisters lived their entire lives in faith, but to me, it seemed that they needed to whisper barely a word about their theology because the integrity of their work said everything.

After spending time in a place of such care and love, I came to understand that when we see self-righteousness it is often an expression of self-doubt and self-hatred. In a place where people are able to accept themselves, love themselves, and know that they are loved, there is no need to criticize or compare, cajole or convince. The sisters concentrated, instead, on loving their neighbors.

When I traveled to Cambodia in the spring of 1998, I visited a hospital outside Phnom Penh where the rooms were packed with men who had recently lost limbs to land mines planted during decades of warfare. Families cooked rice in the hallways, and the half-dressed children of injured soldiers lay crying in the arms of their mothers. Patients lay crowded one next to another. Most of the men had lost legs, a few had lost arms, and some had taken shrapnel to the face and had bright white bandages over their eyes. Mosquitoes buzzed in the patients' rooms as nurses in surgical masks dabbed at bleeding stumps. Groups of newly injured men sat together on blankets laid over the ground. Some of them held the stumps of their legs over buckets as their friends — themselves missing limbs — attempted to clean their wounds.

When I photographed at a clinic run by the British charity the Cambodia Trust in Phnom Penh, I saw a girl — not more than seven years old — lean back on an examination table on one elbow while an orthotic brace was fitted over her right leg. Then she stood and walked with confidence the length of the clinic floor. Polio had shriveled her leg; still she walked with strength.

My travels took me from Cambodia to Chiapas, Mexico, to an orphanage in Albania. By the time I finished my dissertation, I had seen many kinds of humanitarian work, and I had read about many more. Yet for all the compassion and power and beauty I had witnessed, I continued to believe that aid alone was not enough.

• • •

I had become an advocate for using power, where necessary, to protect the weak, to end ethnic cleansing, to end genocide. But as I wrote papers to make this argument and spoke at conferences, my words seemed hollow. I was really saying (in so many words) that someone else should go somewhere to do dangerous work that I thought was important. How could I ask others to put themselves in harm's way if I hadn't done so myself?

I don't remember ever thinking about joining the military as a kid. I had an awareness of military service only because of the grandfather I never met. My father, Rob Greitens, was born on November 26, 1947. His father, August Robert Greitens, was a chief petty officer in the United States Navy, and died on September 11, 1953, when my dad was five years old. My father grew up the child of a widowed single mother in Springfield, Illinois. As kids we called our grandmother, Jeanette Greitens, "Granner." She worked as a shoe saleswoman, and she raised my father and his two sisters.

We always celebrate my father's birthday when the family gathers for Thanksgiving. One Thanksgiving as we sat around the dining room table, Granner handed my dad a gift wrapped in tissue paper. My two younger brothers and I walked over to watch him open it. As my dad pulled back the tissue paper, we saw a framed photograph of my grandfather in his Navy uniform. Medals from his service in World War II hung on either side of the portrait. It was the first time I saw my dad cry. The portrait of my grandfather still hangs over my father's dresser.

When I was a kid, if you'd asked me what I wanted to be when I grew up, it's unlikely that I would have said "soldier" or "sailor." Like most boys, my brothers and I pretended to shoot each other with Wiffle ball bats and we lobbed plastic bowling pins as pretend grenades. I remember liking the movies *Top Gun* and *Rambo,* and I was intrigued by the idea of special operations, but only because I associated it with camouflage. In other words, I was just a boy. I don't know that as a child I really had any more interest in the military than I did in dinosaurs or outer space or the St. Louis Cardinals.

When I worked in Croatia, however, and sat in a shelter and listened to the man who'd been victimized by torturous militiamen, and when I worked in Rwanda and stood at the open door of a church full of skeletal remains, it became more and more clear to me that all of the articles, dissertations, protests, and policy papers in the world had their limits. Sometimes, talking, negotiating, and volunteering to bring food just didn't cut it. It took people with courage to protect those in need of protection. I had written a 441-page dissertation about international assistance.[7] I could keep talking or I could live my beliefs.

So between reading articles about land-mine-clearing projects in Afghanistan and microfinance programs in Bangladesh, I also researched the U.S. Navy SEALs. The Sea, Air, and Land commando teams promised an intensely physical, demanding life, and the test of the training and the camaraderie of the teams appealed to me. The SEALs offered not only the chance to jump out of airplanes, scuba dive, and ride fast boats, but at a deeper level, they offered an opportunity to lead and the chance to serve my country. By the time I finished my dissertation, I was twenty-six. The cutoff age for the SEAL teams was twenty-eight. It was now or never.

I'd learned that all of the best kinds of compassionate assistance, from Mother Teresa's work with the poor to UNICEF's work with refugee children, meant nothing if a warlord could command a militia and take control of the very place humanitarians were trying to aid. The world needs many more humanitarians than it needs warriors, but there can be none of the former without enough of the latter. I could not shake the memory of little kids in Croatia drawing chalk pictures of the homes that their families had fled at gunpoint.

I took the bus to London and met two SEALs who were working there. We sat down to talk. At the time, I had an offer to stay at Oxford and begin an academic career. I also had an offer to join a consulting firm, where I would have earned more money in my first twelve months of work than both of my parents combined had ever earned in a year. I thought about all of the freedom that Oxford promised, and I thought about all of the wealth that a consulting firm had offered me, and I listened to the deal that the United States Navy put on the table.

If my application was accepted—and they'd accept fewer than ten that year—they would send me to Officer Candidate School. The Navy would pay me $1,332.60 per month. I would submit to the Navy's rules and regulations, and in my first months in the military I would have zero minutes per day of privacy. If I graduated from Officer Candidate School, the Navy would make me an officer, but in turn I would owe them eight years of service. They would offer me one and only one chance to pass Basic Underwater Demolition/SEAL training. If I passed, I'd be on my way to becoming a SEAL officer and leader. If I failed, as over 80 percent of the men who entered SEAL training did, I would still owe the Navy eight years, and they would tell me where and how I would serve.

When I returned to Oxford, I attended a fancy dinner at Rhodes House, built in honor of Cecil Rhodes, who had established the Rhodes scholarships. When we arrived, I pushed open a heavy black door with an iron door knocker cast in the shape of a lion. My date's heels echoed off the white marble floor.

The main dining room of Rhodes House feels like the inside of a small cathedral. At one end of the room a balcony holds pews, and at the opposite end, a wood-paneled wall holds a portrait of Cecil Rhodes. The house was sumptuous in a way that was unlike anything I'd ever seen before Oxford. Thick wooden beams, iron and white glass chandeliers, portraits of former Rhodes scholars, massive black marble fireplaces, woven tapestries on the walls, wood-paneled rooms, leather-bound books, grandfather clocks, paintings of the rugged South African plains, marble floors, a grand piano. A long rectangular table was draped with a thick tablecloth and set with wineglasses, silverware, plates, and napkins folded to look like bishops' hats. Wooden cane chairs with woven seat bottoms creaked when we sat down.

Here was everything that Oxford offered: luxury, rest, time, freedom, wealth.

Yet in the rotunda, I looked up and saw that the stone walls were etched with the names of Rhodes scholars who had died during the two world wars. Seeing those names reminded me that the intention of the scholarship was to create public servants who would "fight the world's fight." Many had left the comfort of Oxford for the trenches of Europe in World War I, or for combat across the globe in World War II. If they had chosen to stay at home rather than to serve, I knew that I wouldn't be standing in Rhodes House, looking up at them.

The philosopher John Stuart Mill once wrote, "War is an ugly thing, but not the ugliest of things. The decayed and degraded state of moral and patriotic feeling which thinks that nothing is worth war is much worse. The person who has nothing for which he is willing to fight, nothing which is more important than his own personal safety, is a miserable creature and has no chance of being free unless made and kept so by the exertions of better men than himself."[8]

I had no desire to see my name etched into any wall anywhere. But I felt a sense of obligation. My family was not wealthy. My parents had worked every day of their lives to support me as a kid. People before me had endowed scholarships that allowed me to pursue eight years of higher education and never have to pay one penny. What was all of that investment for?

Oxford could give me time. The consulting firm could give me money. The SEAL teams would give me little, but make me more. I thought, *I might fail at BUD/S; I might find myself miserable; but I'd live with no regrets.*

I signed the papers as soon as they were set in front of me.

# Part III ★ ★ ★
# HEART AND FIST

# 8 ☆

# Officer Candidate School

L ANDING IN PENSACOLA, FLORIDA, on January 20, 2001,
I looked down at the papers in my hand, a printed list of the
"General Orders of the Sentry." The Officer Candidate School
website had recommended memorizing the orders before I arrived.

> General Order no. 2: To walk my post in a military manner, keeping al-
> ways on the alert and observing everything that takes place within sight
> or hearing.[1]

I was going to OCS to take up my new "post," but after signing my
papers, I now had my doubts. A few things were certain: I knew that
I wanted to serve my country. I knew that I wanted to be tested. The
strong often need to protect the weak, and I believed that rather than
talking about what should be done, I should do it. I should live my values by serving. At the same time, I was leaving a life of extraordinary
freedom that I absolutely enjoyed, and I was reluctant to sacrifice that
freedom.

At Oxford I had done pretty much as I pleased. Walking the ancient
streets of the city one overcast day as mist hung in the air, my girlfriend
and I talked about how nice it would be to go on a beach vacation. On
the next street over we saw a poster hanging in the window of a travel
company that advertised bargain vacations to Greece, and we booked

the trip. At Oxford I'd spent whole days reading novels—*The Grapes of Wrath, The Color Purple*—in the University Parks. When I wanted to serve at one of Mother Teresa's homes for the destitute and dying, I left for India. I trained nine times a week with the boxing team, but every time I showed up I did so by choice. I had days, weeks, months, years at my disposal. At Oxford I learned and trained and lived and served on my own schedule.

My Oxford routine included an early-morning workout and a leisurely breakfast filled with reading for pleasure before I started my day. At OCS, I knew that I'd be lucky to steal two minutes to myself. I had read that entire classes were run through the showers and fought two at a sink to shave in just a few minutes a day. My material possessions had always been minimal—bed, books, boxing gear—but I had been living in comfortable places with time on my hands.

General Order no. 3: Report all violations of orders I am instructed to enforce.

I had never really had any rules to follow, beyond the dictates of my own self-imposed discipline. I was entering a world where every candidate was issued a thick rule book that he was instructed to study, memorize, and obey. The rule book was to be placed on the desk such that the right side of the book ran parallel to the right side of the desk exactly one half inch from the edge, and the bottom of the book ran parallel to the bottom of the desk exactly one half inch from the edge. In the Navy, there were rules about rules.

In my first few days at OCS, I wondered whether my decision to join the military had been a mistake. Once on base, I was greeted by candidate officers—officer candidates in the final two weeks of the thirteen-week program, who were put in charge of the incoming officer candidates. One of these guys—sweating, slightly pudgy, his head shaved—yelled at me to "Walk faster!" as his face broke out in red blotches. *Is he kidding?*

I lined up on a sidewalk with other recruits. I was wearing jeans, hiking boots, and the same faded safari shirt I'd worn to China eight years earlier. I dropped my red duffle bag at my feet. The candidate officers walked up and down the line doing their best imitation of General Patton. "Look straight ahead!"

One candidate officer was sweating and the cracked timbre of his voice gave away the fact that he was nervous. "You want to be a Navy officer?!" he yelled repeatedly. We were marched around the base in our civilian clothes. We were yelled at to stand straight and yelled at not to put our hands in our pockets. There was a tremendous amount of yelling, and it all seemed immature to me. Earl and Henry had demanded extraordinary performance, and I had never once heard them yell at or berate one of their fighters.

The candidate officers collected our orders and started our military service records.

GREITENS, ERIC R.
Initial Date of Entry to Military Service: January 20, 2001.

The yelling continued. "Drink water! Drink more water! Every fountain you pass, you will stop and drink water!" I had boxed for years. I knew exactly how much water I needed to drink. "Drink more water! You will empty a full canteen!" A candidate officer shadowed us. "Do what you're told, and you'll have nothing to fear!"

I must not have looked sufficiently panicked, because a candidate officer put his face next to mine and yelled, "Just wait until your drill instructor shows up, you'll be doing pushups until your arms fall off!" I allowed myself the small rebellion of cocking an eyebrow at him and frowning slightly.

The candidate officers had been in the Navy exactly eleven weeks more than I. They were twenty-two years old. I was only twenty-six, but I felt two decades older than these just-graduated-from-college-and-joined-the-Navy kids who were now yelling at me to look straight ahead. Thanks to Hollywood, I had expected to be greeted by wizened drill sergeants, hard-driving veterans who would push exhausted recruits to their limits. That would have been a test. I looked forward to being pushed by people who had served and earned the right to train me. These guys, strutting around in their recently issued black Navy windbreakers, just seemed like jerks. As they walked up and down the rows of recruits, Napoleon complexes in full bloom, I wondered, *Is this the kind of leadership the military produces? All yelling and ego?*

As I stole glances at my fellow classmates, I became even more disappointed. Many of them were so intimidated, their hands shook when they bent to tie their shoes. *Didn't they see that this was a joke?*

We were issued a set of ill-fitting plain green fatigues—"poopy greens"—and wearing those fatigues, I sat down in the chow hall across from another candidate. The yelling had gotten to him, and after forcing down water all day, he promptly puked a full canteen's worth of bile across the table and soaked my fatigues.

From the chow hall, the candidate officers ran us into our barracks and lined us up in the hallway. Finally, someone from central casting arrived. Our drill instructor, Staff Sergeant Lewis, was a pure green comic-book-like figure of Marine Corps perfection striding down the hall, his face hidden beneath his Smokey Bear hat, his biceps emerging from his perfectly rolled sleeves, boots shining, baritone booming. "Get out of my passageway! Stand against the bulkhead!"

As he walked down the hallway, I remember watching with anthropologist-like fascination and thinking, *This is interesting, watching these college kids get indoctrinated in the U.S. military; you can see that they're afraid. I wonder if the drill instructors practice this, the walking-down-the-hallway moment. I wonder what's going to happen next.* Staff Sergeant Lewis grabbed me by the green collar of my fatigues, walked me back three steps, pressed me against the wall, and yelled, "Join the rest of this sorry group!"

I realized then that I was actually in the Navy.

Staff Sergeant Lewis was a squared-away, hard-core Marine and—I would later come to believe—a great drill instructor. But as I watched him march up and down the hall, yelling and shoving and barking commands, the whole thing struck me as comical. We were instructed to run around the barracks. One woman in her panic ran the wrong direction down the hallway. Staff Sergeant Lewis flew into a rage. "Get over here now!" He grabbed her by her lapels and threw her down the passageway.

We were instructed that after hearing a command, we would yell, "Kill!" and then execute the command. "Eyes right!"

"Kill!"

"Forward, march!"

"Kill!"

During one of these kill-yelling moments I looked across the hallway to see if any of the other candidates also thought that this was ridiculous. Only one of them rolled his eyes in a gesture of shared endurance.

"Kill!"

I had very little confidence that my new class would have been able to kill anything. We had a few "priors"—men and women who had previously been enlisted in the Navy and were now here to become officers—but other than those few, it was largely a group of untested and almost uniformly out-of-shape college grads.

"Your name is on your room. Get there!"

I ran to find my room, which I shared with three roommates, and once we were finally clear of the candidate officers and the drill instructor for a moment, I sat down and started to laugh. I glanced at my new roommates, all of them wide-eyed with fear, and I could see them thinking, *Oh no, the pressure's got to this guy, he's cracking already.*

I went through the next several days unimpressed. We were issued workout clothes that were as dysfunctional—swim trunks with no drawstring—as they were unfashionable, and I began to learn some basic Navy lingo. A door was a "hatch," a wall was a "bulkhead," a bathroom was a "head." Women were not to be referred to as women, but as "females." To say something was to "put the word out." To be quiet was to "lock it up."

We sat down in the chow hall to meals of overcooked food. Teams of drill instructors swarmed as we ate. They walked on top of the tables and kicked silverware and glasses onto the floor with their boots. As candidates walked through the chow hall carrying trays, drill instructors who saw minor infractions of the rules knocked the trays out of their hands and sent spaghetti flying through the air.

A great deal of our time was focused on clothes. We spent hours folding our shirts and shorts and pants. We actually sprayed starch—a lot of it—on our underwear, and then ironed our underwear into perfect squares, and then set these flat squares in our lockers for inspection. We were issued two pairs of running shoes, but the word came down to avoid wearing one pair so that they would be clean for inspection. They were anti-running shoes, apparently. It all seemed absurd.

I had anticipated runs so fast my lungs would be on fire. Instead we ran in formation as a class. I was used to running six-minute miles in my training. Now I was jogging twelve-minute miles while singing silly songs.

> Mission top secret, destination unknown
> We don't know if we're ever coming home
> Stand up, buckle up, and shuffle to the door . . .

And the cadence would ring out, "Left, left, leftee right, lay-eft." As we shuffled down the road I felt my physical conditioning actually slipping away—*When were we going to train hard? Is this really my life?* I'd joined the Navy for a challenge, but at night I held a bottle of fingernail polish in my hands. We were told to cut any loose strings—"Irish pennants"—from our uniforms, and then to dab the spot with fingernail polish so that the strays would not reemerge. *This is my challenge? Fingernail polish?*

Wong was a thin, short, Asian American member of my class who had recently graduated from college with a degree in engineering and whose ambition was to be a civil engineer in the United States Navy. One morning during physical training, we were doing pushups when a drill instructor began yelling at Wong. "What are you doing to my gym floor, candidate?" Wong had been instructed—as we all had—to keep a straight back during pushups, but Wong could not do a single correct pushup. With his arms fully extended, his back sagged so that his crotch pressed into the ground. The drill instructor continued, "What are you doing?! You are defiling my gym floor! Are you lonely here?!"

Wong swiveled his hips in an attempt to straighten his back, but this only incensed the drill instructor. "Oh my goodness! That is one of the most disgusting frickin' acts of violence against a piece of United States Navy property that I have ever seen!"

By this time, Staff Sergeant Lewis, United States Marine Corps, had walked over to Wong. "Wong, what is the matter with you!" And then he yelled out, "Where is that Gritchens!"

*Did he mean me?*

"Gritchens, get over here!"

I jumped up and ran over to Staff Sergeant Lewis.

"Yes, sir!"

"Gritchens, Wong here just became your personal project, do you understand me?"

"Yes, sir!"

"You are going to teach Wong how to do pushups! You are going to teach Wong PT! You are going to move rooms and you are going to live in the same room as Wong, wake at the same time as Wong, and you will teach Wong in every spare moment so that Wong *will* pass the final physical fitness test. I am going to hold you responsible for Wong's PT, do you understand?!"

"Yes, sir!"

I had to make my peace with OCS. I wanted to serve, and I couldn't change the school. I couldn't make us actually run, instead of jog while singing. I couldn't change the curriculum so that we ran the obstacle course instead of polishing belt buckles. I couldn't change the schedule so that we learned to use a shotgun instead of folding our underwear into starched squares. None of that was in my control.

OCS produced Navy officers, and those officers were supposed to be leaders. I had imagined that my leadership would be built at OCS through difficult physical tests—obstacle courses, runs, rescue swims—through hard classroom learning, and through precision military maneuvers—learning how to march, to drill with a rifle, to shoot a pistol. I was wrong on all counts—but I now realized there *was* an opportunity here. I had the chance to lead others, to be of genuine help to my classmates. OCS would be easy for me, but for some of the men and women in my class it was the test of their lives, and if I had joined the military to be of service, here was my chance.

I threw myself into the school. Wong and I began to take breaks every ten minutes while working on our uniforms to knock out fifteen pushups. I became the "PT Body," the person in charge of the physical training of the class. I grew to respect Wong in particular. OCS was hard on him. He must have known that it would be hard when he signed up, but still he signed up.

When we were issued rifles, I worked as hard as I could to master the drill. OCS offered a recognition—a white badge called a snowflake—to any man or woman who graduated with excellence in all three areas of endeavor—physical training, academic tests, and military proficiency. I decided that I might not like the course, but I would master it. We worked together as a class and we made it our goal to graduate with more snowflakes than any other class in our year. We started to cooperate in small ways. I was, for example, never very good at shining shoes, so I made deals with classmates: I washed their sneakers and they polished my shoes. Our class was given a "guide-on," a flag, and we marched with it everywhere we went.

The school remained disappointing. Our classes seemed irrelevant, and in one of the most ridiculous traditions in the Navy, the instructors would stomp their feet when they said things that would be tested. "Buoys are considered an aid to navigation"—and they would stomp their feet two times. Someone explained to me, "That means that'll be a question on the test."

"Why don't they just say, 'This is going to be on the test'?"

"'Cause they're not allowed to tell us what's on the test."

We often stayed up late at night preparing our uniforms, and fell asleep in classes during the day. We continued to polish belt buckles, and almost everyone slept in a sleeping bag *on* their beds rather than *in* their beds because we didn't want to have to take twenty minutes in the morning to prepare our beds again for inspection.

Wong and I continued to take breaks during uniform-prep sessions to do pushups. One night we had a mishap. Guys used different strategies to remove the Irish pennants from their uniforms. Not everyone used the scissors-and-fingernail-polish method. Some guys—Wong being one—actually used a lighter to burn stray strings. The night before an inspection, Wong's technique failed, and he burned a three-finger-sized hole in one of his khaki uniform shirts.

On the morning of the inspection, the drill instructors pulled out Wong's shirt with the black burn ring in his official Navy uniform. They exploded. "Wong, drop down!" With Wong in pushup position, they proceeded to pull every item out of his locker—starched underwear, starched socks, laundry bag, knit cap, pants, belt buckles—and throw everything onto the floor. Three screaming drill instructors worked our room over.

"What is the matter with you people?" one of them yelled. "How are you going to let Wong over here *burn holes* in his uniform? What did you think was going to happen when we walked in here?!"

We had no response.

The drill instructor continued. "Oh, Wong, your uniform looks great except for this *fist-sized hole* that you burned straight through your shirt."

We were all standing at attention, and I bit the inside of my mouth harder than I'd ever bit it before in an attempt not to laugh.

He yelled at Wong: "How do you expect to stand in front of your sailors as an officer, a leader, when you do not have common sense enough to not burn holes in your uniform!"

When Staff Sergeant Lewis walked into the room, which now looked like it had been hit by a hurricane, and saw Wong in the pushup position sweating a puddle on the floor, he immediately looked at me. "Gritchens! What is going on here?"

Another drill instructor answered for me. "Wong here has got all creative, a one-hundred-percent individual, and I think that Gritchens enrolled him in a goddarn contemporary frickin' fashion class!" He held up the burned uniform. "That is some avant-garde frickin' runway model trash right here!"

Staff Sergeant Lewis boomed, "Gritchens, I told you to watch out for Wong! What is going on?!"

"No excuse, sir!" I said. "It's my responsibility, sir!"

Staff Sergeant Lewis ordered the other two men in the room to leave and join the class for chow, and told me to walk into the hallway with him.

The other drill instructors were still going crazy around Wong. "How do you expect me to trust you with a billion-dollar Navy ship if I can't trust you with a goddarn shirt?!" They had turned his bed completely over, and then they went around the room and turned over the three other beds and ripped the well-folded sheets off and threw the sheets in a pile in the middle of the room.

One of the drill instructors asked Wong, "Wong, have you ever played a goddarn sport in your life?!"

They weren't expecting an answer and were surprised when Wong yelled from the ground, "Yes, sir!"

"Really?" the drill instructor asked. "What sport did you play?"

"Football, sir!"

Looking through the door frame I saw two drill instructors look at each other in disbelief. "Really, Wong, you played football? What position did you play?"

Wong yelled, "It was John Madden Football, sir!"

I watched as one of the drill instructors walked out of the room trying to control a laugh. The other drill instructor bent down close to Wong's ear and yelled, "Computer games are not a sport! Do you understand me!"

"Yes, sir!"

I thought that Staff Sergeant Lewis was going to yell at me, but for the first time, he addressed me like a human being—albeit a gruff human being. "Gritchens, Wong is going to miss breakfast. I want you to run down to the McDonald's and buy him something to eat."

"Yes, sir!"

From where we stood in the passageway, Staff Sergeant Lewis could not see Wong, though I could. He yelled, "Wong, Gritchens is going to McDonald's to get you breakfast, what do you want?" And then I saw the drill instructor who was bent down near Wong's ear whisper to him. The drill instructor whispered, "You better tell him, 'Lewis, go get me a goddarn frickin' Egg McMuffin.' Say exactly that or I will beat you for days."

Wong yelled, "Lewis, go get me a goddamn fuckin' Egg McMuffin!"

Staff Sergeant Lewis exploded into the room and together with the other drill instructor they worked Wong through a series of pushups and squat thrusts until he'd laid a huge pool of sweat on the ground.

Staff Sergeant Lewis slowly whipped the class into shape. We marched as a class, trained as a class, studied as a class. We passed inspections and we passed exams and for a group that had never marched together before, soon the movements of our rifles were synchronized on the parade ground. We managed, eventually, to get in and out of the chow hall without trays being knocked out of our hands.

I also started to have a good time with my classmates. We earned the freedom of our Saturdays, and we'd all head out—dressed in our goofy candidate uniforms—and laugh for hours over plates of hot wings and burgers. We'd run for miles on the beach. I got to know my fellow candidates better, and I liked them even more. They'd all come to serve. We became one—same uniforms, same haircuts, same military language—but we all retained a rich diversity of thought and perspective and humor and philosophy. They were—almost to a person—kind and thoughtful, and it was through them that I began to rediscover America. One day while driving off base with my friends, I realized that if I counted the years from the time I became an adult at age eighteen to the time I'd joined the military at nearly twenty-seven, I'd spent more time outside the United States than I'd spent in it. My time away had afforded me an invaluable education about the world, but now, back at home, I was being reintroduced to my fellow Americans by some of our best people, people who had dedicated themselves to serving our country.

I often found myself playing the role of counselor. One man's mother became very sick and he broke down crying as he thought about leaving the Navy to return home. Another man who'd grown up hardscrabble fell apart seven weeks into OCS, thinking that he wanted to quit. He'd just never believed in himself before.

I still found the underwear folding and the keep-your-sneakers-clean-for-inspection stuff ridiculous, but I began to see some of the wisdom in what the drill instructors were doing. Some of the people in my class had never been screamed at before. Now they had two trained drill instructors screaming at them and putting them through what were—for some of them—demanding physical exercises while they were forced to recall answers to essential military questions. This did not necessarily approximate the stress of what they would experience as ship commanders, but it did begin to teach the candidates that they could, that they had to, manage their fear and perform while under stress.

Uncontrolled fear rots the mind and impairs the body. Navy officers have to perform in situations—an incoming missile, a sinking ship—that could cause people to become paralyzed by fear. I'd learned in boxing and in my work overseas that human beings can inoculate themselves against uncontrolled fear. When I first stepped into a boxing ring to spar, my heart rate was high, my adrenaline pumped, my muscles were tense—and I got beat up. After years of Earl's training I could get in a ring with an appreciation of how dangerous my opponent was, and I could keep my heart rate steady, my muscles loose, and I could fight well. The same thing happened as I became more comfortable working in dangerous situations overseas. I didn't dismiss the dangers—in fact I became even more finely attuned to the dangers around me—but I was able to operate in those fear-inducing environments without my fear interfering with me. OCS was—for many—their first taste of chaos and confusion.

Likewise, while I found the unrelenting inspections of our uniforms to be mind numbing, it did teach attention to detail. If one man had lint on the back of his coat, we'd all pay. We learned to look out for each other, quite literally.

As we progressed, Staff Sergeant Lewis started to show a human side. We weren't allowed junk food on base, and when it was mailed to us in care packages, candidates sometimes were forced to eat it. During one mail call, one of the candidates was shoving Ding Dongs in his mouth and doing jumping jacks. As the Ding Dong scarfer tried to shout, "Yes, sir!" shards of Ding Dong flew down the hallway. Staff Sergeant Lewis had his head bent forward underneath his big Smokey Bear hat, but the slightest vibration of the hat gave away the fact that he was trying not to laugh out loud.

My friend Matt DiMarco and I organized an extravagantly named "Deathwish PT," and in the evening we would take a group from our class outside for extra physical training. No one came close to death, but we did have a lot of fun. We'd knock out pull-ups and blow off steam by laughing about the day. We competed in an all-OCS tug of war, and our class flag was held high on the victory stand.

Even Staff Sergeant Lewis started to take a bit of pride in our class. He would call out, "One-Five" (we were class 15-01), and we would shout back, "Hell yeah!"

Wong—like all of us—was required to complete forty-seven push-ups in two minutes on the final physical fitness test. In the end, he knocked out more than ninety, stood up, and said, "Guess that's how it's done." By graduation day—our class now dressed in choker whites, marching in formation, executing sword salutes—we had become Navy officers.

I walked off the parade field with orders to report to SEAL training in Coronado, California.

# 9 ☆

# SEAL Training

THE SILVER STRAND stretches for seven straight, beautiful miles along the ocean, connecting Imperial Beach, California, and the peninsula of Coronado. Waves rolling in from the Pacific crash at Naval Amphibious Base, Coronado, home of Naval Special Warfare Command and Navy SEAL training.

As I turned onto the Silver Strand, I thought about the relatively brief but rich history of the Navy SEALs. The original frogmen were the Underwater Demolition Teams of World War II. Before the Allied landings at Normandy, the Germans placed obstacles underwater and on the beaches to deter landing craft and obstruct tanks and vehicles. The Underwater Demolition Teams were sent in to scout the landing zones, blow up the obstacles, and clear a path for the invasion. If the obstacles hadn't been cleared, landing craft would have been stopped in water too deep for the soldiers to wade ashore, and German guns would have torn them apart. Without the frogmen, the Allied invasion on D-day would have literally been dead in the water.

The training I was about to undergo was built on the same principles—often we learned the very same tactics—as those of the men who led the invasion onto the beaches of Normandy. Rangers, Army Special Forces, Marine Force Recon, Air Force Pararescue Jumpers: all are incredible special operations forces that produce dedicated and capable warriors. Each unit has a different mission and different skill sets. All go through incredibly difficult training. Basic Underwater Demolition/SEAL training is, however, universally recognized as the hardest military training in the world. BUD/S lasts a grueling six months. Candidates are pushed to their physical and mental limits. As I drove through the gate in 2001, I knew that only about 10 percent of BUD/S students graduated with their original class. Ninety percent failed or were rolled back to another class. Around 250 men graduated from BUD/S every year, and even then, not all of those survived the additional six-plus months of advanced training it takes to become a Navy SEAL.

To put this in perspective, consider that the National Football League drafted 255 men in 2010. An NFL draft pick who is signed by a team is guaranteed a salary of $325,000, which does not include the bonus money that many of the top draft picks receive (which for some players equals tens of millions of dollars).[1] In the same year, the starting salary for an enlisted Navy man undergoing SEAL training ranged from $19,464 per year for an E-2 (less than two years experience) to $24,744 per year for an E-5.[2] In both cases, tremendous athletes of great courage are put through years of testing to become members of an elite group. I know and admire some of the great people who have played professional sports, but in the course of my training I would come to believe that the 250 men per year who become SEALs are far more richly rewarded.

A young sailor dressed in camouflage fatigues stood up from behind the desk to greet me. "How are you, sir?" Dustin Connors was a physical training phenom in BUD/S—he could fly over the obstacle course and run through soft sand like he was running on asphalt. He later served with SEAL Team One in Iraq and is now a father and an engineer living in California. We would endure a lot together.

"I'm great. How are you?" I shook his hand.

"You gonna be in Class 237?"

"I don't know," I said. Dustin explained that he was in a previous class, broke his leg during training, and rolled back into Class 237. He told me that 237 was "classing up"—getting ready for the initial indoc-trination phase of training. He said that we'd probably be in BUD/S together.

He stamped my orders and told me that I should come back in the morning. I'd be issued my gear and I'd receive a final medical exam be-fore training started.

We had to stencil our names on everything that they gave us in BUD/S: every T-shirt, every knife, every fin. The next morning I was handed my fins, and on them I clearly saw the names of men who'd been issued this gear before me.

~~Walker~~
~~Rodriguez~~
Herman

None of them had made it. I took out a stencil kit, crossed out "Her-man," and wrote "Greitens." Would somebody be issued these fins in a few weeks and have to put a line through my name?

We began the first official day of BUD/S at 0500 on the beach. Under any other circumstances, it would have been a morning to enjoy. Small waves crashed on the shore and rolled up the sand. As we ran onto the beach, I looked up for a split second and thought, *This is beautiful;* the sky was still a deep dark blue, and stars were shining over the ocean.

But we didn't have time to enjoy the scenery. When the instructors came out, they'd want a muster report, a full accounting of our class. The other officers and I bent our freshly shaved heads together and used a small red-lens flashlight to read the clipboard that held a full list of the names of the men in our class who had survived the pre-BUD/S indoctrination course. We had started with 220 names. Now, due to quitting and injury, we were down to just over 160.

Our first task would be to run four miles in soft sand. We were all wearing boots, camouflage pants, and white T-shirts. We milled around the beach nervously before the instructors came out. One guy tried a joke—"Is this when the Charger Girls come out to cheer for us?"—but we were too nervous to laugh. Every man knew that most of the men on the beach that morning wouldn't make it.

"Drop!" The instructors walked onto the beach and we all fell and pressed our hands into the sand. As a class we knocked out pushups in unison:

"Down."

"One!" we boomed.

"Down."

"Two!"

"Down."

"Three!"

An instructor dragged his boot through the sand to make a starting line, and the instructions were relayed over a bullhorn: "There is a truck parked two miles down the beach. Run down the beach. Run around the truck. Then run back here. You have thirty-two minutes. And gentlemen," the voice paused, as we were about to hear for the first time a line that we would hear thousands of times in BUD/S, "it pays to be a winner."

Just then a truck cracked on its headlights, and the beams tore through the black morning. The truck looked impossibly far away.

"Fuck, that's not two miles," someone grumbled.

"This is bullshit."

"I heard they make it impossible to make it on the first run; sometimes it's more like five miles."

From the bullhorn came: "Ready." We all took in a breath. "Begin."

The pack of men started sprinting. The class was in a panic. White T-shirts went flying past. Men kicked up sand as they sprinted through the morning. I yelled, "Be steady. Be steady," but fear ruled that morning, and the class flew down the beach.

The classmate I was running beside was an accomplished triathlete, and we looked at each other in disbelief at the panic around us. As we reached the half-mile mark, the sprinters had slowed desperately, and some were already at a jog. They were jogging, then sprinting, then coughing and stopping, then running again. We still had three and a half miles to go, and already these guys were in trouble. These were athletes: high school and college football players, water polo players, state champion wrestlers. Many of them would later ace the runs, but as we'd learn over and over again in BUD/S, physical fitness mattered little without the mental fortitude to deal with fear.

As we approached the turnaround truck, the beams of the headlights cut through the morning and lit up a small group of us running tight together near the front of the pack. We ran half-blinded into the headlights and could hear the instructors yelling, "Take off your shirts! Take off your shirts! Throw 'em in the back of the truck!" We peeled off our shirts as we ran, tossed them in the back of the truck, and ran for the finish line.

The instructors had all been through BUD/S before. They knew every trick. They knew that in the dark, in the confusion of 160 men, it would have been easy for any one man to make a quick turn on the beach short of the truck and start running back to the finish. Our shirts, however, had our names stenciled on them, and they would provide the proof that we'd made it to the halfway point.

We ran swiftly back down the beach, and those of us who ran across the line in the sand under the cutoff time were sent to stretch.

As the thirty-two-minute mark came closer, desperate trainees sprinted for the finish. Instructors prowled near the line in the sand, and as the watch ticked past the time limit and men raced in late, the instructors yelled, "Hit the surf! Straight to the water!" And the exhausted men went stumbling into the 50-some-degree water of the Pacific Ocean.

When the men came out of the waves soaking wet, the instructors yelled, "Get sandy!" and the men dropped and rolled until every inch of their bodies was covered in sand. "Pushups—knock 'em out!" the instructors yelled. And the men did pushups until they were exhausted, and then they were made to flip over and do flutter kicks, and then it was back to pushups, back to flutter kicks, back to pushups. "Stand up. Grab a partner. Fireman's-carry drills down the beach. Run to Instructor Wade. Now!" Men whose quads were already shot picked up other soaking two-hundred-pound men and ran down the beach.

One of the instructors walked over to those of us stretching and said, "Gentlemen, observe this closely. It pays to be a winner at BUD/S." The "losers" were now running back into the water, diving in, then running back out to the beach. Running in; running out. Running in; running out. "You fail. You pay. You fail. You pay," an instructor yelled from the shore.

The instructors circled around a man who'd failed the run and was now covered in salt water and sand. He was in the pushup position, his butt in the air. His arms were shaking and they were failing him. One instructor yelled at him, "You know what the prize is for second place in a gunfight?"

"Negative, Instructor."

"It's death. There is no prize for second place. Now do your pushups properly."

The man's arms were shaking and drool was hanging from his lip as he tried to spit the sand out of his mouth. He must have said something like, "I'm trying," because the instructor exploded: "There is no *try*. We do not *try*. Your teammates do not need you to *try* to cover their backs. Your swim buddy does not need you to *try* to rescue him on a dive. Your platoon does not need you to *try* to shoot straight. There is no *try*. There is only *do*. *Do*, or *do not*. There is no *try*." By the time we ran to breakfast, several men had quit.

The instructor staff made it easy to quit. They encouraged it. If at any moment in the training a candidate said, "I quit," or, "I D.O.R." (drop on request), he was removed from training immediately, and often we never saw him again.

The quitters would later have to "ring out" by ringing a bell three times. They then set their BUD/S helmets on the ground. As each day passed, the line of helmets grew longer.

In an effort to provide "excellent customer service," the instructors would sometimes bring a bell out with us while we trained, and you could "express quit" by going straight to the bell.

I arrived every morning at the base before there was any hint of sun. As I pulled in, I often heard hard, angry rock music blaring from the barracks—*Shut up! Shut up! Shut up!*

The screaming lyrics reflected the musical tastes of a few of our young hard-chargers. Men dressed in camouflage with shaved heads milled about the courtyard trading guesses about what the day might entail.

"Hey, Mr. G."

"What's goin' on, Lipsky?"

"Just another morning in paradise."

I smiled as I walked in to work. If I had stayed at Oxford to teach or gone to work for a consulting firm, it's hard to imagine that I would have been up this early and having this much fun. I realized also that if I'd stayed at Oxford or gone to work for a Fortune 500 company, I could have lived my entire life with the same kind of people who went to Duke or Oxford, or worked at fancy law firms. There was a "diversity" of people at each of those institutions: they had men and women from Indonesia and Zambia and Turkmenistan, and they had people of every color there—but in truth, the backgrounds of the people at these "diverse" institutions were often remarkably similar. Almost all of them understood what it meant to be a professor or a lawyer, but few people there understood what it meant to be a police officer or to have a job where you depended on the strength of your back. They easily thought of themselves as cosmopolitans, as "global" citizens, while these men at BUD/S thought of themselves simply as Americans.

The men in our class didn't fit the Hollywood vision of what it meant to be a Navy SEAL. There were few Hollywood physiques. These guys weren't flashy. They were just tough. Andrejus Babachinas was a member of the Lithuanian Special Forces who came to train with us. I watched him pull his 250-pound body up a rope using only his arms.

Aftermath of the suicide truck bomb in Fallujah, Iraq. The crater in the foreground is where the truck exploded. The blast blew off the entire western wall of the barracks.

JOEL POUDRIER

All uncredited photographs appear courtesy of the author.

The shifu smashing bricks over the heads of kung fu students in a test of their strength and willpower.

Survivors of the ethnic cleansing in Bosnia, in the Gasinci refugee camp. These families had lost all of their material possessions; many had lost friends and family.

Refugee boys in the Puntizela camp played soccer in the afternoon. These moments of recreation and joy helped children and their families to maintain hope.

Mothers and children outside a health care clinic in Rwanda. I hesitated to take photographs until the women welcomed me.

Boys and girls whose parents died during the genocide in Rwanda were sheltered in centers for unaccompanied children. Here a volunteer brings some joy into their lives.

Sitting with some of the younger children at the Mano Amiga home in Bolivia. Spending time with children of the street in Bolivia convinced me that in some ways, a background of abuse and abandonment was harder for children to overcome than the violence of war.

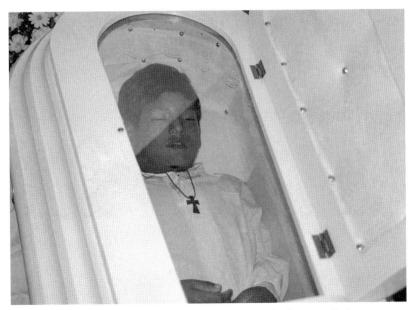

Juan Carlos, one of the children of the street, died as a result of poor medical care.

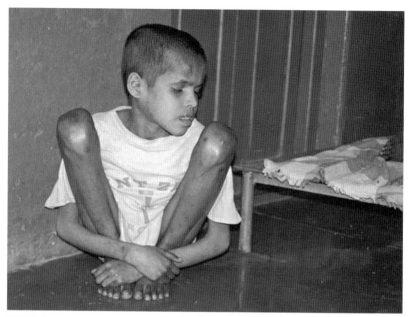

A boy in Mother Teresa's home for the destitute and dying in Varanasi, India. He had squatted and begged for so many years that his legs became deformed.

With an orphan named Fjorda in Albania. Many of the children were severely underdeveloped.

The Oxford boxing team, 1998, after we beat Cambridge, 5–4. The victory was part of the longest winning streak in the history of Oxford sports.

Landing an uppercut in my first Varsity Match.

The grinder: the famous concrete compound where men crank out thousands of pushups and sit-ups. With the exception of the week after Hell Week, all students at BUD/S are required to run from place to place during training. RICHARD SCHOENBERG

As indoctrination at BUD/S begins, classes often start with over two hundred men learning how to run with boots on, in soft sand. By the end of training, only two or three out of every ten men will graduate. RICHARD SCHOENBERG

An oddity of BUD/S is that part of the brutal training takes place on one of the most beautiful beaches in the country. Here, students run toward the Hotel del Coronado, a famous luxury resort. RICHARD SCHOENBERG

Drown-proofing is one of BUD/S's most feared evolutions. With their feet tied together and their hands bound behind their backs, these men will swim fifty meters, then perform a series of exercises, including retrieving a face mask from the bottom of the pool with their teeth. RICHARD SCHOENBERG

The principle of surf torture is simple: Lie in fifty-degree water. Stay there as your core body temperature drops. RICHARD SCHOENBERG

Boat races. The goal is to get the boat out past the surf zone before the waves crash down on you. Boats that fail to make it can send seven two-hundred-pound men flying through the air. RICHARD SCHOENBERG

Log PT is a truly painful evolution. Spiritual training by physical means, it tests teamwork as much as endurance. RICHARD SCHOENBERG

A student reaches for the wall at the end of his fifty-meter underwater swim. Notice the instructor swimming several feet above him, ready to pull him to the surface if he passes out. Because of the difficulty and danger of BUD/S, instructors watch over students every step of the way. RICHARD SCHOENBERG

Fifteen feet down, a student (right) performs underwater knot-tying in front of an instructor. During this evolution, one of our classmates passed out and had to be revived on the pool deck. RICHARD SCHOENBERG

Instructors blast rounds at the beginning of Hell Week. Water from hoses, smoke from grenades, insults from bullhorns, and the whine of air raid sirens bombard trainees. The instructors aim to sow chaos and confusion. RICHARD SCHOENBERG

During Hell Week the instructors always made sure the bell was nearby. Men who quit "rang out" by ringing the bell three times. RICHARD SCHOENBERG

The instructors lined us up on the sand berm to watch the sun go down at the beginning of the first full night of Hell Week. At night, the water gets colder, the hours get longer, and the instructors become more vicious. RICHARD SCHOENBERG

In the demo pit at BUD/S, students practice taking cover during incoming artillery fire. Practice creates habits, and I fell into this position when we were hit by the suicide truck bomb in Iraq. RICHARD SCHOENBERG

James Suh and Matt Axelson were both in my boat crew during SEAL Qualification Training. When Axe was later pinned down in a firefight with the Taliban in Afghanistan, James boarded a helicopter to fly in for a rescue mission. Both men died that day, June 28, 2005.

With James Suh before a training evolution in the California desert.

Our Mark V detachment outside our base in Zamboanga, Philippines.

Riding an elephant with my BUD/S classmate and fellow boat detachment commander Kaj Larsen in Thailand.

The Mark V special operations craft. Commanding two of these boats in Southeast Asia was one of the highlights of my military service.

Outside the government center in Fallujah, Iraq. Note the American Humvee beside me and the Iraqi police trucks in the background. We were most effective when we were able to work well with our Iraqi allies.

At the opening of The Mission Continues in 2008. With me are Matthew Trotter, whose fellowship was named in honor of Travis Manion, and Travis's mother, Janet Manion.

Drew Bolton was the son of a logger from northern California. Drew was unbreakable. He was also an avid reader and a fan of Ralph Waldo Emerson. And then there was Jordan Maywell from Texas. Jordan's twin brother, Jason, went through BUD/S a few classes before, and one day Jordan slipped into Jason's uniform and did a day of training while his brother took the day off. At the time, Jordan was a civilian. What he did was crazy, not to mention illegal, but it showed that he had guts, and that he'd do anything for his brother.

Much of our BUD/S training took place at the combat training tank, a specially designed 164′ x 82′ Olympic-sized pool that had sections of varying depth levels: fifteen feet, nine feet, and three feet.

We ran to the training tank dressed in camouflage shirts, camouflage pants, black boots, and our green "first phase" helmets. We all wore a "web belt"—a thick belt made for carrying gear. Attached to the belt was a canteen, and tied around the top of the canteen was a piece of white rope.

In any free moment—waiting for chow, waiting our turn to run the obstacle course—we'd practice tying knots. We learned how to tie knots because we needed to be able to attach explosives to obstacles underwater. Knot tying is a skill as old as the frogmen themselves. The men creeping up the beaches at Normandy had to tie knots in the dead of night, their hands stiff with cold, to blow up the Nazis' obstacles, and now we were going to be tested.

When we arrived we saw that the instructors had strung a line in the water in the fifteen-foot section of the tank, just inches from the bottom of the pool. I jumped in the water with a swim buddy and we swam to an instructor treading in front of us. We both took a deep breath, made a fist, and pointed our thumbs down to indicate that we were about to dive. As we kicked to the bottom of the pool, pressure built on my eardrums. Using the Valsalva technique we'd been taught, I grabbed my nose and blew hard until I felt my ears pop and the pressure equalize.

When we reached the bottom of the pool I pulled out my rope and started to tie a knot around the line in the water. The knots were easy to tie on dry land, but at fifteen feet underwater I was floating upward as I tied, and I had to keep releasing my hand from the knot to paddle myself down again.

When my swim buddy and I finished tying our knots, we gave the instructor the OK? sign. He twisted his face into a question behind his mask. He exhaled, and a few bubbles ran for the surface. He looked at the left side of our knots, then the right side. He tugged on both knots, and just as I felt that I couldn't stay down there much longer, he gave us both the OK sign. We untied our knots and made for the surface.

Treading on the surface, we took five big breaths, and then our instructor said, "Let's go," and we swam down to tie the next knot. We had to tie five knots, and it got harder with each trip to the bottom.

One of the men in our class swam down and, after tying his knot, started floating up to the surface, his body limp. The instructors grabbed him and swam him to the surface. The rest of us were ordered out of the pool. We were made to sit down and face away from the casualty, but we could hear their efforts at CPR—the body being dragged out of the water, the chest being compressed, the breaths taken—as they worked to revive our classmate. The man was revived on the pool deck and lived. He also suffered brain damage and left BUD/S.

Lieutenant John Skop, the officer in charge of the BUD/S class two classes before ours, had not been so lucky. Pulmonary edema occurs when the extreme stress of training causes fluid to be pushed into the lungs. This reduces lung capacity. It's like drowning on dry land. Symptoms include chest pain, a feeling of drowning, and coughing up blood. Most BUD/S trainees were in such good physical condition that even with reduced lung capacity, they could perform at a high level. So it was possible for someone with pulmonary edema to keep training, keep pushing himself, keep anyone from knowing that he was in trouble.

The instructors warned us over and over again to tell them if we were coughing up blood. In that same combat training tank, Lieutenant Skop had been doing caterpillar races. In those races, teams of men wearing lifejackets line up in the pool. Each man—buoyed by his life-jacket—wraps his legs around the man in front of him. The men then begin to row with their arms—looking like an ungainly caterpillar—as they race against other teams the length of the pool. The lieutenant had kept his pulmonary edema a secret, and when he started to struggle through the caterpillar race, his lungs finally filled with fluid. He died on the pool deck.

When I first heard Skop's story I thought, *That was stupid. I would have let the doctors know. I would have just rolled back into another class and completed my training later.*

My thinking changed when I was actually in the middle of BUD/S. When in BUD/S, the last thing in the world you want is to be rolled out of your class for medical reasons and have to start training all over again with another class of men you don't know.

A few weeks later, a friend and fellow member of BUD/S Class 237 would watch me spit out what felt like a lungful of blood after I'd come up from tying a knot at fifty feet. I turned to him and said, "I'm fine." All he said then was, "Come on. Better not let the instructors see you."

As the weeks progressed, our original mass of 220 men contracted to a smaller class of men we knew, liked, and trusted. Men quit as the runs continued and the swims got longer. Men quit in the pool and were hurt on the obstacle course. One man fell forty feet from the high-tower obstacle and broke his legs. We learned how to row our boats as a team and we learned how to make our backpacks float so we could pull them through the ocean at night. We learned how to sharpen our knives, and we learned how to patrol as a team. Many of the evolutions were painful.

One thing we all enjoyed, however, was working with the helicopters. We ran to them as their rotors flew, and the first time we climbed inside we all had on smiles a mile wide. As my helo lifted free of the ground, I leaned over and yelled to Greg Hall—one of the petty officers in my boat crew—"This is cool!"

He thought I was giving him some kind of last-minute instruction, and he tapped his ear to indicate that he couldn't hear me. "This is COOOOL!" I yelled. His face broke into a wide grin, and he gave me a thumbs-up as we flew over San Diego Bay.

The helo slowed to ten knots. We flew ten feet above the water of the bay, and the rotors whumped and churned the water into a wild froth. I was in charge of a boat crew of seven men and we all stood and formed a line. When the instructor pointed out the door, the first man jumped. The helo continued to fly, and we jumped at intervals one after another, inserting a long string of swimmers in the water. Hall was the second-to-last man to jump.

Hall was a former Marine and a former college football player. He was only about five nine, but he must have weighed 215 pounds. Greg Hall was a rock. He had a ready sense of humor, but he was also dead serious about getting done whatever job was set in front of him. I'd come to trust him completely. In a class full of young and inexperienced men who weren't used to being tested and weren't used to taking authority, Hall was a beacon of strength and maturity.

After Hall, I was the last man out of the helo. The instructor held his fist in the hold sign, then he pointed out the helo and I jumped. We were now a line of men afloat in the water. The helo flew a wide circle around the bay and dropped its ladder as it approached us again. Now the test began. The helo would fly over us—again at ten feet, again at ten knots—and each man in our boat crew had to grab the ladder as it was dragged through the water, and then climb up the ladder and into the helo.

We were practicing a method of inserting and extracting SEALs on an operation. A helo would fly in and drop off a team in the water. The team would conduct a mission, swim back out into the ocean, and the helo would lower a ladder, fly by, and pick up the team.

Hall spun around in the water to check our alignment. We were all in one straight line, and he held his arm high out of the water and gave me a thumbs-up. The first man in our crew grabbed the ladder and started to climb. He had stepped up three rungs—this was perfect—when the ladder hit the second man. Yap was a commando from Singapore who had come to BUD/S to train with American special operations, and the ladder twisted as he grabbed it. By the time the ladder hit the third man, Yap had climbed only one rung, and now the ladder was in a spiral all the way down and men were being dragged through the water. Still the helo kept flying and the men kept climbing.

I adjusted my mask over my eyes. The helicopter threw up a swirling mess of water as it approached. I knew that in this mechanical storm of wind and water it wasn't uncommon for men to miss the ladder altogether, an offense that would be severely punished by the instructors.

As the rotor wash of the helo approached Hall, I could make out only three bodies clad in black wetsuits hanging on to the same twisted ladder. Hall was swallowed by the rotor wash, and then the helo flew toward me. I had my eyes on the ladder as the whine of the engines grew louder still, and the mechanical storm approached.

Suddenly, I was floating in a very calm San Diego Bay. I punched the water in anger. I thought I had missed my grab.

I looked up and saw the helo climbing at thirty, forty, fifty feet, with two of our men still clinging to the ladder. Just then one of them let go—and I knew that it was Lucas, a former Marine and the only African American in my boat crew. I watched him fall through the air, his arms spinning, until he brought them to his side and crashed into the bay. The other man, who I later knew to be Greg Hall, was still holding on.

I later learned that after Hall grabbed the ladder, and as the helo approached me, a critical failure occurred in one of the engines. The helo had come a foot or two from crashing into the bay, and the pilots turned to make an emergency run back to Naval Air Station North Island. The instructors had yelled at Lucas to jump—he was safer in the water than in a disabled helo—and so Lucas let go of the ladder and plunged into the bay.

But as Lucas jumped, he freed the ladder of his weight, and as the twisted ladder righted itself, hanging on to the bottom was Greg Hall.

Now the helo was at eighty feet, then one hundred. The instructors yelled to Hall over the whump of the rotor and the whine of the engine, with the symbol of a closed fist, "Hold! Hold! Hold!"

Hall later told me that as he watched the world below him fly by at sixty knots from over 150 feet in the air, and he looked up at the instructors yelling, "Hold! Hold!" he thought to himself, *Well, no shit!*

Hall held on to the ladder as the helo flew over the 200-foot-high Coronado Bridge, and I can only imagine what those morning commuters thought when they looked through their windshields, coffee in hand, and saw stuntman Hall flying overhead. Hall had a wild ride, but the helo landed safely back at North Island, and Hall was unhurt.

Throughout BUD/S, whenever we failed to do something that we should have done, we had to do pushups. If you should have sharpened your knife, but failed to, you did pushups. If you should have inspected your lifejacket for saltwater corrosion, but failed to, you did pushups. As Hall was walking away from the helo, the instructors yelled, "Hall, drop down!" Hall dropped into the pushup position. "Hall, you should have died. Do pushups for being alive."

Greg Hall knocked out twenty happy pushups and yelled, "Hooyah for being alive!"

Our confidence grew with each passing day. Not only were we still alive and still at BUD/S, but we learned we had a team we could count on. We learned that we could do things we might once have thought were impossible.

I stood with five other men next to the ledge of the combat training tank as our swim buddies tied our feet together so that we could not kick free. We then put our hands behind our backs, and our swim buddies tied our hands together.

"How's that?" My swim buddy asked.

"Feels good."

He tugged at the knot to check it a final time. A knot that came undone meant automatic failure. The five of us on the pool deck exchanged glances and then, with our feet tied together and our hands tied behind our backs, we jumped into the pool. It was time for drown-proofing.

The first test was to swim fifty meters. We dolphin-kicked toward the other end of the combat training tank, rolling to our sides every few kicks to catch a breath. After that, it was time to "float." Using a small dolphin kick, we floated about a foot below the surface, kicking up to the surface for air every twenty seconds or so. After five minutes of this, our instructor yelled, "Now bob!"

I blew the air out of my lungs and sank to the bottom of the pool along with the other men around me. As I felt my feet hit the bottom, I crouched into a squat, then pushed off hard. Shooting up through the water, I blew all the remaining air out of my lungs, and as soon as my head broke the surface, I inhaled for an instant and then began to sink again.

Calm was key. If your mind ran to thoughts of your bound feet, or you struggled to free your hands tied behind your back, problems compounded quickly. Timing was also key. A mistimed breath could mean swallowing water, which could lead to panic, which could lead to forgetting to blow all the air out of your lungs. When that happened, men ended up suspended—limbs bound—several feet from the life-giving air, and feet away from the bottom of the pool.

Drown-proofing required intense concentration. During training one day before the test, our hands were bound, but instead of our feet being tied, we were instructed to press them together to simulate them being bound. As we bobbed, my thoughts wandered for a moment. As I came to the surface I mistimed a breath, swallowed water, and went sputtering back to the bottom of the pool. I pushed hard for the surface, but I was out of air, and my mind was running in circles of fear. I pulled my feet apart and started treading water. "Whatsa matter, Greitens? Oh, no, looks like we got another officer panicking on us." I took in a breath to calm myself and let my body sink back down again to the bottom of the pool.

Unwavering mental focus was essential. I came to learn that in SEAL training and on deployments, the greatest distractions for men were not physical challenges, but family issues. The military can place a great strain on family life, and problems in family life can place a great strain on people serving in the military. Men in good relationships were not just happier men, they were also better trainees, and—I'd later come to believe—better SEALs and better public servants. Like drown-proofing, service overseas often demanded total concentration. Walking down an Iraqi road on patrol, men need to be thinking about what's happening in the alley on their right, not about an unhappy wife at home. On deployment, I've had men whose wives left them, a man whose child was diagnosed with autism, men whose homes were broken into, men whose parents died. Life doesn't stop when a service member heads overseas.

I learned how difficult it can be to stay focused when you're worried about someone that you love, and for that learning I'm grateful. I think that it made me a better officer on deployment. I'd check in with guys: "You call home recently? Everything good?" Usually guys would just brag about how great their kids were doing. But on a few occasions, I had guys wake me up in the middle of the night to tell me that they feared their marriage was falling apart, or to tell me that their kid was sick. Strong guys would break down crying. Of course, just like life doesn't stop at home, the mission overseas doesn't stop either, and those same men had to wake up the next day and get back to dangerous work. Emerson once wrote that concentration is the secret of strength. You can't chase two rabbits at once. And for men to perform overseas while their lives kept running at home, absolute concentration on the task at hand is essential.

During the actual drown-proofing, after the bobbing we moved on to flips. Again we blew all the air out of our lungs. As I touched the pool bottom I kicked my bound legs over my head and did a back flip. I pushed off the pool bottom and went to the surface for a snatch of air and then I sank again, blowing bubbles of air until I felt the bottom of the pool. This time I did a front flip underwater.

I pushed off the pool bottom. When I next broke the surface, I saw my swim buddy standing on the pool deck holding my facemask. As I sank back down, he threw it into the nine-foot-deep water. I watched the mask float to the bottom of the pool, and on my next push to the surface I grabbed a breath of air and rolled forward. I dolphin-kicked for the mask on the pool bottom, and when I'd made it to the bottom of the pool, I moved the strap of the mask into place with my nose, then bit the strap tight, swung my feet to the bottom of the pool, and pushed again for the surface. I bobbed five more times, breathing at the surface as I held the mask with clenched teeth.

The men at BUD/S wanted to be SEALs for a wide variety of reasons. Some were inspired by relatives, some were inspired by movies, some had played "special operations" video games. Some sought the respect of their parents and their friends. Some wanted to impress a girl. Some just wanted to test themselves. Many of the men had grown up in a culture where they'd inherited ideals about manhood from beer commercials and sitcoms. And whether the men they saw on TV were portrayed as overgrown and selfish boys, or as wimpy doofs forever outwitted and always ineffective at accomplishing anything worthwhile, the men who came to BUD/S knew—even if they might not have articulated it—that there had to be more. They knew that there had to be more to being a man and a responsible adult, and they knew that they wanted to become someone worthy.

We sometimes ran north of the BUD/S compound and onto the civilian beach in front of the Hotel del Coronado—an architecturally spectacular hotel and a popular vacation destination. One day during one of these runs—we still had about sixty men in the class and we were sick of looking at each other—the bikini-clad women lying out on the beach captured our attention.

Senior Chief Salazar led the run that morning. Senior Chief was a shorter man, powerfully built, who had a long history of honorable operations in the SEAL teams. He was also the epitome of an excellent trainer, unapologetically demanding and relentlessly positive. Every man in our class admired Senior Chief Salazar. I suspect that he knew this, and he used his power to teach important lessons, not just about combat, but also about how to live. "You know what, guys? I want to tell you something about women. And I want to tell you something about what it means to be a real frogman. You know how a real frogman treats women?" We kept running, none of us with any idea what Senior Chief would say. "If you're a real frogman, then every time a woman leaves your side, she'll feel better about herself."

In a culture where so many had been fed a steady diet of shallow macho posturing that involved degrading women, here was a simple message: "Every time a woman leaves your side, she'll feel better about herself." Many men had come to BUD/S not only to learn what it meant to be SEALs; many of them had come because they needed to learn what it meant to be men.

Waiting wasn't going to make the pool any shorter, so I stood with one of the first groups. There were five of us lined up on the pool deck, with five instructors treading in the water. We were standing at the deep end of the combat training tank. The water was fifteen feet deep, and the pool was twenty-five meters across. Our task was straightforward: jump in the pool and execute a front flip underwater, then swim underwater to the other side of the pool and back again, for a total swim of fifty meters underwater.

Standing on the pool deck, my mind started to race: should I try to jump in as far as possible, and save myself an extra foot of swimming, or will that use too much energy and oxygen? Should I do the front flip as soon as I hit the water, or wait until I sink a few feet?

I grabbed control of my thoughts and tried to concentrate on only three things: take a deep breath before I jumped, go deep, and stay relaxed while I swam.

I could feel the eyes of the men in my class on my back. I was being watched because I was one of the first students to swim, and because I was one of the class leaders. They were watching to see if I was worthy to lead them.

I took a very long, very slow, very deep breath, and I jumped. I did the front flip immediately, and I started swimming for the other side of the pool at a steep angle, hoping to get as deep as I could as quickly as possible.

Boyle's law states that at a fixed temperature and within a closed system, pressure and volume are inversely proportional. The deeper you go, the higher the partial pressure of oxygen in your system. The bottom line is that it's actually easier to swim fifty meters at fifteen feet deep than to swim the same distance at five feet deep. Mr. Boyle was very far from my mind just then, but I knew that I wanted to be deep. I pulled, kicked, and glided about three inches above the bottom of the pool.

As I came to the turnaround at twenty-five meters, I touched the wall, set my legs, and pushed. The water rushed past me, but the other side of the pool looked very far away, and I was out of air.

As I put my hands out in front to start the next stroke, I thought to myself, *Stay* . . . and as I pulled my arms back, I completed the mantra: . . . *relaxed.* I repeated this: *Stay . . . relaxed . . . Stay . . . relaxed.* I was out of air, and my body was desperate for oxygen, but thousands of men had done this before me. Thousands more would follow.

I had to keep my heartbeat steady. *Stay . . . relaxed . . .* The faster your heart beats, the more oxygen you use.

I pulled again, and then I was there. An instructor launched me onto the pool deck as I touched the finish wall, and I crashed onto the deck between two other students, each of us on our hands and knees, breathing hard. A corpsman bent down and looked in my eyes. I held up the OK sign with my right hand and said, "I'm OK."

"Good job, sir."

Was that it? Was that the swim I'd been worried about for months? I stood up and walked over to my boat crew. "Guys," I took another deep breath, "just go deep, and stay relaxed on the way back. We can all do this."

The guys looked up at me and nodded their heads, but I'm sure it wasn't the most inspirational speech they'd ever heard.

"Oh my, folks, looks like we've got a funky chicken," one of the instructors said.

One of the men that swam in my group was doing the funky chicken on the pool deck. When underwater and desperate for oxygen, your body will sometimes start involuntarily convulsing. It's awkward and painful as your body jerks and spasms. Sometimes when this process has started, the spasming and jerking will continue even when you've made it out of the water.

Men quit every day, and our boat crews—the groups of seven that we used to organize ourselves—changed every day. That morning a very quiet man named James Suh had joined my crew. He looked nervous watching the funky chicken on the pool deck. I said, "You too, Suh. You got this."

Suh looked at me. "I got it, Mr. G." And Suh did get it. He aced the fifty-meter swim that day, and while the class shifted and changed around us for months, for the most part, Suh remained part of my platoon or part of my boat crew for well over a year. I never once heard Suh raise his voice. He was utterly dependable. He had an undergraduate degree in mathematics, and he was one of the smartest men in our class. He would later help dozens of his fellow classmates with dive physics, and if it weren't for Suh's tutoring, many of our men wouldn't have passed the tests that required us to calculate the explosive power of demolitions. Suh was as good on the rifle range and underwater as he was in the air under a parachute. I remember Suh relating a few stories of fights that he'd had in college. He knew how to fight, and he could fight when he needed to, but he never provoked violence. We suffered a lot together, and we became good friends.

Suh would later die as a Navy SEAL in Afghanistan. He was flying on a helo that was shot down by the Taliban in the middle of a firefight. He was flying in to rescue another man—Matt Axelson, "Axe"—who was sitting with us on the pool deck that day.

"I got it, Mr. G."

Yes, Suh. Yes, indeed.

Hell Week was coming. Training up to this point had been a challenge, but Hell Week is the hardest week of the hardest military training in the world, and in a class of Golden Gloves boxers, state-champion wrestlers, international-quality water polo players, and collegiate swimmers, we all knew that we'd never been tested in the way that Hell Week would test us. We were sitting in the first-phase classroom, and Instructor Harmon stood behind the podium. Instructor Harmon had a philosophical streak in him, and he said this:

"Each one of you is like an earthen vessel—a beautiful piece of pottery—prettied up by your fathers and mothers and teachers with tender loving care. In a few days, Hell Week is going to begin, and we're going to take every one of you out onto the grinder and we're going to smash you on the ground, break you open, and we're going to see what's inside each one of you. With many of you, we'll find nothing. There's just air. You are empty men without substance. For others, when you break we're going to have to turn away from the smell, because you live in a weak culture that has allowed you to get by on charm and pretty talk and backslapping and you have practiced dishing manure for so long that it almost seeps out of your every pore, and now, that is what you are. For others, when we smash you, we'll find inside a sword made of pure Damascus steel. And you are going to become Navy SEALs."

# 10 ☆

# Hell Week

EVERY MAN HAS a different story of Hell Week; they remember particular classmates, particular instructors, their own most difficult moments. But in a larger sense, every Hell Week story is the same: A man enters a new world with the aim of becoming something greater than he once was. He is tested once, twice, three, four, five times, each test harder than the last. Then comes the most difficult test of his life. At the end of the week, he emerges a different man. He has met the hardest test of his life, and he has passed or he has failed.

Hell Week normally begins on a Sunday night, but the instructors vary the start time, so we didn't know exactly when the trial would begin.

We arrived at the base early that weekend for a nerve-racking wait. Men carried their favorite movies and their favorite music to pass the time. They carried a set of civilian clothes to wear in the event that they quit and were sent home. They carried pillows to sleep on and food to eat. Our class was restricted to a few general-purpose tents on the beach, and inside these long, green-tarped tents, we were sardined with dozens of other men on packed cots.

We passed around food: protein bars, sports drinks, pizza. One guy's wife had made oatmeal raisin cookies and we picked morsels out of the tinfoil. We knew that we'd be burning close to 8,500 calories a day. We also knew that the water temperature was in the fifties, and we knew that the body burned calories to produce heat. We ate as much as we could. As night came, we sat up talking.

Our boat crews were always shifting as men quit and the class got smaller. Raines had been in my boat crew in the first weeks of indoctrination, and now—right before Hell Week—he was with me again. Raines was a kind of BUD/S wise man. He'd been in Class 234, was injured, and as he recovered he saw Classes 235 and 236 pass through before he joined our class, 237. Raines was in his late twenties: old for a BUD/S student. He was married: this put him in a small minority of BUD/S students. And he was African American: this put him in another minority of BUD/S students. Raines was about five foot ten. He was in great shape relative to most people, but by the standards of BUD/S he had a small gut. He was slower than most in running, and slower than most on the swims. He was slower than most on the obstacle course, and slower than most to knock out fifteen pull-ups.

Eddie Franklin, Greg Hall, and Old Man Johnson (who was probably thirty-one) were all in our crew, and all previously served as Marines. We also had a young guy named Lipsky and another young athlete named Martin. We had a solid group of hard-charging athletes and disciplined Marines, and then we had Raines. The athletes kept us strong. The Marines kept us disciplined. And Raines, he kept us wily—Wile E. Coyote wily. Things don't always work out so well for the coyote, but he's got an endless bag of tricks.

Raines's wife had packed him a brick of brownies, and we were eating Raines's brownies sitting on the cots and waiting for Hell Week to begin when he started to tell us a story from his time serving on the Florida Highway Patrol.

"So, I get a call on the radio, that there is this cow standing in the middle of this two-lane highway, and it has traffic stopped. I asked the dispatcher was she serious, and she tells me yes. So I start driving out that way, and traffic is backed up for miles in both directions, people just barely creepin' along. I have to drive on the embankment of the road, and I go flying past all of these people of the great state of Florida that have summoned me to remove this bovine obstruction from their midst. Now, you got to understand, these people are hot. Pissed off. They been sittin' on this road goin' nowhere. So, I get up to the cow, and I see that there is another officer already on the scene.

"Now it's important to tell you that it's another black officer from the city for a couple of reasons, but one of 'em is that I know for damn sure that my man has never dealt with a cow in his entire life. And he is standing there. And there in front of him is this cow, and the cow simply will not move, standing smack in the middle of the highway. A few people could drive by the cow on either side of the road real slow, but the cow has traffic stopped in both directions.

"And then of course, all the drivers—who ain't never touched a cow before either—they have all become experts on the movement of cows, and they are yelling at my boy and tellin' him, push the cow with your car, hit it with your baton, pull it by the ear, all kinds of craziness.

"Now I walk up to my man, and I can tell, he is super-fuckin'-crazy-fragilistic-expi-alla-docious pissed off, out there sweatin' in the sun, and a huge traffic jam, suckin' on exhaust, and all those people honking and yelling at him, and this crazy motherfucker is yellin' at the cow. He told me to get something, so I walk back to my car, and I got my trunk opened, and just then I look up, and that crazy motherfucker is drawing his weapon from his holster. He points it straight at the cow, shoots, and the cow drops dead in the middle the road.

"Now I'm watching this, and I see this little old white lady step out her car, and pull out a car phone. I didn't know who she was calling, or what she was saying, but I knew that this was going to be a mess, and I knew that I didn't want to be anywhere near it, and so I got right on in my car and I drove off."

The whole tent is laughing because it's classic Raines: pain is coming down, and he knows just where not to be.

"So, next day, I get called over to the chief of patrol's office, and I'm sitting outside his office next to the man who shot the cow, like two kids getting called into the principal's office. Then the officer turns to me and he says, 'Hey brother,' and I'm thinking, *Oh, now I'm your brother.* Well, he says to me, he says, 'You got to help me out.' I'm thinking, *Help you out? What the hell am I supposed to do? You shot a cow dead in the middle of a pack of witnesses on a highway in broad daylight.* So I said, 'What do you want me to do?' And that motherfucker looked at me straight in the eye, and he said, 'Tell 'im,'"—and Raines paused—"'that the cow attacked me.'"

We all busted out laughing. Somebody yelled to Raines, "So what did you do?"

And Raines says, "When they called me in that office, I didn't even wait for 'im to ask me anything. I walked straight up the desk of the chief of patrol, and I said, 'That motherfucker shot that cow for no goddamned good reason whatsoever,' and I turned around and I walked out of there."

The tent roared with laughter—a group of men letting go of tension before the test. There were a lot of men in the tent that night. Only a handful of us would make it through BUD/S, but of all the traits that would be essential to our success, it turned out that this one—a sense of humor—would prove to be more important than I would have imagined.

Men drifted off to sleep, each with his own thoughts. I rehearsed our plan in my mind. As a boat crew leader, my most immediate responsibility was for six other men. I'd instructed our crew to sleep fully dressed, boots on. We knew that we'd wake to chaos—instructors firing automatic weapons, artillery simulators exploding, sirens, bullhorns—and our plan was simple: drop to the ground and crawl out under the east side of the tent. Stay down. I would get a full head count. Hall would grab the back of my collar, the man behind him would grab Hall's collar, and so on, until we were all connected. We couldn't plan to be able to hear each other, and if they threw smoke grenades we might not even be able to see each other. Other men and instructors would be running and crashing around us. Connected, we'd start to move. I wondered, *Was there anything else I should say to my guys? Anything else I should do?*

Almost as soon as I fell into sleep, I woke to the sound of a Mark-43 squad automatic weapon. The Mark-43 has a cyclic rate of fire of 550 rounds per minute. It is the primary "heavy" gun carried by SEALs on patrol. A blank round is not nearly as loud as a live one, but when the gun is rocking feet away from your ears in an enclosed tent, it still sounds painfully loud. I rolled to the ground. For a moment—certainly less than a second—I was on my knees and elbows in the sand, about to crawl out of the tent. A huge smile broke across my face. The wait was over. The test had begun.

I—like all of the others in the tent that night—had grown up in a modern America that offered its young men few tests. As a kid I read about the Spartans, the Romans, the Knights of the Round Table. I studied Native Americans, aboriginal cultures, and ancient Jewish tribes. Past cultures all seemed to offer young men some orderly set of trials that allowed one to progress into manhood. America offered very little. I'd seen Earl Blair—in the Durham boxing gym—constructing trials for boys who otherwise would have constructed their own trials for themselves in gangs. Men came to BUD/S for many reasons, but to some extent we all shared at least one reason: We wanted to be tested. We wanted to prove ourselves worthy. We wanted a good fight, and now it had started.

The plan worked perfectly. The seven of us crawled out the side of the tent, avoiding the packs of instructors waiting for students at the entrance and exit. The night was dark, and in the confusion we felt unseen. We had a precious few seconds to make sure that we were all together. I stood, Hall's hand on my collar, and we ran. Instructors yelled at us, "Drop!" "Drop!" "Drop down!" but I kept running. Air raid sirens blared, artillery simulators exploded, guns ripped through endless rounds of ammunition, and I decided to use the chaos of the night to our advantage.

We ran off the beach and past a group of instructors who had a fire hose trained on another boat crew as they did pushups. The instructors yelled at us, "Drop!" "Drop down!" and we kept running. We knew that the instructors were going to beat us, but we weren't going to make it easy for them.

Students were being corralled into the famous concrete compound known as the grinder for a murderous session of physical training under the assault of hoses and prowling instructors. The intention of the instructors was to start Hell Week in chaos. Break the teams apart. Sow confusion. As the seven of us ran for the grinder, I turned left and ducked us behind a dumpster, where we all seven crouched to a knee.

The instructors were screaming, guns firing, and the other boat crews were running back and forth.

"Mr. G, what are we doing?" We weren't swimming in the river of craziness around us, and it was actually the calm that made some of my guys nervous.

"Be cool. We're just gonna hang here for a bit," I said.

The river of madness ran past us into the grinder, and we could hear the other boat crews getting soaked, the instructors shouting at them for pushups, flutter kicks, squats, sit-ups.

Raines said, "My man, this is beautiful." We waited.

"Stay low." I peered around the side of the dumpster: clear. I stood and we ran back to the beach.

We all seven stood on the beach together. We caught our breath. No instructors. Then we started to laugh. It was the laugh of the happy nervous. *Were we really making this happen?*

Raines had learned from stories of previous Hell Weeks, and we'd planned our first moves together. He'd said, "A lot of the officers want to be tough. They get all excited. Go charging into the mouth of the cannon. Get soaked. Get beat. Show everybody how tough they are and start the whole week beat and exhausted." We talked about a different approach.

I'd briefed my guys before the week. "There's going to be a tremendous amount of pain that we cannot avoid. Whatever comes, we'll stay strong and we'll keep smiling. We'll have fun with it and we will enjoy it, because every moment that passes is a moment that takes us closer to becoming SEALs. We'll work together, and we'll remember that we're in this together. But we're also going to be smart, and whenever there is pain that we can avoid, we're gonna do a little sidestep."

Standing on the beach, we listened as sirens blared, whistles shrieked, and smoke grenades spread a menacing pall over the ground. Speakers had been strung up around the grinder and they amplified the sound of shrieking air raid sirens. For added confusion, fifty-gallon barrels exploded with artillery simulators and flashbang grenades.

We stood on the beach, almost giddy with laughter, for a good ten minutes. A few stars shone through the clouds and waves rolled up the beach. We kept a loose lookout, our eyes on every possible avenue of approach that the instructors might take to the beach. But no one came. I felt that we'd pushed our luck about as far as it could go. Pretty soon someone would do a head count, and I didn't want to be caught on the beach and have my crew singled out for torture. I said to my guys, "Gentlemen, let's go join the party. Stay connected. Hold on tight to the man in front of you. We are about to have a great time."

We ran onto the grinder into a whirling mix of chaotic pushups and flutter kicks and hoses and men soaked and exhausted and sirens blaring and instructors yelling. I ran straight for the middle of the grinder. Our crew ran through the chaos, and as we ran we tapped our fellow classmates on the head, a feint we'd discussed on the beach. The instructors yelled at us, "What the hell are you doing! Drop down!" and I yelled back, "Hooyah, Instructor Jones," and I kept on running and we kept on with the head tapping. "Mr. Greitens, what are you doing?"

"Hooyah," I yelled, and we kept on running.

"Mr. Greitens, what the hell are you doing?!"

"We're doing a head count of the class, Instructor Jones." The instructors were running coordinated chaos, and they didn't know if we'd been ordered to do a head count by another instructor. They assumed that we had, and I was willing to let them assume, and my crew kept running around the grinder tapping other guys on the head. A few guys in the class saw what we were doing, and they jumped up to join us, and soon we had a long line of guys running through hoses and smoke and chaos, tapping other guys on the head.

It was a beautiful way for us to start the week. It's unlikely that we had really outwitted the instructors; they knew all of the tricks, and they probably turned a blind eye to what we did. SEALs were supposed to take advantage of chaos, and we felt that we had won the first round. We couldn't avoid 99 percent of the pain that was going to come our way, but we'd avoided a little, and we had a sharp psychological edge heading into the week.

The inflatable boat, small (IBS) is a hundred-some-pound black rubber boat, thirteen feet in length. Each crew had been assigned to a boat, and it stayed with us through every minute of Hell Week. At mealtimes we left a guard on the boat. Instructors who found unguarded boats would steal oars and deflate spray tubes. Unguarded boats led to beatings. Our boat crews were divided by height so that if we ran as a team, each man could carry a portion of the weight of the boat on his head. Many BUD/S students leave training with neck injuries. As we sprinted away from the chaos of the grinder, we picked up our boats, and they bounced on our heads as we ran through the soft sand.

As we ran down the beach I could hear the boat crews on either side of us yelling at each other. "I told you not to—" "You need to listen!" "Shut the fuck up and run." The men were soaked and beaten from their time on the grinder, and now they were uncomfortable under their boats, and they had begun to snipe at each other.

"Let's be cool," I said as we ran. "We're off to a good start, but the whole week's not gonna be like this. Not everything is going to go our way. Listen, though, to the other boat crews right now, tearing each other up. We're gonna stay positive, stay together, and have fun with this. We can all make it through together."

As we ran on the soft sand in the middle of the night at the start of the hardest week of the most grueling military training in the world, Greg Hall said, "Not bad. Not bad at all, Mr. G. We got this." A few men had already quit. Our crew was solid, and our confidence grew with each step we ran in the sand.

When I had first checked in to BUD/S, I had walked onto the grinder, where thousands of BUD/S trainees had done millions of pushups, sit-ups, jumping jacks, and flutter kicks. Small, webbed feet are painted onto the concrete, designating a place for each man to stand during physical training. A wooden sign hangs over the grinder: "The only easy day was yesterday."

I had been sent to meet the officer in charge of the indoctrination phase of training. Warrant Officer Green was a broadly built, respected man who wore a thick mustache and had nearly two decades of service in the SEAL teams. We sat on a bench outside his office overlooking the grinder.

"BUD/S is hard for everybody, but we're going to make it even harder on you, and harder on all the other officers," he said. "Everyone will be looking to you for leadership. You have to lead your men in BUD/S because, if you make it through this, we're going to expect you to lead in the teams, and you can't lead from the back. We expect you to be at the front of the runs, the front of the swims. We expect you to be an example and to set the standard."

One of the great virtues of BUD/S training is that officers and en-listed train side by side, and officers are expected to endure the same pain—or more—as the men they lead. Every man wore a helmet in BUD/S, and each officer had a bold white stripe painted, skunk style, from the front of his helmet to the back. Everywhere you went, you could be picked out from the crowd. As a kid I had read that Roman officers used to wear red crests made of horsehair so that even in the chaos of battle they could be seen and followed.

At Officer Candidate School, our drill instructor used to say, "Lead from the front or get the hell out of the way." That message echoed here. I don't think that I realized it at the time, but one of the reasons the military can sometimes produce exceptional leaders is that mili-tary training clearly emphasizes the most important leadership quality of all: setting the example. Sometimes that example is physical: "You better be at the front of the run." More often, and more importantly, the example is set by the actions you take that express your values. So, for example, SEAL officers eat last, after the men they lead. Captain Smith, the commanding officer of the Naval Special Warfare Center when I was a trainee, gave all of the junior officers a copy of the 1950 edition of *The Armed Forces Officer*. In its first paragraph, leadership through character is placed at the heart of the officer's duty: "Having been specifically chosen by the United States to sustain the dignity and integrity of its sovereign power, an officer is expected to maintain himself, and so to exert his influence for so long as he may live, that he will be recognized as a worthy symbol of all that is best in the national character."[1]

Running in soft sand down the beach, our boat bouncing on our heads, I realized that what Warrant Green had said was true, but it wasn't the whole truth. He was right, of course, that the officers were watched closely, and he was right that we had to be at the front, and that we had to set an example. But he was wrong about BUD/S being harder for officers.

What Warrant Green didn't tell me, but what I came to learn, was that when you are leading, it can in fact be *easier*. For fear to take hold of you, it needs to be given room to run in your mind. As a leader, all the room in your mind is taken up by a focus on your men.

I got to a point where my senses were attuned to every physical, verbal, emotional, even spiritual tremor in the crew. Who looks like he's about to lose his temper? Who is worried about his kid? Who's limping? Who's feeling sorry for himself? Who needs to be coached? Who needs to be challenged?

As we ran down the beach, another one of my guys huffed as we ran, "Nice job back there, Mr. G." It was the greatest affirmation I could have ever asked for.

Before I joined the Navy I knew that BUD/S would be a test, but by the time I was running down the beach that night, I'd learned—at least in part—what the test was for. The test wasn't about me.

The purpose of the test was to create a man who was capable of leading some of the best men in the world on the most difficult missions our country could ever ask anyone to undertake. Under my boat that night I ran with fathers and husbands and former police officers and former Marines and kids fresh out of school. BUD/S students came from Virginia and California and from middle-class midwestern families and from poor single-parent homes. They were a diverse crew, but they all shared in common a willingness to serve their country, a willingness to sacrifice their own pleasures and comfort and even their lives, in service of others. They deserved to have leaders who had been tested, leaders who had suffered, leaders who were willing to sacrifice in service of others. Once I came to know these men, leadership in BUD/S wasn't really that hard at all; it became easy because I had no place for my own pain, my own misery, my own self-pity. The test wasn't about me; it was about them. Running that night with my men under our boat at the beginning of Hell Week was one of the greatest nights of my life.

After we had run several hundred yards south, the instructors started surf torture. We ran into the ocean until we were chest-deep in water, formed a line, and linked arms as the cold waves ran through us. Soon we began to shiver. I could be wrong about when on the first night this happened. While I can vividly remember moments from Hell Week, the order of those moments is a jumble. Did we dig a pit in the sand, build a fire, and run back and forth into the ocean on Wednesday night or Thursday night? Did we have a King of the Hill pool fight on Tuesday? Thursday? I don't know. I am sure, however, that they got us in the ocean, and they got us very cold, very early, and they kept us cold and wet for a week.

As we shivered in the ocean, instructors on bullhorns spoke evenly: "Gentlemen, quit now, and you can avoid the rush later. You are only at the beginning of a very long week. It just gets colder. It just gets harder."

"Let's go. Out of the water!" We ran out through waist-deep water and as we hit the beach a whistle blew: whistle drills. One blast of the whistle and we dropped to the sand. Two blasts and we began to crawl to the sound of the whistle. We crawled through the sand, still shaking from the cold, until our bodies had warmed just past the edge of hypothermia. Then, "Back in the ocean! Hit the surf!"

Some men had quit after the opening session on the grinder. Others quit after the run down the beach, and others quit after they sent us into the water. The men who quit then—I believe—were trapped in a cage of fear in their own minds. We woke to the sound of blanks being fired through machine guns. We got wet. We did pushups and flutter kicks. Instructors yelled at us. We ran on the beach. Every man in the class had endured at least this much before, so it could not have been the physical pain that made them quit. No. They lost focus on what they had to do in the moment, and their fear of this monster—Hell Week—overwhelmed them like a giant wave that had crashed and washed away their sense of purpose.

During whistle drills I crawled with Raines. One of my favorite instructors, Instructor Wade, started to yell. "Oh OK, Mr. Greitens, you don't want to crawl on your own. You want to wait for Mr. Raines here? Then both of you, hit the surf!" Raines and I took off for the waves, dove into the cold water, and ran back and fell again to the sand. Instructor Wade was an incredible swimmer. He taught the combat sidestroke classes, and when he kicked with fins underwater, it was like watching a sea lion fly through its natural environment. Wade had served numerous tours in South America, and he taught our basic classes on patrol. He was also wickedly smart. When Raines and I fell back on the sand, he yelled, "I guess you two just don't get it. Hell Week is an *individual* evolution. You two keep trying to work together." What Wade meant, of course, was that Hell Week was a team evolution—only teams could survive—and he wasn't yelling at me and Raines so much as he was letting the whole class know we better work together.

As we crawled, soaking wet, we became covered in sand. The skin on our elbows and knees grated, and just when we reached an instructor who had blown one whistle, another whistle would sound—two blasts—thirty yards away, and we would begin to crawl again. "Only five more days! You guys tired yet? You cold? You haven't even started!"

We ran into the surf and back out again, and then we were lined up on the beach. The instructors asked me, "How many men do you have in the class?" Men had been quitting in all the confusion, and I had no idea how many remained. "Mr. Greitens, how the hell are you going to lead when you don't even know how many people you have?" They asked the other officers: "Mr. Fitzhugh? Mr. Freeman?"

"Pathetic!"

We counted off—*one, two, three*—and as we went down the line we realized that we had already lost a half-dozen men. And Hell Week had hardly begun.

Ordered back to the cold water, we stood at the ocean's edge. The waves crashed and flowed around our soaked boots. We were instructed to turn toward the beach, our backs to the waves, and, with arms linked, to lie down. Waves crashed over us. "Kick your boots over your head and into the sand!" the instructors yelled. With our legs kicked over our heads, our breathing was constricted; as each wave crashed over us, we held our breath.

Men stood up shaking, their will collapsed, and walked to the instructors. The instructors would often ask them, "You sure?" They always were. Once they let quitting become an option—a warm shower, dry clothes, a return to a girlfriend or wife, an easier job, perhaps a chance to go back to school—they had no use for a future of cold and wet and pain and misery. We heard the bell ring—ding, ding, ding—as they chose another life.

We ran to our boats, which were rigged for sea at night with bright red and green chem lights tied to the spray tubes. We had chem lights attached to our helmets as well. In the event that we were knocked unconscious in the water at night, the chem lights would mark the position of our bodies in the water. As we stood next to our boats, the instructors yelled, "Prepare to up boat!" and all seven of us grabbed our boat and yanked it into the air, and then we all seven stood underneath the boat with its weight pressed over our heads at an extended-arm carry. Often we held this position until our arms started to shake. Then: "Down boat!" In one motion we all stepped out from under the boat and brought it back to the sand. Then again: "Up boat"—we pressed. Down boat. Up boat. Down boat. Up boat. Down boat. As a team we lifted and lowered our boats hundreds of times over the course of Hell Week.

We began a series of races. We ran our boats into the water and paddled out past the surf zone, and there we "dumped boat"—flipped the boat over so that it rested upside down on the water, soaking every man in the process. We then flipped the boat right-side up and paddled back to the beach through the breaking waves.

Over and over again, we rowed out into the ocean through the waves, got soaked, then rowed back in. The instructors kept everyone rowing fast and hard by rewarding winners and punishing losers. The crew that won a race was often allowed to sit out the next race. The crew that came in last was often tortured with a series of exercises: team sit-ups with the boat on your head or pushups with your feet raised on the spray tubes of the boat.

At some point we traded our boats for 150-pound logs and did "log PT" on the beach. As a team of seven we ran down the beach with the logs bouncing on our shoulders, and then we ran over a fifteen-foot-high sand berm, with the logs held at our waists. Straight-armed, we held the logs over our heads, then brought them down to our shoulders, then lowered them to the ground, and then we lifted the logs back up to our shoulders and pressed them up over our heads again. We ran with our log into the ocean to "give it a bath," and then we picked up our soaked, slippery log and ran back out of the water and through the soft sand.

It's difficult to describe the physical pain of log PT. This did not compare to training in a gym. It was not like setting yourself at a bench press, cranking out ten repetitions, and then waiting for your muscles to recover while chatting with a friend. The pain of log PT was unlike any kind of muscle pain I'd ever experienced before; muscles didn't burn, they seared. This was not really "physical training" at all; it was spiritual training by physical means.

After log PT we ran onto the obstacle course and, exhausted, as a crew we ran our boats over the obstacles. All seven of us worked to-gether to haul our bulky rubber crafts up the high wooden walls, across the logs, and over the course.

Then we ran our boats back to the water again. I ran at the stern — the back of the boat. My six crew lined up three on each side, and as we ran into the water and the water reached waist height for the men in front I yelled, "Ones in," and the two front men scrambled into the boat and began to paddle as the waves came toward us. Then I yelled, "Twos in," and the pair mid-boat jumped in, then "Threes in," and the last pair of men jumped in and began to paddle, and then finally I scrambled into the boat, grabbed my paddle, and began to steer as our crew stroked furiously to make it out and over the surf line.

Timing was essential. Boats that mistimed the waves were often flipped, and seven two-hundred-pound men and their oars would go flying into the surf. We wore helmets, but injuries happened — usually just cuts, bangs, and bruises, but sometimes badly twisted ankles or knees, and occasionally a broken bone.

We paddled north for one of Hell Week's more dangerous evolu-tions — rock portage. Coronado beach has a large outcropping of jag-ged black rocks. Waves roll in and crash on the rocks. The objective of rock portage was for us to "insert" our team — as if on an operation. We had to land our boat on the rocks, jump out, and carry the boat over the rocks to dry land.

In 1991 during the first Gulf War, Saddam Hussein's commanders expected a major amphibious assault of thousands of men. Instead, the Navy inserted a team of SEALs. The explosions the team rigged were so convincing that Saddam diverted almost two full divisions to respond. Saddam fell for the diversion, and as his troops moved, allied forces in-vaded Kuwait from Saudi Arabia. That SEAL team, which helped thin Saddam's defenses in a critical area, comprised just six men.[2]

During practice for rock portage prior to Hell Week, we had learned that it was essential to time the waves. When we got close to the rocks, our bowman would jump out of the boat and onto the rocks. He held a rope attached to the bow and he would attempt to anchor himself in the rocks as we continued to paddle. As the waves rolled in they could crash with tremendous force; a man trapped between the boat and the rocks was in trouble. Dustin Connors—the first man I met at BUD/S—had broken his leg during rock portage.

As we paddled north before the landing, we were exhausted, and we were not even through the first night of Hell Week. But rowing in the ocean, away from the instructors, the night was suddenly peaceful. There was no yelling, and for a full twenty minutes we did nothing but row. But we rowed worried. Rock portage held the possibility of real injury. We each had it in our power to quit or endure; that we could control. But no one could control a fierce wave, a tossed boat. No one's muscles were harder than rock. No man's hands could hold back a wave. Few of us feared injury itself. We'd all suffered broken bones before. What was frightening was the prospect of being rolled out of our BUD/S class. We would have to spend months recovering, and then we would have to start all over again.

We rowed our boats together in a bobbing flotilla outside the surf zone one hundred meters from the rocks. The waves seemed small as they rolled in, but that could be deceiving; they might be crashing with fury near the beach. We watched as the first two boat crews paddled for the rocks. The crews landed and we could see their helmet lights bobbing as they carried their boats up and over the rocks.

Now it was our turn. We paddled. As we closed, it looked as if the waves were breaking and crashing before reaching the rocks. The tide was out. If we timed it right, we could hit the sand and then carry our boat over the rocks, rather than having to land on the rocks themselves. We scrambled over the rocks with our boat, and as we made it to the other side, the instructors yelled at us to drop down and then beat us with pushups for a dozen small offenses. But when we picked our boat back up and ran, I said, "Great job, guys," and I think it was Lipsky who said, "Thank God," and we ran on, the boat bouncing on our heads. Exhausted after hours of punishment, we felt like the luckiest crew in the world.

They tortured us through the night. Run into the surf, run out of the surf. Take your camouflage top and T-shirt off, then lay back in the fifty-some-degree water again. BUD/S taught us funny things. Skinny guys are cold. Fat guys are warm. Better to be stuck in the surf next to a fat guy. "Fat" of course is a relative term; there weren't really any fat trainees, but I remember Eddie Franklin saying to Lipsky, "Get your fat ass over here and warm up the ocean."

Eventually the sky started to lighten. Dawn light? We'd made it through the first night. With our boats on our heads we ran along Tarawa Road for the other side of the base and the chow hall.

At the battle of Tarawa during World War II, U.S. Marines were sent to dislodge twenty-six hundred Imperial Marines, Japan's elite amphibious troops, from a tiny island. Even with intelligence gathered from aerial photography, observations by telescope, submarine soundings, and interviews of merchant sailors, the Americans still misjudged the tidal range. Amphibious landing craft packed full of Marines ran aground on the reefs surrounding the island seven hundred yards from shore. The ramps of the landing craft were lowered and men stepped out. Laden with packs and waist-deep in water, they walked through machine-gun fire that tore through bodies and dropped men into the ocean. Hundreds of Marines and Navy personnel were shot and killed. Many died in the shallow water before they made it to the beach. In just over seventy-six hours of fighting, over 990 Marines and 680 sailors were killed, battling for a thin sliver of island just four miles long and a quarter mile wide.[3] Today, U.S. Marines still call it "Terrible Tarawa." After Tarawa, the U.S. Navy determined never again to allow faulty intelligence to lead to that kind of slaughter. Men would have to be sent in ahead of time, men who could have eyes on the ground and in the water, human beings who could do reconnaissance of landing zones and rig demolitions to blow obstacles. It was in the bloody waters of Tarawa that the Underwater Demolition Teams were born.

In the chow hall we had a few minutes of relative peace to eat as much as we could. A lot of SEALs had given us the advice, "Just try to survive from meal to meal."

Inside the chow hall, Hell Week students rolled through a special section of the line cut off from the other diners. We pushed our trays. Scrambled eggs? Yes. Sausage? Yes. French toast? Yes. Hard-boiled eggs? Yes. Fruit? Yes. Tomatoes? Yes. Beans? Yes. I stopped for two glasses of water and a mug of hot chocolate. Every calorie was energy to be spent running, lifting, swimming, energy to burn for heat. I sat down with my boat crew at the table, all of us with a mess of food on our plates. I ate fast. Hash browns and scrambled eggs fell in my lap. I wiped syrup with my sleeve, and bits of tomato and sausage fell to the floor.

At BUD/S it helped to be able to run and swim on a full stomach. As an officer who ate last and usually had little time to get a full meal, I was used to running away from my tray with a mouth full of pancake and an apple in hand.

The instructors generally left us alone at meals. They insisted that men drink plenty of water. A few men had trouble shoveling food when they were exhausted, and the instructors prodded them to eat. Later in the week—when we would fall asleep during meals—the instructors would sometimes load a sleeping trainee's plate with hot sauce, and then wake him up and tell him to eat. Dazed, guys would shovel in a forkful of food, and their eyes would pop open as the hot sauce hit their throats.

After the meal we ran with the boats on our heads over to the BUD/S medical compound for our first medical check. The doctors examined cuts to look for flesh-eating bacterial infections and they checked temperatures to test for hypothermia.

The med checks always presented a dilemma: the instructors left us alone as we ran through medical, and medical was warm. This meant that it was tempting to stay in medical for as long as possible. On the other hand, we all tried as hard as possible to hide any ailments from the doctors. A swollen knee, an infection, pneumonia, any of these might lead to being medically rolled, and if you were rolled, you had to start all over again. Most of us elected to rush through as fast as we could. We ran through wearing nothing but tri shorts—black spandex underwear that we wore to help prevent chafing of the legs—so it was hard to hide injuries, but still we tried.

"You feel OK?"

"Yes." They'd put a stethoscope to our backs.

"Any trouble breathing?"

"No."

"Any injuries?"

"No."

After medical, we sat at the "foot station." Brown Shirt rollbacks —BUD/S trainees who made it through Hell Week, but were later rolled out of their classes for injuries and were waiting to class up again— sprayed our feet with antibacterial medicine. They applied tape and bandages and Vaseline where necessary.

It could have been peaceful at the foot station, but the instructors set up a boom box that played a loud, shrill, nonsensical scream-chant:

*What day is it? What day is it? Is it Thursday? No? Shoes-day? Tuesday? What day is it? Will someone please tell me? No, no, no! Is it yesterday, or already tomorrow? Someone please tell me, what day is it?*

We left the foot station and its psychological torture and ran in our tri shorts to a set of milk crates. Each of us had a milk crate with a piece of duct tape stuck to it with our name scrawled on it. A set of dry clothes sat in the crate, and we took a blissful thirty seconds to pull on dry socks and pants and a T-shirt. As we ran out of the changing station, an instructor waited for us with a hose.

Later in Hell Week after a med check, one of the instructors yelled at me to drop down. I dropped to the concrete and started doing push-ups with a hose in my face, and as I lowered myself, I felt something in the chest pocket of my shirt. On the next pushup I let myself down to the concrete ground again, and as I did so I could feel the shape and weight of a candy bar; one of the Brown Shirt rollbacks had slipped a candy bar in my pocket. I smiled as the fire hose soaked me, thinking, "A free people can never be conquered!" and "Long live the resistance!"

and a bunch of other fiery, half-goofy inspirational phrases that were very meaningful to me at the moment, and were also an indication that I was exhausted.

The next day is a blur. We ran a four-mile timed run in boots in the sand, and then, I believe, we prepared for a long swim in the ocean. Standing on the beach in our wetsuits prior to a knife inspection (we carried knives when we swam, and our knives and lifesaving equipment were inspected before every swim), we started to get warm.

All told, we were awake and under near-constant assault for the first eighteen hours of Hell Week. There was no break: Long timed runs. Marathon swims. More pushups. More everything.

My swim buddy and I knew that we were going to freeze all week, so we talked about diving into the water rather than walking in. They could torture us. But, we thought, we'd show them; we would act like we *enjoyed* it. You want to freeze us? Ha. We'll freeze ourselves. We ran to the water and dove in, and somehow we felt like we'd won something.

The two-mile swim was usually a dreaded, all-out, kicking-and-pulling race for at least seventy minutes. But during Hell Week, swimming two miles in the ocean was relatively pleasant. Our bodies were warmed by the exercise, and though the instructors patrolled the pack of swimmers in kayaks and yelled at us with bullhorns, there was actually very little torture they could inflict on us while we swam.

Men continued to quit as the day wore on. Two quit after the swim. When it was announced that we were going to put on forty-pound rucksacks and march, two more men quit, and then it turned out that we didn't even do the rucksack run. Instead, we were ordered to our boats and then ran to chow.

After the first night, we got four meals a day: breakfast, lunch, dinner, and midrats — midnight rations — and it seemed true that we could just survive from meal to meal. At lunch on Monday, Friday might as well have been five years in the future. But dinner didn't seem that far away.

We ran into the chow hall that day already showing signs of wear.

Our feet were swollen. Our hands were swollen. Anyone who had a tight knee, an injured hamstring, a tender ankle, ran limping toward the chow hall. We were hosed down before we went inside, but still we carried sand in our hair and sand in our ears and sand around the collars of our T-shirts.

Most of the men who ran into that chow hall also carried ambition, but it's a kind of ambition that is often misunderstood. In his first published speech, Abraham Lincoln wrote, "Every man is said to have his peculiar ambition. Whether it be true or not, I can say for one that I have no other so great as that of being truly esteemed of my fellow men, by rendering myself worthy of their esteem."[4] The men at BUD/S carried that same ambition; they wanted to make something meaningful of their lives. They wanted to leave a worthy name.

At the pass of Thermopylae, where three hundred Spartans gave their lives to hold off several hundred thousand Persians, an epitaph marks the place of their death with the elegiac couplet:

> Go tell the Spartans, stranger passing by,
> that here obedient to their laws we lie.[5]

Most of the men in my class had come to BUD/S convinced that they wanted to fulfill their lives' ambition as modern-day warriors, as SEALs. Now many of them were starting to question this. As we sat down to lunch we had little energy. Two guys bumped trays and glasses of water crashed to the floor. "Watch what the fuck you're doing!" Tempers were short. Men frayed at the edges. Humor helped to repair the damage.

We sat at our table: "D'you see Instructor Jones with that bullhorn? He looks like he wants to eat it."

"No, he fuckin' kisses that thing."

"He fuckin' loves that thing."

"Is he single?"

"Yeah."

"No, he's not. He's married to the bullhorn."

"I bet he takes that thing home with him at night."

"He's probably got a bunch of pet names for it. Oh, bully, oh, bully, oh, bully."

"I bet he doesn't let any of the other instructors touch that thing."

"I bet they don't want to."

Instructor Jones walked past us in the chow hall and someone started to hum the melody to Wagner's Bridal Chorus in a very uneven tone, and another guy sang softly, "Here comes the bride, all dressed in . . ."

We chuckled and turned back to our food. It didn't matter to us if anything we said was actually funny or mature or even made any sense. It was hilarious to us, and just then being able to laugh reminded us: *We can do this.*

We fought our way through Monday afternoon. We endured the tortures, completed the exercises, ran the races. Usually any moment that passed in Hell Week was a good moment, but on Monday afternoon, we still had Monday night hanging over us.

"OK, gentlemen, just a few more hours until the sun goes down." Laughter rolled through the bullhorn. Monday night was infamous. The hardest night of all. "Steel piers" was coming. We'd heard that steel piers would freeze you like a soaked and naked man left to die at the North Pole. Monday night was feared. Monday night was the killer night. Monday night would be the worst night of your life.

As the sunlight weakened, the instructors ran us out to the beach. We stood there in a line, and as we watched the sun drift down, they came out on their bullhorns:

"Say goodnight to the sun, gentlemen, say goodnight to the sun."

"Tonight is going to be a very, very long night, gentlemen."

They reminded us that tonight was going to be our first full night of Hell Week.

"And you men have many, many more nights to go."

We watched the sun slip lower and make contact with the ocean.

Then, when they really wanted to torture us, they said, "Anybody who quits right now gets hot coffee and doughnuts. Come on, who wants a doughnut? Who wants a little coffee?"

As we watched the sun slip away, something broke in our class. Out of the corner of my right eye, I saw men *running* for the bell. First two men ran, and then two more, and then another. The instructors had carried the bell out with us to the beach. To quit, you rang the bell three times. I could hear it ringing:

Ding, ding, ding.

Ding, ding, ding.

Ding, ding, ding.

A pack of men quit together. Weeks earlier, we had started our indoctrination phase with over 220 students. Only 21 originals from Class 237 would ultimately graduate with our class. I believe that we had more men quit at that moment than at any other time in all of BUD/S training.

Who would have thought that after having to swim fifty meters underwater, endure drown-proofing and surf torture and the obstacle course and four-mile runs in the sand and two-mile swims in the ocean and log PT and countless sit-ups and flutter kicks and pushups and hours in the cold and the sand, that the hardest thing to do in all of BUD/S training would be to stand on the beach and watch the sun set?

Each man quits for his own reasons, and it might be foolish to even attempt any general explanation. But if men were willing to train for months before ever joining the Navy, and then they were willing to enlist in the United States Navy and spend months in a boot camp and months in specialized training before they came to BUD/S, and if they were willing to subject themselves to the test of BUD/S and endure all of the pain and cold and trial that they had already endured up to this point, then it seems reasonable to ask, why did they quit now?

They quit, I believe, because they allowed their fear to overwhelm them. As the sun went down, and the thoughts of what was to come grew stronger and stronger, they focused on all of the pain that they thought they might have to endure and how difficult it *might* be. They were standing on the beach, perfectly at ease, reasonably warm, but they thought that they might be very cold and very pained and they thought that they might not be able to make it. Their fear built and built and built. The mind looked for a release, and the men who quit found their release in the bell.

Others found their release in the self-detachment of humor.

"You think all this sand on my face is a good exfoliate?"

"Yeah, you're lookin' pretty *GQ* smooth."

"They call this look Hell Week Chic. I don't know what they call the way I smell."

"You know, my girlfriend actually goes to a spa to pay for shit like this, where they scrub you down with sand and stuff."

"Yeah, this is like a spa, but we're getting paid to be here. Can you believe this? Awesome fucking deal."

"I want to get a job at one of those spas."

Others simply didn't let fear come to rest in their minds. They'd learned to recognize the feelings and they'd think, *Welcome back, fear. Sorry I don't have time to spend with you right now,* and they'd concentrate on the job of helping their teammates.

"How's your foot?"

"Fine."

"Good. Keep an eye on it. Tonight's gonna be a good night for us. Dinner should be pretty soon."

Still others just focused on the moment. What a pretty sunset. This is all I have to do to make it through Hell Week right now? Stand on the beach. This is great.

One of my favorite guys in my crew was Eddie Franklin, former Marine, who had a very low tolerance for BS and a wicked sense of humor. Eddie would always joke about quitting. "I'm quitting today for sure. Right after the run. Then I'm gonna go up to Pacific Beach and surf and hang out and eat tacos." We'd finish the run and Eddie would say, "Hey, anybody want to quit with me after breakfast? I gotta eat, but then I'm gonna quit." We'd finish breakfast, and Eddie would say, "PT, I love PT, I'm gonna quit after PT." After PT, "I'm gonna quit right after lunch. But they've got burgers today, and I'm crazy for those Navy chow hall burgers." And so he could go on—sometimes to the annoyance of others who were truly thinking about quitting—but in Eddie's humor there was wisdom. I can quit later if I have to, but this, whatever this is that I have to do—hold this log over my head, or sit in the freezing surf, or run down the beach with the boat bouncing on my head—I can do this for at least ten more seconds, and that's really all I have to do.

Finally the bell stopped ringing and the sun slid beneath the ocean and the night was upon us. We formed into boat crews and started running again. The steel piers were located on the San Diego Bay side of the Naval Compound. The water was calm and cold and dark and we jumped in wearing boots and cammies. We all spread out and began to tread water.

After the cold grabbed hold of our bones, the instructors yelled, "Now take off your T-shirts and blouses." Treading, we took off our T-shirts and camouflage tops and threw them onto the steel piers. "Boots!" We struggled in the cold water as we treaded and we untied our boots, teeth chattering and hands shaking, and we threw our boots onto the piers. "Out of the water!" We climbed up on the quay wall, and we stood on the concrete on feet numb with cold. "Pushups!" We felt our blood begin to flow again. "Get down to the piers!" We stood on the piers. The instructors were oddly silent, and we all heard our teeth chattering. Then a voice came over the bullhorn. "Some of you might be here because you thought that being a SEAL was cool, or glamorous. You thought that you could be tough, Hollywood. You should know right now that *this* is what being a SEAL is about. A whole lot of misery. You can leave here and go on to serve your country in a lot of other ways. You don't all need to be SEALs."

We stood on the steel piers. "Enter the water," and we all jumped into the black cold water again. We treaded water with our teeth chattering and our hands and feet numb.

I knew that men had survived Hell Week ever since John F. Kennedy signed the Presidential Order on January 8, 1962, commissioning the first SEAL teams.[6] Kennedy was a major proponent of special operations. His "flexible response" defense strategy rejected the idea that the U.S. should rely only on nuclear weapons to respond to Soviet challenges. The U.S. could not order a nuclear strike if the Soviets were funding a Communist regime in Africa, supporting rebels in South America, or sending military advisors to Southeast Asia. President Kennedy believed that we had to be able to respond *flexibly*, and that meant having a variety of tools of national power, including special operations teams that could conduct a wide range of clandestine operations. One of these special operations forces was the Sea, Air, and Land commando teams of the U.S. Navy, or Navy SEALs. Men had been doing this for over forty years. Now it was my turn.

SEALs are frequently misunderstood as America's deadliest commando force. It's true that SEALs are capable of great violence, but that's not what makes SEALs truly special. Given two weeks of training and a bunch of rifles, any reasonably fit group of sixteen athletes (the size of a SEAL platoon) can be trained to do harm. What makes SEALs special is that we can be thoughtful, disciplined, and proportional in our use of force. Years later, in Iraq, I'd see a group of Rangers blow through a door behind which they believed there was an al Qaeda terrorist, take aim at the terrorist, assess that he was unarmed, and then fight him to the ground and cuff his hands behind his back. They did this while other Rangers, at the very same time, in the very same room, positioned themselves over a sleeping Iraqi infant girl to protect her and then gently picked her up and carried her to an Iraqi woman in another part of the house. As Earl used to say, "Any fool can be violent." Warriors are warriors not because of their strength, but because of their ability to apply strength to good purpose.

The night went on. One evolution, "Lyons lope," consisted of a series of cold runs and swims in the bay. Then we ran over to the combat training tank. As we ran the instructors reminded us that a man had died in the pool just a few classes ago. "Anybody want to quit now?"

At the pool we started with a few games. The instructors told trainees to dive off the one-meter platform. Guys that performed awesome belly flops or dives were given a few minutes to rest in the warm locker room. Weak performers were sent to "decon," where they stood under a collection of high-pressure hoses that shot cold water down on them.

We broke into teams and did caterpillar races across the pool. After the races, the instructors sent a crew out to grab several of the boats. We threw the boats into the pool and the instructors told us to climb in. As we sat floating in our boats in the pool, an instructor held up a bag of McDonald's hamburgers, saying, "King of the Hill. If you get thrown out of your boat, swim to the side of the pool; you're out. Last man standing wins his crew a bag of burgers. Ready. Begin."

The dozens of us that remained in the class started wrestling in the boats. Everything started friendly. We were a class, a team, and while we'd wrestle each other for the burgers, we weren't going to hurt one another or exhaust each other. But as men were thrown out of the boats, the battle intensified. The boats could barely bear the weight of all the men fighting. I was wrestling when I heard, "Franklin!" then, "Franklin!" then ten seconds later, "Franklin, help me!"

I glanced over my right shoulder and saw Greg Hall's face underwater, his eyes wide open. Greg was a Division I collegiate football player and one of the strongest men in our class. In the melee—probably because he had taken on four guys on his own—Greg had been forced to the bottom of our boat, and now there were five or six men fighting on top of him, oblivious to his position. The boat had taken on water, and Greg was pinned to the bottom. As the fighters fought, the weight in the boat shifted back and forth, allowing Greg to grab a quick breath and yell before again being pushed back under. Franklin had been fighting beside him, but in the commotion he didn't hear Greg.

I grabbed Greg by the shirt just under his chin and yanked to pull him up, but both his arms were pinned down; two men were on his chest and another two were on his legs. I couldn't move him. I erupted. "Get the fuck off! Get the fuck off!" I grabbed a man and shoved him into the water. I punched another in the ribs who had his back turned to me and then kicked him into the pool.

I think it's fair to say that I had a reputation for calm. Raines used to say, "Mr. G's cooler than the other side o' the pillow. That man's cooler than a fan." So when the guys saw me explode like that, many of them backed away or dove into the pool—not because they feared me, but because it was obvious to them that something had gone very wrong.

I pulled Greg Hall up and he coughed the water out of his lungs. We were the last two men in the boat.

"Mr. Greitens, get the fuck over here. Get over here right now!"

I jumped out of the boat and swam to the instructor at the side of the pool. As I pulled myself out of the pool, the instructor grabbed me by my camouflage shirt and threw me against the wall. "What the hell is a matter with you? What are you doing!" I started to speak, but the instructor yanked me toward him and then slammed me against the wall again.

From poolside, it looked like I'd gone crazy for burgers and started attacking my men. I explained that Hall had been trapped at the bottom of the boat. They called Greg Hall over, and he confirmed what had happened. "All right, you two, go eat a fuckin' hamburger. But just one. You don't get the whole bag."

The rest of that night is a blur. We ran around the base with the boats on our heads. We got wet and sandy. We did whistle drills and jumped up and dropped and crawled and jumped up again and crawled again through the sand. When we next ran through medical I saw that Raines had been pulled aside. He was sitting on an examination table. We were too far away from each other to talk, but I raised both hands and mouthed, "What?" and Raines lifted his left leg. He formed his two hands like he was holding a camera, and snapped his index finger down as if he were taking a picture. They were taking him for an x-ray. I'd noticed Raines limping, but I figured that he'd fight through it. That was the last time I ever saw Raines.

The mass of quitting happened Monday night, but as the sun rose on Tuesday we continued to lose men to injury, and we still had others who quit. After Hell Week, I'd come to know many men who had attempted BUD/S and failed, and without exception they fell into one of two categories. First were the men who'd come to terms with it. They would talk about their BUD/S experience, maybe laugh a bit about it, and then they'd say, "But it just wasn't for me. I respect those guys and I had a good time, but it wasn't the right way for me to serve." Then there were the tortured men. They spoke in half sentences and back-slaps, still wanting, years later, to pretend that they had made it. "I made it, but the instructors didn't like me and forced me to quit." Or, "I would have made it, but my girlfriend started college and moved away while I was in BUD/S, so I had to follow her." I always felt with them as if I were talking with men who had fragile balloons inflated in their chests. They twisted and turned in conversation to keep the balloons from popping. The men who told the truth were able to move forward. Those who lied to themselves dragged their BUD/S experience with them like an anchor through the rest of their lives.

Tuesday and Wednesday and Thursday were also a blur. Days on end. More cold. More running. Endless surf torture. One night we dug a pit in the sand with our oars and were allowed to rest for fifteen minutes at the bottom of the pit. We then built a fire, and in an insane game, the instructors had us run circles around the fire until we were warm, then made us run down to the ocean and jump in, after which we ran back to the sandpit. Imagine a hot tub near the snow—jumping in the snow is fun once, perhaps, but they beat us with exercises as we ran back and forth over and over and over and over and over again.

As our mental faculties grew foggy, the instructors chased us through the night with a bullhorn, which played an incessant laugh track. We paddled our boats north, then south. We ran to chow and we ate and we ran through medical and got soaked.

My hardest moment came at what should have been the easiest. Our crews were gathered at the dip bars (parallel bars where we did exercises to build our triceps). A man from each crew competed, and the winning team was allowed to run to the general-purpose tents on the beach for a rest. It was Wednesday. We'd been up for three nights straight. We were so tired that men fell asleep standing up.

Sleep—I thought—would be immediate and blissful. I ran into the tent with my crew. Already men were asleep around us. I lay back hoping to pass out instantly, but I found that I was very awake. I shut my eyes and took in a long breath through my nose. *That* should put me out.

Nope. My left foot had been wrapped on my last trip through medical and with each pump of my heart I could feel the blood pulse in my foot as if it were wrapped in a tourniquet. I sat up. Everyone else was asleep. I took off my boot and unwrapped my foot and threw the bandage to the ground. I put my boot back on and laced it up. (We knew that if we slept with our boots off, our feet would swell so badly we'd never get them back on.)

I lay back on the cot. There was an open flap in the ceiling of the tent and the sun was at an angle such that it cut a beam of sunlight that landed right on my chest and face. After a week of freezing, the tent packed with bodies was now oppressively hot. I sat up again. I tried to move my cot, but I was wedged between two men who were dead asleep. I was stuck.

And pissed. This wasn't fair. The Brown Shirts had bandaged my foot badly. I had the worst cot. Everyone else was asleep. What if I can't sleep? Will I be able to make it? My mind started to run in circles of fear. I stood up and walked out of the tent. Two of the Brown Shirts saw me.

"You all right, sir?"

"Yeah, I'm fine."

But I wasn't. The week, though punishing, had been going well, but I needed this sleep and I couldn't get it. Would they let me sleep later? No. What a stupid question. What was I going to do, ask for a nap? How could I sleep? Should I go somewhere else? No, I had to sleep in the tent. What if I can't sleep?

I walked over to a faucet mounted on a wall at about shoulder height. The last thing I would have thought I wanted was to be wet again, but I twisted the faucet with a sandy, swollen hand. Water poured out and I stuck my head in. I let the water wash over my head. It cooled me, and I stood up. I took in a deep breath. *If I can deal with everything else, I can deal with this. I'm going to be fine.* Then for a moment as I stepped back to the tent on swollen legs I had an overwhelming feeling of compassionate thankfulness. So many men had quit, so many men had been injured. I had thought about this particular test on a hundred nights, and now here I was in Hell Week. I was halfway through now, and at this very moment I had been granted an opportunity that almost no one ever received. I had a moment of absolute calm, completely to myself. I was able to stand in the middle of a week of trial alone on the beach to enjoy everything that I had been granted. "Thank you, God," I said, and I walked back into the tent and fell asleep.

We woke to chaos. I believe that they were firing blanks again, or it could have just been screaming and bullhorns, but it was an immediate and shocking awakening. We stumbled into the sun, and they made us run for the surf. Most of the men in the class were still half-asleep and stumbling and tight and pained. When we were shoulder-deep in water they told us to run south. We ran an awkward floating pace in the ocean, making little progress. They were getting us cold again. I looked back, and the faces of the men in my class wore expressions of pain. I can't remember if I started to sing a song or yell for our class or shout defiance at the instructors, but I remember booming at the top of my lungs, and the class joining me in an outburst of some kind. The attitude of the class turned—as if we all decided to stand up at once after being knocked down—and soon we were shouting with joy. That was the moment of my greatest personal victory over Hell Week. I had at least two full days more to go, and the possibility of injury still hovered over us, but I knew that I'd lived through the worst of it.

When I reflect back on it now, I realize that my hardest moment was also the only moment in all of Hell Week when I was alone, focused on my own pain. It was the only moment when I began to think that things were unfair, when I started to feel sorry for myself.

Hell Week continued. Through a fog, I recall running with the boat on our heads and IBS races and games in the pool and running back and forth to the chow hall. The intensity was unrelenting. "Prepare to up boat. Up boat," and we stood at extended-arm carry until our arms shook. "Let's go," the instructors yelled, and we walked down the beach, and walked, and walked, the boat bouncing on our heads for miles until we felt that we could not take one more step. We did runs over the sand berm until men in the crew—powerful runners—had to crawl on hands and knees.

And this was one of the great lessons of Hell Week. We learned that after almost eighty hours of constant physical pain and cold and torture and almost no sleep, when we felt that we could barely even stand, when we thought that we lacked even the strength to bend over and tie our boots, we could in fact pick up a forty-pound rucksack and run with it through the night.

After several days without sleep, our mental faculties deteriorating rapidly, the instructors began to toy with us. After a medical check we ran out onto the beach and played a game of Simon Says.

"Simon says lift your right leg. Simon says lift your left leg. Simon says lift your right leg. Now your left leg." The instructor shook his head in disappointment. "This is very simple, gentlemen. I give the instructions, and you listen and follow orders. Children can do this. Did I say 'Simon says'? No, I did not, so all of you goofballs standing there who had your left legs raised, go hit the surf."

We were all standing now on both legs, each of us wondering if the instructor had seen *us* with our left legs raised. "OK, you guys want to play games? You don't want to have an honest game of Simon Says? OK, I see how it is. Why don't you all go get wet and sandy."

We trudged down to the beach, jumped into the water, jogged out, flopped around on the sand, and then lined up for more Simon Says.

We did the Hokey Pokey. On the fourth day of Hell Week, we limp-ran to the beach and our instructors yelled, "Put your left leg in, put your left leg out, put your left leg in, and you shake it all about."

A few guys were less than enthusiastic about the Pokey, and this gave rise to one of the most ludicrous threats I have ever heard: "You guys better shape the hell up and get serious about this Hokey Pokey!"

I chuckled to myself. Next thing I knew, in my delirium, I couldn't control myself and I started laughing hard. I crossed my left arm over my face to muffle the laughter.

"You think this is funny, Mr. Greitens?"

I tried to steady myself, and I wanted to say hooyah or no, but when I took my arm from my face, I said, "Yes, Instructor."

I thought that he'd send me into the surf, and I was worried for a moment that he'd make the whole class pay for my laughter, but instead he said, "Well if you think this is so damn funny, why don't you get up here?!" I ran to the front of the class.

"Now, Mr. Greitens. You went to Oxford right, and you were a Rhodes scholar?"

"Hooyah."

"Then you should be pretty damn smart, right?"

I felt like I was being set up, but I didn't know what to do. "Hooyah?"

"Well, then I want to see the best damn Hokey Pokey I've ever seen, you got it?"

"Hooyah!"

"OK, guys, you put your left elbow in, you put your left elbow out, you put your left elbow in, and you shake it all about. You do the Hokey Pokey and you turn yourself around," and then—overcome with the joyful absurdity of the moment—I yelled, "AND THAT'S WHAT IT'S ALL ABOUT!"

I led the class through right elbow in, right elbow out, left foot in, left foot out, and we all began to shout at the end of each turn, "AND THAT'S WHAT IT'S ALL ABOUT!"

When I'd finished, the instructor turned to me. "Mr. Greitens, that was the best damn Hell Week Hokey Pokey I've ever seen. You guys all get five minutes' rest."

We sat down next to our boats. We were too tired to joke now, almost too tired to breathe deeply, but as the guys in my crew leaned against the side of our boat and fell immediately asleep, I sat in the sand, very proud of myself. I was not the fastest runner, not the fastest swimmer, not the fastest man on the obstacle course, but at least for the moment, I was the world's greatest living Hokey Pokey Warrior.

We learned that we could hallucinate and still function. We learned that we could take turns passing out and still function. And we learned that we could fight off mind games.

The games continued. Was it Thursday afternoon? I ran out onto the beach and was greeted by Darren Harrison, then a member of my boat crew. "Mr. G, Mr. G, get over here." I ran over to him. He put his hand on my shoulder and leaned in as if he were going to share with me a very important secret. "Franklin has a lock." And then he turned and pointed down the beach.

"What?"

"Franklin has a lock."

Harrison was tottering in front of me, his mind gone now that he'd been awake for a fifth straight day. "Darren," I said, "what are we supposed to do?"

"Franklin has a lock, and he's down there."

Harrison's mind was fried. Franklin had been given a closed padlock, told the combination, and sent some hundred yards down the beach. The rest of our crew was instructed to spread out on the beach in intervals of about fifteen to twenty yards. The race was set up so that Franklin would crawl through the sand to the next man in our crew, hand him the lock, and tell him the combination. The next man had to memorize the combination, crawl through the sand fifteen yards, then hand off the lock and relay the combination, and so it would go until the last man in the crew got the lock, turned and crawled for the finish line, and then—in order to win—had to open the lock. By the time the lock got to me, my guy handed me the lock and said, "Go, Mr. G, go!"

"What's the combination?"

He stared at me. "I don't know, but we have to win, Mr. G! Go!"

"We need the combination to win."

"Oh. Well, just make something up."

I turned and crawled. Harrison was an incredible runner, an incredible swimmer, an incredible athlete. At the moment of the padlock game, he probably still could have picked up Greg Hall in a fireman's carry and run him two hundred yards down the beach. Harrison had also started to lose his mind. We had other guys in the crew who were limping so badly that at full speed they might have been able to run no more than a ten-minute mile. Those same guys, however—some of them—remained mentally sharp.

When doing surveillance, SEALs would often have to remain in position for days, watching, observing, reporting. BUD/S tested us in this way as well. The instructors summoned a representative from each boat crew and gathered them around a wooden board covered with a cloth. They pulled the cloth back and we saw seven objects: toothbrush, $CO_2$ tube, penny, safety pin, piece of gum, watch, 550 cord (a type of string). They gave us thirty seconds to observe before covering the board and sending us back to our crews to write down what we had seen. After five days without sleep, most of the trainees' memories were impaired: "Penny, and a piece of gum, and, and, and maybe a watch?" But other guys would come back, "Penny, safety pin, watch, $CO_2$ tube, toothbrush, did I say watch? Oh, a piece of gum . . ." They were incredibly sharp after five days without sleep.

On Thursday night, we ran to our boats, rowed out past the surf zone, and began the around-the-world paddle. Coronado is a peninsula, connected to Imperial Beach by a thin sliver of land. In the around-the-world paddle we rowed all the way around Coronado. The beginning of our paddle was glorious. We stroked with a fresh shot of adrenaline because we knew this was the last night of Hell Week.

We paddled to different stations around the island to check in with the instructor staff. We paddled hard, but our boat was leaking air and the extra drag through the water slowed us. We checked in to each station near the back of the pack of boats. As we approached the instructors, we heard, "OK, you guys, you don't want to put out, go ahead and chilly dip," and we had to jump out of the boat and into the cold bay.

Martin fell asleep as he paddled, and he half-fell out of the boat and crashed into the cold bay. Another man and I grabbed him by his lifejacket and hauled him back in. As the boat crew leader, my job was to steer. I used my oar as a rudder, and I remember my guys turning back to me—"Mr. G!"—and waking me up because I'd fallen asleep and turned us off course.

I remember the lights of San Diego swirling as I fought to stay awake. The crew kept at it. None of us could have made it around the island alone, but working together through bouts of consciousness and sleep, we managed to keep moving forward as a team. As we paddled, some of the chatter had become nonsensical.

"Mr. G, it's you, did you see? Did you call those guys?"

"What?"

"The lights of the green and the red sabers, see how they're attacking and bumping each other?"

"What?"

"Oh my God, it's like a squirrel there and he had the water in him!"

"Martin, wake up!"

He didn't wake, but Franklin started to chuckle as Martin chattered. "Damn, it's over, those cans and the MRE rolls, I mean the Tootsie Rolls, because I have one here, you want one? I had one, I can ask for another one, it's OK, really, it's all good, Mr. G, you just keep us going straight, I've got to pee, but it can be warm, and the sabers are here now anyway."

We finished the paddle that night. I walked out of chow on Friday morning and thought, *We made it, last day.*

The instructors played with us: "Prepare to up boat. Up boat. OK, let's begin walking, gentlemen. Tomorrow'll be your last day of Hell Week, just one more night to go."

My guys asked me under the boat, "Mr. G, it's Friday, right? It's the last day, right?"

"Yeah, yeah, it's Friday, I'm sure." I yelled over to my friend and fellow officer Mike Fitzhugh. "Mike, it is Friday, right?"

"Yeah, I think so."

We ran our boats out into the ocean and we paddled south for the "demo pits." We'd heard about what was coming from previous Hell Week classes. The area known as the demo pits is really just one huge hole in the ground surrounded by a fence. During Hell Week, they pumped the hole full of seawater until it created a muddy slurry of dirt and grease.

As we ran into the demo pits, a whistle blew and we dropped to the ground. Smoke grenades exploded and artillery simulators boomed. Two whistles blew and we started to crawl. Barbed wire was strung a foot off the ground, and we crawled under it, just barely able to make out the boots of the man in front of us through an acrid haze of purple and orange and red-green smoke. Tunnels were cut into the demo pit, and we crawled down the tunnels into the slurry of water and smoke. The pit became a scum pond of muddy salt water, sweat, and bubbles that popped with orange residue.

The stench of sulfur was strong. I blew my nose and caught a wad of purple snot on my sleeve. We all crawled into the pit, immersed up to our armpits. Two ropes were stretched across the pit, one of them strung about a foot over the scum; the other was five feet higher than that. We each had to climb onto the ropes and then—with our feet on the bottom rope and our hands on the top rope—slide our way across the scum pond while the Brown Shirts shook the ropes. No one made it past halfway before crashing into the pit.

The demo pits—we knew from Hell Week lore—were the last evolution of the week. As my fellow students climbed across the ropes, we sat in the muddy water, the sun beaming, and I was very, very happy. Hell Week was about to end.

Then a whistle blew. Then two whistles. We started crawling out of the demo pits. "Get back to your boats. Get back to your boats. Paddle down to the compound." *Were they serious? Weren't we finished?* In my haze of exhaustion I started to get angry. *These instructors have screwed this up! We were supposed to finish back there; they don't know that we're supposed to be done!*

We ran to our boats, paddled out through the waves, then rowed north back to the compound. My crew was running on frayed nerves. "What the fuck is this! What the fuck!"

We turned our anger on the instructors. "Did you see his fat ass chewing tobacco and spitting in the pit? Fat fuckin' bastard!"

When we had rowed to the compound, the instructors started to beat us again. "Hit the surf, go get wet and sandy." We limp-ran. We held on to each other to keep standing. We could no longer dive into the ocean. We simply fell over in the water, got soaked, and then fought our way back to our knees and then made it to standing and then ran back onto the beach.

We were made to drop down and knock out pushups. By this point, for a "pushup," we would lower our bodies an inch and drop our heads, and then pull our heads back up. It was about as much as we could do.

"Drop down! Face the ocean!" We did another set of pushups, and then the instructor yelled, "Recover." When we stood up and turned around, every instructor and all of the SEAL staff of the Naval Special Warfare compound were standing in one line atop the sand berm.

The commanding officer called down to us. "BUD/S Class 237, you are secured from Hell Week!"

We stood there. *Really?* We looked down at our boots, up at the instructors. Was this a trick? Then Franklin leaned back open-chested and let out a roar, and we all started to shout. We turned and hugged each other. We'd made it.

We shook the hands of every one of the instructors and then we walked over the sand berm to medical. After a final medical check we walked out into the sun, and there laid out for us were two large pizzas and a bottle of sports drink for every man.

I sat on the concrete next to my guys. We were too tired to talk. Too tired to shout. It was the most delicious pizza and the best sports drink that I have ever had in my life.

People always ask me, "What kind of people make it through Hell Week?" The most basic answer is, "I don't know." I know—generally—who *won't* make it through Hell Week. There are a dozen types that fail. The weightlifting meatheads who think that the size of their biceps is an indication of their strength; they usually fail. The kids covered in tattoos announcing to the world how tough they are; they usually fail. The preening leaders who don't want to be dirty; they usually fail. The me-first, look-at-me, I'm-the-best former athletes who have always been told that they are stars and think that they can master BUD/S like they mastered their high school football tryouts; they usually fail. The blowhards who have a thousand stories about what they are going to do, but a thin record of what they have actually done; they usually fail. The men who make excuses; they usually fail. The whiners, the "this is not fair" guys, the self-pitying criers; they usually fail. The talkers who have always looked good or sounded good, rather than actually been good—they usually fail. In short, all of the men who focus on show fail. The vicious beauty of BUD/S is that there are no excuses, no explanations. You do, or do not.

It is, however, hard to know who will perform. I thought that Greg Hall would make it, and he did. I thought that Eddie Franklin would make it, and he did. I thought that Mike Fitzhugh would make it, and he did. I also thought that Darrell Lucas would make it, but he did not (failed for drown-proofing). Yet at the same time, some men who seemed impossibly weak at the beginning of BUD/S—men who puked on runs and had trouble with pull-ups—made it. Some men who were skinny and short and whose teeth chattered just looking at the ocean—made it. Some men who were visibly afraid, sometimes to the point of shaking—made it.

BUD/S—like Instructor Harmon promised—smashes the shell and reveals the inner man. I was reminded of the stories that people in Bosnia and Rwanda had told me about their neighbors. They told me stories of people who took extraordinary risks to save the lives of others, and they told me stories of people they had known all their lives who—when tested—decided to save themselves. Who could have known?

BUD/S was the same way: who knew until the test came?

It's important, however, not to overstate the significance of Hell Week. Hell Week is in many ways only the beginning of BUD/S. It is the test you pass so that the SEAL community will say: "You are worthy of being trained."

You emerge with swollen hands and swollen feet and cuts and bangs and bruises. You emerge weak and beaten. But the week does not transform you. While Hell Week emphasizes teamwork and caring for your men, it does not necessarily produce good people. Some of the best men I've known in the world are SEALs, but there are also some jerks, abusive boyfriends and husbands, men who fail to care, fail to lead, men with a few moral screws loose, who also make it through Hell Week. Hell Week tests the soul, it doesn't clean it.

Yet Hell Week does offer this, at least—after it, for the rest of your life, you have this point of comparison: *I've been through Hell Week; I can face my current trial.*

After the final medical check we walked—or did they drive us?—the two hundred yards to our barracks. I opened the room and walked to my bed. I sat down on it. I had half a pizza left and I set the box on the ground. *That'll taste good in the morning, or whenever I wake up—will I sleep until Saturday?* I set a pillow at the foot of my bed and kicked my feet up on the pillow. I wanted to keep my feet raised to reduce swelling. I set another pillow behind my head.

I smiled. Hell Week was over. It was the best time I never want to have again.

# 11 ☆

# Advanced Combat Training

I woke after a long sleep. Was it twelve hours? Eighteen? My body felt heavy and numb, but when I held up my hands I saw that the Hell Week swelling had gone down. We rose from our bunks and ambled out of the barracks. We shuffled like a file of corpses to medical. We were checked again for cellulitis (flesh-eating bacteria), for pneumonia, for broken bones. After passing through medical we drove to a local restaurant and sat down to a breakfast of stacked pancakes, sausages, crispy hash browns, cheesy eggs, sparkling fresh fruit, and biscuits covered in gravy.

I was still swollen—head, hands, feet—and I moved slowly when I pulled up to my house and stepped out of my car. My neighbor's sprinkler was on, and just a few drops were landing on the sidewalk, but I walked wide around it. I wanted, for a day, to be nothing but warm and dry.

On Monday we began to train again. We trained in hydrographic reconnaissance, learning how to conduct a detailed examination of a surf zone before an invasion. We trained in basic techniques of the combat patrol, and we exercised to rebuild our strength. We did physical training on the grinder, runs on the beach, and we continued our weekly two-mile ocean swims.

One early Tuesday morning my swim buddy and I came out of the ocean after a two-mile swim, and as we ran up the beach, a man running in the other direction shouted something to us as he passed.

"What did he say?" I asked.

"I don't know. Something about a plane crash in New York."

As the rest of the team finished the swim, stripping off wetsuits and donning boots and camouflage uniforms, word was passed through the class: A plane had crashed into the Twin Towers. No, it was two planes. One of the buildings collapsed. Both buildings collapsed. Thousands of people died.

"Four ranks!" We formed into four lines and ran for chow. Rumors were traded on the run. At the chow hall the TV was on, and sailors dressed in whites and in fatigues stood next to cooks and servers wearing plastic gloves, holding serving spoons. "Get your food." We hustled through the line and then gathered at the tables near the corner of the hall so that we could be close to the TV. We ate fast. Usually we ate with some banter, but that morning we ate in silence, except for occasional single words of profanity and prayer.

We had sat down for our meal thinking that we were members of a peacetime military. When we stood up, we knew that our class was going to war.

A new energy inhabited the men of Naval Special Warfare. We all knew men who were on active SEAL teams, and in the team buildings up and down the beach, lights burned on and coffee was brewed into the night as men crowded around maps of Afghanistan. Men pushed bullets one by one into magazines; they disassembled and cleaned weapons; rifle scopes were checked and then checked again. Teams left for advanced mountain warfare training. Small adjustments were made to uniforms, wills were updated, and letters to loved ones written and sealed.

I and the other men in my class weren't SEALs yet. We were, however, the first class that would go through every phase of SEAL training in the knowledge that we were going to war. Guys asked questions while we ran to chow: "Mr. G, you think that they'll speed up our training and send us to Afghanistan?" It was in those conversations that I learned just how different, just how distinct my men were from the rest of the population.

We all remember our own story of 9/11, and I think that most Americans experienced the attack with a mixture of shock at the horrific violence, sympathy for the victims, a surge of patriotic feeling, and some desire for revenge. We grieved. We celebrated the heroism of those who gave their lives in service to others.

My class shared those sentiments, but it was also true that every man in the class had one very visceral, very real wish. They all said, in their own way, "I wish that I'd been on one of those fucking planes." This wasn't bravado, and it wasn't just talk. They had signed up to fight for their country, and now the fight was on. They had no illusions that they were supermen. They might not have saved the day. But they wanted, more than anything, to be there at the country's critical hour.

SEALs fight from the sea, from the air, and from the land. We serve as the nation's elite commando force, and suddenly it looked like our country had an immediate need for us. We trained hard, and over the next several months we were shaped into warriors.

In dive phase we learned to be combat swimmers. Up to that point I had never taken a single breath underwater. In dive phase, I learned how to use scuba gear, and I trained in a way that only SEALs would. While swimming scuba, we were repeatedly attacked. Instructors jerked our mouthpieces from our mouths, tore off our facemasks, ripped off our fins, flipped us in circles, turned off our air, tied our hoses in knots, and then swam away. Starving for oxygen underwater, we had to wrestle our twisted tanks and hoses in front of us, turn on our air, untie our hoses, and try to reestablish a line to life-giving oxygen. As soon as we caught a breath of oxygen and straightened our tanks, we were hit again.

Later we swam to the bottom of the combat training tank with a swim buddy. We swam down with one scuba tank and one mouthpiece between us, and we wore facemasks completely covered in tape. Both blind underwater, we shared oxygen back and forth as we transferred all of our dive gear from one man to the other. Still later we treaded water for five minutes with our hands in the air while wearing sixty pounds of gear. Men whose hands touched the water failed. Dozens of men failed different tests, and our training moved forward without them.

We executed a five-and-a-half-mile ocean swim, kicking north into a fierce current. We dove twice a day, and air often became trapped in our inner ears and expanded at night so that it made us temporarily hard of hearing. We woke every morning after a few hours' sleep with our alarms blaring and we blew our nose hard into our fist and cleared our ears for another day of diving.

We dove in the bay and I learned how to count my kicks in the pitch-black water fifteen feet deep while following a compass bearing underwater. By counting my kicks, I could tell when I'd traveled exactly one hundred meters. Nine weeks after I first entered dive phase, my swim buddy and I descended into the water at night wearing a Draeger combat diving system that emitted no bubbles. We kicked underwater for several hours. We adjusted our course several times according to the dive plan we had built by studying the chart, tides, and currents. With a series of hand gestures we communicated underwater and confirmed our plan until we reached our target, placed our simulated mine, and swam away.

We moved to land warfare and weapons training. At Camp Pendleton, we fired thousands of rounds from a Sig Sauer 9mm pistol and thousands more from our rifles. We began with single shots on target, and weeks later we were executing immediate action drills in teams of sixteen men, running and shooting and shouting and firing hundreds of bullets on target in a synchronized kill ballet.

Given a box of mixed parts, we had to assemble our rifles and pistols. We learned how to shoot a submachine gun, a shotgun, and an AK-47. We fired light antiarmor rockets and antitank weapons and we planted claymore mines. We were issued basic gear and we learned how to patrol quietly wearing ammo pouches and canteens, and how to black out every bit of metal, every piece of gear that might reflect light. We learned the basics of using demolition and we set explosive charges of C4 and TNT and we learned how to rig explosives under-water. We threw grenades, and as a class we were tear-gassed, learning that, though in pain, we could fight while in a cloud of gas if we had to. We lined up on the range at night and we learned to fire our rifles using night-vision goggles and lasers. We learned how to clear jammed weapons, we learned how to rappel, and we learned how to gunfight as a team. We learned how to navigate over mountains and we learned how to use radios. We spent weeks in the woods, and we learned the basics of reconnaissance.

Men kept dropping out of the class—one man couldn't handle the land navigation, another had trouble with demolitions. The in-structors kept up the four-mile timed runs, the two-mile timed ocean swims, and the timed obstacle-course runs, and as the required times got faster, some men failed and were dropped from the class. Toward the end of BUD/S we went to San Clemente Island—"Where no one can hear you scream"—and we executed a night ocean swim. The in-structors liked to tell us that San Clemente is home to one of the larg-est breeding grounds for great white sharks in the world, and they reminded us of this as they stepped onto safety boats with loaded shotguns—"to repel a shark attack"—and told us to enter the water and swim. We swam very fast.

The physical trials never ended. On the island we had to earn our meals with a lung-exploding sprint up a mountain, wearing full gear. Men who failed to meet the cutoff time ate their meals soaking wet and covered in sand.

On San Clemente we brought all of our skills together. Given a folder full of information on a simulated target, our platoon devel-oped and briefed a plan. We were dropped off in the ocean, did re-connaissance of the beach, swam in to shore, patrolled through the mountains, and set up an ambush that we initiated with demolitions. Firing blanks, we swept down on men playing the enemy, ripped them from their vehicles, gathered intelligence, and then melted back into the underbrush. We made our way to the other side of the island for a planned extraction, and once there we were ambushed and the beach exploded in towers of flames as we had to simulate fighting our way out. Six months before, we'd just been a bunch of guys with freshly shaved heads waiting in the early morning to begin our first four-mile timed run.

We graduated from BUD/S and then went to advanced training. We went to Fort Benning, Georgia, for Airborne School, and we learned how to jump out of a plane. The concept seemed very simple to me, but it took three weeks to learn: open door, green light, go! We learned that parachutes are deceiving. We do not float to the ground but crash, like human lawn darts. We learned the specifics of the "parachute landing fall" maneuver, which was supposed to ensure a smooth landing. You hit the ground with the balls of your feet, then roll to your calves, keep rolling to your hamstring, then onto your rear end and back. When executed properly, the fall mitigated the impact of crashing into the earth. The first time I hit the ground, I got to my knees in a daze and started to collect my parachute, now depleted on the ground. One of my guys yelled, "Mr. G, nice parachute landing fall. You crashed feet, ass, head!"

We went to Survival, Evasion, Resistance, and Escape school and starved for five days. We learned how to build shelters for warmth and how to evade capture behind enemy lines. Eventually we were all caught, and for days we lived as prisoners crouched in small individual cages, let out only for torture and interrogation.

We then returned to Coronado for SEAL Qualification Training. We refined our skills with rifle and pistol until we fired live ammunition just feet from our running teammates, tracer rounds burning through the night. We advanced our work with demolitions and we learned how to build booby traps and how to set ambushes. Into the mountains, we patrolled through thick brush and slept on open ground on our ponchos as we completed ever-longer courses of land navigation. We jumped into the night-dark water of the bay again and again wearing our bubble-less diving systems as we executed ever more challenging combat dives. We went on long rucksack runs on the beach and in the mountains. We learned to apply our camouflage and we learned how to build a good hide site. We traveled to the desert and we learned to fight there. We ran a thirteen-mile combat conditioning course with a rifle and a forty-pound rucksack, and we stopped to shoot rifle and pistol, throw grenades, and launch rockets at various checkpoints along the way. In our close-quarters defense course we learned how to subdue, handcuff, and control prisoners. In our combat medicine course we pulled our buddies over our backs in a fireman's carry, ran with them hundreds of yards, and then threw them in the backs of pickup trucks. We then climbed into the trucks, and as they raced and swerved across broken desert roads, we attempted to start IV lines in the veins of the sweaty, dust-covered arms of our friends.

During maritime operations training, we drove Zodiac boats for miles through a churning ocean, five men bouncing as the engine whined over black waves. One night we came over a wave and cut the motor to idle to study a form lying on the black surface of the water. *What is that?* We motored closer, slowly, until we saw that we'd come upon a graveyard of deflated balloons. Hundreds of helium balloons of all colors had been released from some party or wedding and had blown out over the ocean. We sat for a moment, bobbing in the water, and then drove slowly away like we were leaving a body to rest in peace.

Men who failed to meet standards continued to be dropped, including one man who was failed after a year and a half of training, just three days before graduation, because he wasn't sufficiently proficient with his rifle. We had all grown. I had started training relatively late, at age twenty-six. I was now twenty-eight. Other men had started training when they were nineteen. They were now twenty-one. They had literally grown up in SEAL training.

The class graduation was spartan. We stood in a nondescript concrete bay known as the boat barn. An American flag was hung, but nothing else adorned the open bay. No band, no streamers. We stood not in dress uniforms, but in starched fatigues. We each walked to the podium and a few words were said as a golden Trident was pinned over our heart.

"The Trident has been the badge of the Navy SEALs since 1970. It is the only warfare specialty pin that is the same for officers and enlisted. It symbolizes that we are brothers in arms—that we train together and we fight together. There are four parts to the Trident. Each one symbolizes an important facet of our warfare community.

"The anchor symbolizes the Navy, our parent service, the premier force for power projection on the face of the planet and the guarantor of world peace. It is an old anchor, which reminds us that our roots lie in the valiant accomplishments of the Naval Combat Demolition Units and Underwater Demolition Teams.

"The trident, the scepter of Neptune, or Poseidon, king of the oceans, symbolizes a SEAL's connection to the sea. The ocean is the hardest element for any warrior to fight in, but we must be masters of the sea.

"The pistol represents the SEAL's capabilities on land—whether direct action or special reconnaissance. If you look closely, it is cocked and ready to fire and should serve as a constant reminder that you, too, must be ready at all times.

"The eagle, our nation's emblem of freedom, symbolizes the SEAL's ability to swiftly insert from the air. It reminds us that we fly higher in standards than any other force. Normally, the eagle is placed on military decorations with its head held high. On our insignia, the eagle's head is lowered to remind each of us that humility is the true measure of a warrior's strength."[1]

After we all had our Tridents pinned on, we turned as a class and ran down the pier and jumped into the bay. As trainees, we had jumped into the water a thousand times. This was the first time we hit the water as Navy SEALs.

We swam across the bay and then ran a six-mile course around the island of Coronado. We finished our run at a beach, where we grilled steaks, told stories, and wished each other well. Like every great passage, it was a celebration of our achievement that was also marked by some sadness. We were leaving men who had become our brothers. In the dark of night, faces covered in camouflage, I could tell my men apart by the way they carried their rifles. On patrol, I could tell by the turn of their heads if they were listening hard. I knew their families, and I could tell by the way they sat down to load their magazines if they were distracted by something at home. We knew each man's brow, eyes, smile, when each man was angry, afraid, triumphant. We'd laughed a thousand crazy laughs motoring on the ocean, climbing in the mountains, before jumping from planes. Standing on the beach, this was our last moment as a class together, and we knew that all of us would be deployed, and some of us might not come back. For all of the incredibly difficult training we'd done, no one had ever shot real bullets at us with the intent to kill.

# 12 ☆

# Afghanistan

I WAS LYING in a hammock flying into Afghanistan. The hammock hung from two carabineers, one clipped to the metal wall of the aircraft and the other clipped to a cargo box full of weapons. The plane flew full of a tangle of men and boxes packed with gear. Men read in hammocks, slept on crash pads, and sat in the webbed seats of the aircraft with their feet up and headphones on as we flew into a combat zone. I was rereading a book about the Taliban.

On September 11, 2001, I don't know that I'd ever heard of al Qaeda before. In graduate school I had studied—briefly—the history of Afghanistan. I knew that the Russians had invaded the country and I knew that they had failed. I knew that Afghanistan was littered with unexploded ordnance and land mines and that these weapons often exploded and left civilian men, women, and children without limbs. I knew that Afghanistan was ruled by a vicious tyranny called the Taliban and that the Taliban was famous in the West for its brutal treatment of women. In 2001 that was about all I knew. If you'd pressed me then, I don't think that I could have even named all of the countries that border Afghanistan.

As a kid, I had read with awe about Alexander the Great. He had conquered a territory stretching from Macedonia to Egypt and across to the northern territories of modern India. After September 11, when

I started to educate myself about Afghanistan, I read that Alexander's toughest battles took place in the Hindu Kush Mountains on the border of modern-day Afghanistan and Pakistan, where thousands of his men were slaughtered. Alexander's fibula was broken when an Afghan warrior shot him with an arrow, and in another battle, he suffered a concussion when an Afghan fighter smashed a rock on his head.[1]

Other foreign armies followed Alexander. Outside East Asia, Genghis Khan and his Mongol warriors suffered their only defeat in the province of Parwan, Afghanistan. The British invaded in 1839 with relatively few casualties, but by 1841 the people of Afghanistan were in open revolt of the British occupation. The approximately 16,500 remaining British troops and their families attempted to retreat in the dead of winter to Jelalabad. By the end of the two-week, ninety-mile journey only a single man stumbled through the gates of Jelalabad. More than 16,000 others lay dead on the roads, frozen by the winter cold or slaughtered by the Afghan tribes in two feet of snow piled in tight mountain passes. By the end of the year, the British withdrew their troops, only to invade again thirty years later.

In 1979 the Soviet Union invaded Afghanistan to prop up an unpopular Communist government on the verge of collapse. Instead of defeating the rebellious tribes, the Soviet troops served only to unite the Afghan warlords into a new movement: the Mujahideen. The sole goal of the Mujahideen was to evict the Soviets from the country by means of raids and ambushes.

With overwhelming force, the Soviets pushed the Mujahideen into the mountains. To root out the fighters, the Russians began brutal aerial assaults to "depopulate" Afghan village hideouts. The Russians carpet-bombed the mountainside. They unleashed fearsome Mi-24 helicopters, loaded with missiles and powerful machine guns that fired thirty-nine hundred rounds per minute. They napalmed green valleys into a naked and fire-charred countryside. They dropped millions of mines onto Afghan farmland, some of the mines disguised as toys to attract children.[2]

The Mujahideen—who fought back with World War II–era equipment—seemed trapped and helpless under the assault of the over-whelming aerial firepower of the Russians. The United States then began to supply the Mujahideen with the Stinger, America's latest heat-seeking antiaircraft missile, and the Mujahideen began knocking the dreaded helicopters, fighter jets, and other aircraft out of the air. The tide of the war shifted. By the time the Soviets withdrew in 1989, they had lost nearly fourteen thousand troops and hundreds of tanks and aircraft.

The Russian withdrawal left a power vacuum, and in 1992 an alliance of tribes wrested the capital city of Kabul from the remnants of the Communist government. Throughout Afghanistan, warlords fought other warlords for territory, looted civilians of their meager possessions, and kidnapped young boys and girls.[3] The opium trade was used to finance military operations,[4] and the people of Afghanistan suffered horribly in the crossfire as tribes and drug kingpins and local warlords fought for money and territory and control of the drug trade.

Out of the chaos arose the Taliban. The Taliban originally gained power because they promised to be a force for good. "Talib" means student, and the Taliban were students of the Qur'an who promised to root out corruption and establish a strong Islamic state. The Taliban defended the general population from the violence, rape, and pillaging of warring tribes, and they spread rapidly across Afghanistan as thousands of young idealistic men joined their ranks.[5] The growth of the Taliban brought stability and order, and the Taliban nearly eradicated opium production by early 2001.[6]

But the Taliban also brought about their own brutal repression. In a Taliban-ruled country, a hungry child who stole bread lost a hand. Women fared worst of all. Communities gathered to watch women accused of adultery be wrapped in white cloth, buried in the ground up to the shoulders, then stoned to death. Thousands packed into soccer stadiums to watch women publicly hung from the crossbars of soccer goals for "crimes" against Islam. The Taliban banned television, music, photography, and kite flying. They beat women who allowed even an inch of their skin to show.[7] The Taliban also famously harbored a terrorist by the name of Osama bin Laden.

By the spring of 2001, the Taliban controlled 90 percent of the territory in Afghanistan. The remaining tribes who opposed them were united into the Northern Alliance, led by the charismatic and brilliant Ahmad Shah Massoud. Known as the Lion of Panjshir, Massoud was the key leader holding the tenuous Northern Alliance together. On September 9, 2001, Massoud was assassinated by al Qaeda suicide bombers posing as Algerian journalists (they had bombs hidden in their fake video camera). Two days later, planes hit the Twin Towers and the Pentagon.

On September 14, 2001, Congress granted President George W. Bush the power to find and kill anyone involved in the 9/11 attacks. "The President is authorized to use all necessary and appropriate force against those nations, organizations, or persons he determines planned, authorized, committed, or aided the terrorist attacks that occurred on September 11, 2001, or harbored such organizations or persons, in order to prevent any future acts of international terrorism against the United States by such nations, organizations or persons."[8] President Bush demanded that the Taliban surrender Osama bin Laden. The Taliban refused.

Paramilitary forces infiltrated Afghanistan. They carried with them stacks of hundred-dollar bills to bribe tribal leaders of the Northern Alliance, and they also promised the assistance of fearsome American air power. U.S. Special Forces arrived in late October and joined their Afghani allies.[9] From horseback, American soldiers called in coordinates for air strikes, and tribesmen of the Northern Alliance galloped in to kill scattered Taliban troops. With the help of a handful of U.S. Special Forces and CIA officers, the Northern Alliance defeated more than fifty thousand Taliban soldiers, pushed the Taliban out of power, and drove them into the mountains. It was one of the most effective campaigns ever waged by the United States. By the time we took Kandahar, we had lost only twelve lives, and the entire effort cost just $70 million.[10] Bin Laden and other senior al Qaeda leaders were still at large, but if we had paused in early 2002, we might well have assessed that we'd already won the war, and that we'd done so with deadly efficiency.

It was now the summer of 2003, and as I flew into Afghanistan, I was worried about the U.S. mission. Afghanistan had always been easy to invade and impossible to conquer. We had already driven the Taliban from power and denied al Qaeda the ability to conduct operations out of Afghanistan. We still had men that we needed to kill, but that required well-placed sources, possibly the cooperation of allies in Pakistan, and well-trained commando forces, not occupation.

We were flying into a huge base that was now manned by tens of thousands of Americans. Even during periods of relative peace and prosperity, Afghanistan had no history of centralized control. If we intended to subdue the country and build a democracy along American lines, that seemed like a mission that would take decades, and it was unclear when or how we'd ever be able to declare victory.

I was with a team of SEAL commandos and our mission was clear: to hunt and kill senior al Qaeda targets. This required local cooperation, intelligence, and a functioning network of allies. It did not require us to build a democracy.

Before we left the States, I received a brief on the rules of engagement—the rules that govern the use of force in Afghanistan. In almost all cases, we could use deadly force only if the enemy engaged in a hostile act or demonstrated hostile intent. There were, however, a few targets who were "declared hostile." I had remembered from my SEAL training what it meant to declare a force hostile:

> *Declaring Forces Hostile.* Once a force is declared hostile by appropriate authority, U.S. units need not observe a hostile act or a demonstration of hostile intent before engaging that force.[11]

Bin Laden and other senior al Qaeda leaders had been declared hostile. Explaining rules of engagement can sometimes be complicated. In this case, it was very simple: if you see Bin Laden or one of his associates, kill him.

We were about to test the proposition that using disciplined force and doing good can go hand in hand in a confusing, chaotic country. When we arrived in Bagram, I walked into a makeshift briefing room and sat on a stack of brown-boxed MREs and listened as a SEAL senior chief gave a brief. "We're here to kill Bin Laden and his chief associates. If Bin Laden is here"—he pointed to an area high on the briefing board—"and we're here"—he pointed low—"and we are able to take down some of his key lieutenants, and get closer to Bin Laden"—he pointed to the middle of the board—"then we will have succeeded."

The group around me nodded their heads. These men were members of an elite SEAL team. They wore nontraditional uniforms with almost no insignia, and the majority of them wore beards. Many of them had served in the SEAL teams for more than a decade. They were the very best special operations commandos in the world. In comparison, I was fresh out of SEAL Qualification Training. Imagine a guy who has just been drafted into the NFL sitting in the locker room at the Pro Bowl. While I had been in field training exercises, assaulting mock compounds guarded by Americans dressed like Afghanis, most of these men had been conducting real operations, spilling real blood. I had a tremendous amount to learn.

I had come to join this mission at the invitation of Captain Campbell, then the commanding officer of the team. I'd come to know Captain Campbell through a friend and colleague, Dr. Aaron Rawls. Rawls and Captain Campbell told me that given my time working in war zones overseas, they wanted me to take a fresh look at our work in Afghanistan and see if there might be ways to improve our interactions with potential allies. SEALs had spent thousands of hours training to kill their enemies, but to win this war we also needed to win friends. Alliances had been key in defeating the Taliban, and we needed allies to help us hunt individual men in Afghanistan and Pakistan. Another key element in defeating al Qaeda was human intelligence. The United States of America had the best signals and electronic intelligence in the world, but we were fighting an enemy that often passed messages via couriers who rode on horseback through the mountains. There was no substitute for intelligence won through interpersonal contact with Afghanis. How could we adjust our operations so that we could win friends?

Before leaving the base, we piled into a convoy of Toyota Hilux pickup trucks. As we drove on a practice range, a small explosive charge went off to simulate incoming fire. Men stepped out of the trucks, took cover, and the mountainside erupted in bullets and rockets as we returned fire against an imaginary enemy.

When we walked back to our barracks, I saw pinned to a board a printed picture of a Navy SEAL operator—a member of this team—who had died fighting in Afghanistan. The men I was driving with had been at the very tip of the spear of American military operations for nearly two years. They had paid a price in blood, but their experience had made them sharp.

Later, as we drove over rocky ground, a tire went flat on one of the trucks. I jumped out and grabbed a lug wrench and squatted on the rocky soil and started to change the tire. I was glad to be useful. My dad had taught me how to change a tire on our Ford when I was sixteen years old. After all my years at Oxford and my experience in SEAL training, it was my dad's lesson on the driveway that allowed me to do my first positive thing serving in the military overseas.

I went to Kabul with the headquarters element of the team, and after a few days of work there I left for a firebase. The firebase compound was surrounded by high mud walls. There was a dirt field inside the compound—just about the size of a baseball infield—and parked there were a dozen Humvees and Hilux trucks. Inside the firebase headquarters, beat-up desks were loaded with computers and the glow of the monitors lit the faces of the men who stood up periodically to move pins on a map to indicate where American teams were moving on the battlefield. Atop the highest wall of the compound, satellite antennas reached into the air beside the flapping flag of the Chicago Bears, a testament to the presence of troops from the Illinois National Guard.

Each day our team, dressed in battle armor, riding military vehicles, carrying our weapons, drove out of the compound to try to make friends. We met with local businessmen, village elders, pharmacists, informants. We worked in a mixed team of SEALs, members of the FBI Hostage Rescue Team, Navy Explosive Ordnance Disposal experts, Air Force Combat Controllers, Air Force Pararescue Jumpers, Army Civil Affairs personnel, and members of other government agencies. Each person brought his own skill set to the team. The FBI agent, trained to speak with witnesses and suspects, was often good in conversation and was trained in evidence collection. The Air Force Pararescue Jumpers were some of the best combat medics in the world. The SEAL teams were incredible assault teams, and in the event that we had actionable intelligence, they could plan, brief, and execute a complex tactical capture/kill operation better than any force in the world.

We tried to put on a friendly face yet be ready for violence at a moment's notice. On one of our first trips out of our compound, our convoy entered a traffic circle. As we drove around the circle, I looked to my left. "Man with an AK-47, passenger seat, white Toyota." The man had black hair, an unkempt beard. He looked back at me with brown eyes and his lips parted to show yellowing teeth. I laid the barrel of my rifle to rest on the open window, and I tilted the muzzle so that I could take a shot if he raised his weapon to fire. We turned right, his car turned left, and he was gone.

We turned onto a narrow road paved not quite wide enough for two trucks to pass each other. Each time we passed another vehicle our convoy ran along the side of the road and our wheels kicked up dust. But for the occasional transmission to let headquarters know our position, there was minimal radio traffic. I sat in the back seat of one of the pickups on a thick green ballistic blanket meant to provide some protection in the event of a blast.

Before us, brown mountains stood in the distance like sentries. The landscape had a desolate beauty: sun, rocks, clean air, mountains. We passed a caravan of camels, their shaggy humps laden with bulging sacks, water jugs, blankets. At the head of the caravan rode a man on a donkey. As we passed him, he turned his head, wrapped in a clay-red turban, and squinted into the sun, and I saw the deep lines etched into his bearded face. We drove past the charred skeleton of a burned-out Volkswagen, and we turned off the paved road and onto a dirt track.

We pulled into a village—a warren of mud-brick homes surrounded by fields sprouting green from the baked brown earth. Here, we acted like Doctors Without Borders. Our team medics unzipped bags of gear and medicine and they listened with a translator as villagers came to them with complaints: "This boy cut his hand," or "This man's elbow is bleeding," and our medic cleaned the wounds and wrapped them in fresh bandages. Our medics could treat minor ailments, but when the translator pointed to an older man—"He says that his chest is in pain, his heart is not strong"—there was little the medics could do but offer the man a vial of aspirin.

I walked around the village with an Army Civil Affairs officer and one of the village leaders. I guessed the village leader to be in his forties. He was thin and wore a broad black turban and walked with sure-footed vigor. He made wide gestures at the land around him as he talked more quickly than our translator could interpret. He talked about his need for a well and the Civil Affairs officer asked some basic questions about how the villagers got their water now. How do they irrigate their crops? Is the drinking water clean? To the elder, we were a potential source of money and services.

The leader asked us about our lives: Did we have children? How long have we been freedom fighters? I told him that I used to do work caring for children and communities, but that now I had become a soldier. He replied to me through the translator, and the translator and two other Afghanis started to laugh. "He says you are the same as him, but backwards. First, he is commander who fight the Taliban. Now, he is to be chief of village. He says much easier to fight the Taliban. There was less yelling and complaints."

Later that day in another village I stood outside a medical clinic with other members of our team on guard. We held security while a meeting took place in the clinic. Children slowly approached us with friendly banter.

"America, good!"

"Afghanistan, good!" I yelled back, and more children came around. For a moment I was reminded of being surrounded by the children in Croatia as I walked into the refugee camp, and of the children in Cambodia who swarmed around us when we stepped into their villages. I felt strange here now, body armor on, rifle in my gloved hands, magazines loaded. There were some older teenagers in the group, and I scanned the crowd for threats, looked for weapons. I made a note of where the other SEALs were standing and I thought, *What should we do if someone shoots at us from that house to the north? What if someone drives by in a truck on that road to the south and opens fire? What if . . .* Only a few years ago I would have been holding a camera and organizing a game. Now I was holding a rifle and planning contingencies in case of attack.

Our convoy left in a cloud of dust. I sat back in the truck next to my "go bag," a small bag containing basic essentials we'd need if we had to make a quick escape—a survival radio, extra med gear, extra ammo. We drove to another village and met with a shop owner who was a former associate of the terrorist we were hunting. His shop had been blown up several months ago, and he described with a few phrases in reasonable English that everything he owned had been destroyed. He was friendly but unhelpful; his eyes darted left and right as he spoke, and I left feeling sure that he was reluctant to talk with us because he was afraid of the consequences of cooperation. We walked out of his shop with few answers and stepped back into our trucks.

Much of our schedule was dictated by members of other government agencies who wanted to meet with potential sources and track down leads. The other government agencies lacked the trucks, weapons, and security they needed to move freely and safely around Afghanistan. These other government agencies sometimes had, however, more language ability, a better cultural understanding of the environment, and, most importantly, more financial freedom than the military.

The military requires stacks of paperwork for even the most meager financial transaction. Members of other government agencies had more freedom to pay for information, to pay local contractors to build wells in villages, to pay for a host of projects that might help to open relationships.

The money worked. You can't buy peace, but you can sometimes make a down payment on it, and it struck me that it was much cheaper to invest money in relationships with potential Afghani allies than it was to house, feed, arm, water, transport, and supply tens of thousands of American troops. Not every investment paid dividends, but if we could pay one man a few hundred or even a few thousand dollars to give us quality information on a high-level terrorist, and we could use that information to capture or kill our target, it was cheaper and more effective than spending millions of dollars on complex signals intelligence collection platforms that cost hundreds of thousands of dollars to operate and rarely gave us a clear line of attack on our targets. If we could pay a local leader a few thousand dollars a month and buy safe passage for our forces, the goodwill of a village, and information on al Qaeda, it was far more effective than sending twice-daily patrols of kids from Missouri rolling through villages to project "presence," in the hope that the people of Afghanistan would become enamored with Americans.

I love American idealism. I love the hopeful spirit of Americans endeavoring to shape the world for the better. A lot of times, though, many Americans—especially those in senior positions in government and the military—who have never spent a day working with people who suffer, can be blinded by the bright shining light of their own hopes. You cruise through a town where you don't speak the language and offer someone a conversation about freedom or fifty bucks, most people will take the cash, thank you very much.

I'd learned, working in Croatia, Rwanda, Albania, Cambodia, and Gaza, the very simple lesson that people were smart enough to know what they needed, and if we wanted to have credibility with them, we had to be able to help them directly.

As we sat in villages under a fierce sun and talked with haggard, scarred, and bearded men who looked to be in their mid-fifties, they often smiled at us and told us that they were in their early thirties. The average life expectancy in Afghanistan was forty-three years old. The infant mortality rate was estimated to be about 257 out of every thousand. In the United States, by comparison, the infant mortality rate was six out of every thousand.[12] In graduate school I had often looked at the United Nations Human Development Index, which ranks countries on the basis of "three basic dimensions of human development: a long and healthy life, knowledge, and a decent standard of living."[13] Full statistics were hard to come by for Afghanistan because of the movement of refugees across the borders and the ongoing war, but generally speaking, Afghanistan ranked approximately 174 out of the 178 countries of the Human Development Index; one of the poorest, harshest, and most brutal places to live in the world.[14]

The men on the SEAL teams were impressive. The days were long, the air full of dust. Often our visits seemed fruitless, and as we drove from one village to another we ate meals of MREs in hot pickup trucks. Yet even at the end of a long day every radio transmission was crisp, every potential threat was noted. We drove one early evening as the sun was fading, when a call came over the radio, "Stop him! White Toyota, the passenger, that's our guy!"

"Get him!"

I jumped out of the truck, stepped into the street, and pointed my rifle at the chest of the oncoming driver. A white compact car with two Afghani men was rushing toward me. I shuffled two steps backward so that I could move behind our truck while firing if the car accelerated at me, but the driver applied the brakes and the car slowed. The passenger and the driver threw their hands into the air. I held my rifle on them as other men on our team opened the doors to their car and pulled both men from the vehicle. We searched their car and emerged with a blue notebook; did it have intelligence value? As we questioned the driver, a crowd began to form on the road. Afghani men approached to see what was happening. They stood with their arms crossed on their chests, and then they would shout and point at us as they yelled to other Afghani men joining the crowd. Eyes narrowed.

"Two cars stopped on the road, one hundred meters south. Men emerging."

"I've got three men on a rooftop, two hundred meters east, one of them with a stick or an AK in his hands."

More people began to step from their stopped cars. Children and young boys inched closer.

"There's a truck stopped on the road to the west, blue truck, about fifty meters back. Has five guys in it, all young, all full beards, all black turbans."

We released the driver and quickly ushered his passenger into one of our trucks. Every man on our team jumped in a truck and one second later our convoy was accelerating away.

I sat in the room while Chris, a professional interrogator working with our team, spoke with the detainee. "Assalaam alaikum," Chris said and shook the hand of the man who was now our prisoner. Chris touched his hand to his heart. Chris handed the man a candy bar, opened it for him, and asked the prisoner if he'd had enough to eat. Yes, he had, he said, thank you.

So tell me about yourself, Chris said, what is your profession? The man said that he was a farmer.

"Where is your farm?"

The man answered. "And what kind of crops do you grow?" The man answered. "And where were you going when my friends stopped you?" The man explained that he was returning to his village in a car driven by the friend of a relative. He had been on a trip to sell something and he was now on his way home.

Chris sat comfortably, and he occasionally asked the man if he needed anything to drink, if he was sure that he wasn't hungry. As they talked, Chris covered the same ground as before, often with slightly different questions: "Do you often make this trip? What kind of crops did you grow last year?"

Chris talked with the man for a few hours, and by the end of the conversation Chris assessed that we had detained the wrong man. Our prisoner was, it seemed, indeed a farmer, who had been on a personal errand when at the end of a long day we mistook him for a terrorist and yanked him from his vehicle. Chris explained to the man that we were very sorry to have caused him this inconvenience. Chris explained that our prisoner looked similar to a known terrorist who had been murdering innocent people in the area, and that we were doing our best to protect the local population. Chris said that the American people have a great respect for the people of Afghanistan, and that we had a desire to work with them. Chris said that we would provide this man money in the morning to help him make the trip back to his village and to pay him for the trouble we had caused him.

I later watched other young Army interrogators try to intimidate detainees into talking, and I never saw one of those interrogators get a single piece of useful information. Chris was a professional, and he knew what worked. The world's best interrogators proceed not by fear and intimidation, but by establishing rapport with their prisoners and learning from them over time. We'd learned in Survival, Evasion, Resistance, and Escape school that the world's most effective interrogators, from World War II to the present day, are men who use their intelligence to establish rapport and gain information.

There is a famous picture from World War II of the legendary interrogator Major Sherwood Moran of the Marine Corps "breaking" Japanese POWs.[15] In contrast to images of dogs held several feet from prisoners to scare them, Moran is sitting on a cloth foldaway chair across from a Japanese prisoner. He is listening intently, his body leaning forward and eyes focused on the prisoner. This practice of highly effective, respectful, intelligent, and noncoercive interrogation has been applied effectively to al Qaeda, too.

Jack Cloonan, a special agent who worked at the FBI's Osama bin

Laden unit from 1996 to 2002 described the following incident of "breaking" a terrorist.

> One man we captured was Ali Abdul Saoud Mohamed, an al-Qaeda operative behind the 1998 bombings of the U.S. embassies in Kenya and Tanzania. Ali Mohamed had fully expected to be tortured once we took him in. Instead, we assured him that we wouldn't harm him, and we offered to protect his family. Within weeks, we had opened a gold mine of information about al-Qaeda's operations.
>
> Ali Mohamed wasn't unique. We gave our word to every detainee that no harm would come to him or his family. This invariably stunned them, and they would feel more obligated to cooperate. Also, because all information led to more information, detainees were astonished to find out how much we already knew about them—their networks, their families, their histories. Some seemed relieved to reveal their secrets. When they broke, the transformations were remarkable. Their bodies would go limp. Many would weep. Most would ask to pray. These were men undergoing profound emotional and spiritual turmoil—the result of going from a belief that their destiny was to fight and kill people like us to a decision that they should cooperate with the enemy.[16]

The professionals who I was working with also understood that the man we had just brought in for questioning was going to go home and tell his entire village about his experience with the Americans. There was a good chance that this man would be the first person in his village to have any interaction with Americans, and he might well live in a village with no newspapers, magazines, or TV news coverage. His story would likely be *the* story of Americans in Afghanistan. What happened to you? How did the Americans treat you? Are they like the Russians? The British? This man—by our best estimate—was a farmer on a personal errand being driven home by a friend when I stepped into the road and pointed my rifle at him and my teammates yanked him from his vehicle. If we were going to be able to catch real al Qaeda targets, we would need the kind of human intelligence that only men like this farmer and his friends and family could provide. In every interaction that we had, we had the opportunity to create enemies or to create friends.

Treating Afghanis well was not only essential to the conduct of the campaign to win the intelligence war. I also began to see that it was essential for ourselves. The Taliban were often well trained, arguably often better trained to fight in Afghanistan than many American troops. So what makes us different from the Taliban? What distinguishes a warrior from a thug? Certainly it's not the quality of our weapons or the length of our training. Ultimately we're distinguished by our values. It would have been easy to abuse a prisoner, but any act of wanton personal brutality is not only unproductive to defeating a group like the Taliban, but on a personal level it degrades the warrior and turns him into a thug. Any man who tortures a prisoner, who shoots an innocent person, might escape formal justice, but he can never escape his own self-knowledge. As I worked with this small group of professionals in Afghanistan, it became clear to me that men need to have the strength to conduct themselves with honor on the battlefield.

Every day the men on this team went out to meet with allies and to hunt enemies, and every moment of every day was filled with a low-grade tension. *Is somebody gonna take a shot at us here? Is this guy telling us the truth? Are we driving into an ambush?*

One day we stepped into our trucks and drove for an hour until we came to a collection of mud-walled buildings that were home to a local leader who had in the past provided information on al Qaeda targets. When we walked into the center of his compound, a few boys wearing skullcaps dashed away. Our contact came striding out to meet us dressed in jeans, a T-shirt, and sunglasses. He talked with one of our colleagues from another government agency, and then he directed us out of the compound—he wanted our help. We walked fifty yards down a dusty lane shaded by overhanging trees. One of the members of our team pointed to opium fields on the hillside. We spread out for security, and I took a knee about twenty yards from a compact car parked under a tree. Our contact and one of our teammates walked up to the car. I watched our teammate bend at the waist and lower his sunglasses to peer through the dust-covered windows of the car, and then he started to walk away quickly while talking with his Afghani contact. The American called for our Explosive Ordnance Disposal expert, and as the EOD tech walked toward the car, I walked away from it. The car was filled with explosives. Old unexploded artillery shells lined the seats. It was unclear if the car had been parked outside the compound as a bomb but had failed to go off. Some of the men from the village had pushed the car down the street to move it away.

"Well, tell everyone not to touch it again."

The man wanted our help to safely blow up the bomb. Our team could destroy small amounts of explosives, but we had only one EOD tech and he assessed that the explosives were too unstable, and the bomb was too close to the village for him to safely blow it in place. We called in to headquarters to have an EOD team sent out to the village to destroy the bomb. By the time we jumped back into our pickup trucks we had information about a possible Taliban bed-down location nearby. Our contact explained that there was a group of young Taliban fighters in the area.

As we drove for the suspected Taliban site, we called back to headquarters and had an unmanned aerial vehicle diverted to look at the campsite for any human activity. As we bounced along the road, our team leader worked at a ruggedized laptop computer to plot our position in relation to the target site. The site appeared empty, but it was daytime. Should the team plan a night reconnaissance, possibly an ambush?

When the UAV had been deployed, we turned and drove to meet with another potential ally in the area. The police station was set on a relatively well-manicured compound that hosted a set of white-painted buildings, and we talked with the head of the local force as he smoked a cigarette. What had he learned since our last conversation? Did he have any information on the targets we were tracking? Had he heard about a suspected Taliban camp in the area? Sitting in a disheveled Afghani police uniform and filling a tray with ashes, the officer talked about how difficult it was to train and feed and equip his men.

Someone from the government had promised him more money, but it had not arrived. He asked, could we help him?

This police chief wanted money, and he probably had information that we needed. At first glance, it seemed a simple question: should we pay him?

Every interaction in Afghanistan was, however, more complicated than it first seemed, and the success of our campaign depended upon tens of thousands of individual human interactions just like this one.

The police chief—and every Afghani we talked with—had his own allegiances, to the government, to the Taliban, to his ethnic group, to his tribe, to his personal financial gain, to his family's honor, to his professional career. He had his personal loyalties, his personal quirks. In order for us to win here, we had to have friends and allies, but building those friends and allies could only happen if we worked through barriers of language and geography and culture and custom.

Most of the professionals I knew had made an effort—as I had—to brush up on their history of Afghanistan. But just when we thought we understood the history of the Taliban, we began to learn that we also had to pay attention to ethnic differences in Afghanistan—between, for example, Tajiks and Pashtuns. And just when we thought we had begun to understand ethnic groups, we learned that we had to understand tribes.

Of course, once we began to understand tribes, we realized that we had to try to understand the particular issues and difficulties of the communities and individuals with whom we were interacting. And of all the incredible men on my team, there wasn't a single one who spoke more than twenty words of Pashto or Dari—the major languages in Afghanistan—or more than twenty words of Arabic—a predominant language among al Qaeda fighters.

The stakes involved in every interaction were incredibly high and we learned fast, but American forces usually deployed for three, seven, or twelve months. Because of the frequent rotation of forces in and out of Afghanistan, knowledge was lost.

I felt like I was just beginning to get a sense of the fight. Afghanistan is about the size of the state of Texas, and depending on how you count refugees, the population is generally thought to be about 30 million people. The population is overwhelmingly rural. If you took twenty-five of the major cities in Afghanistan, they would only encompass about 20 percent of the population.[17] In contrast, 80 percent of America's population lives in an urban/metropolitan area.[18]

The population, moreover, was spread out over one of the most mountainous and inaccessible countries in the world. If we wanted allies, they'd be difficult to find and difficult to supply. And when we did make it to their villages, we'd find a population that was 70 percent illiterate, living in an economy that was—next to Somalia—one of the worst in the world.

More difficult still, this fight involved Pakistan as well as Afghanistan, where at that very moment, much of al Qaeda was waiting, training, organizing, equipping, and rearming, just over the border.

All of this suggested that the mission in Afghanistan would be complicated and difficult, but perhaps the most difficult aspect of the fight was that it was not at all clear what our long-term mission actually was. Was our aim to defeat al Qaeda? Was our aim to defeat the Taliban? Was our aim to build a functioning democracy and prosperous economy in Afghanistan?

I felt that—even in 2003—we had begun to misremember what happened in Afghanistan in 2001. We began to think that *we* had defeated the Taliban and driven al Qaeda into Pakistan. It was true that American financing, air power, and military personnel had been essential to the effort, but the ground forces in that fight were Afghans. Our allies, the Northern Alliance, were the predominant forces that had defeated the Taliban on the ground, and it concerned me that now, just a year and a half later, the American "campaign" didn't seem to have a clear enough plan for recruiting and supporting our allies. We also seemed to confuse the Taliban with al Qaeda.

Al Qaeda was a foreign force, made up of men like Bin Laden, from

Saudi Arabia, and Ayman al-Zawahiri, from Egypt. Of the nineteen hijackers who had participated in 9/11, fifteen of them were from Saudi Arabia. The Taliban, by contrast, was an Afghani force. And it seemed to me that they both required a different approach. Al Qaeda terrorists had attacked the United States. They represented a threat and they needed to be killed. Some of the Taliban also needed to be killed, but the Taliban was a wide and diverse group with many competing interests and a history of shifting allegiances, and it seemed to me that we had better determine for certain who among them needed to be fought before we launched a shooting war with tens of thousands of men spread throughout a mountainous country.

The Taliban and al Qaeda were associated, but not the same, and in order for us to fight effectively, we had to be laser-focused on killing and capturing the right people, and building as many allies as we could.

Some people argued that in order to defeat al Qaeda and secure American interests we had to defeat the Taliban, and that in order to defeat the Taliban we had to build a democracy in Afghanistan. This seemed to me like arguing that in order to rid your house of rats you had to replace the walls in your home and then build an Olympic-sized swimming pool in the backyard. To turn Afghanistan into a country with a highly functioning democracy, a well-run economy, and a prosperous population is a noble vision. But defeating al Qaeda is a more pressing and more modest mission, not to mention a clear mission that we could achieve. But it also seemed to me that it would require us to keep our efforts in Afghanistan focused.

If our strategy to defeat al Qaeda was going to require us to build democracies and economies, then we had to do that work not just in Afghanistan and Pakistan, but in Somalia, Yemen, and a dozen other enclaves and countries around the world.

We returned to the firebase that night while a UAV patrolled over the site of the suspected Taliban camp. Our phone rang, and I answered it. The commander of our unit in Kabul was on the other end. "I talked with Bruce. SEAL Team One and Special Boat Team Twelve want you to go back and take command of the Mark V detachment before the next field training exercise." In other words, they were sending me stateside already.

I shut my eyes in disappointment.

"Yes, sir. I'll be ready to go."

I had spent only a few weeks in Afghanistan. I had only just begun to feel that I had my body armor riding well. Before I had come to Afghanistan, I had taken command of a Mark V special operations craft detachment that was preparing to deploy to Southeast Asia. The deployment wasn't scheduled to leave for several months, and we thought that I'd have all that time to spend in Afghanistan. No luck.

I left Afghanistan through the main base at Bagram, full of the French, Dutch, Polish, and German flags of our allies. I passed the giant chow halls where thousands of meals were prepared for soldiers every day, walked past the huge bunkers, the oversized TVs, and I sat through briefings on counterdrug initiatives, legislative plans, civil affairs efforts. I remembered the village leader who said that it was much easier to fight the Taliban.

When I got back to San Diego, I learned that a SEAL who served in the unit I deployed with had been killed right after I left.

Now, the bullets were real.

# 13 ☆

# Southeast Asia

A S  W E  P U L L E D out of Sembawang Wharves on the northern tip of Singapore, I looked at the radar. Green dots indicated three large tankers in the shipping lanes. Otherwise, it was a quiet night.

"Let's turn the lights off," I said.

The boat captain spoke into the radio, "Lights off," and our two ships went dark. With our running lights extinguished and the internal lights dimmed, we became two black masses rolling over black waves on a black night, white wakes our only visible sign.

As we passed our second checkpoint, the navigator said to me, "Mr. G, that's checkpoint Betty."

"Roger."

The radioman called to headquarters, "Eastgate, Eastgate, this is *Calisto*. I pass Betty. How copy? Over."

"*Calisto*, this is Eastgate. I copy Betty. Over."

Our checkpoints were often named in categories and progressed alphabetically—we used the names of cities: Albany, Buffalo, Colorado Springs, Denver; or of cars: Alfa Romeo, Beemer, Cadillac, Dodge; or, most popularly, girls: Alexis, Betty, Cassandra, Danielle. Guys would sometimes slip the names of their wives and girlfriends into the operation.

We passed checkpoint Betty and the open sea beckoned. The boat captain said, "Bring it up?"

"Bring it up." The boat captain pushed the throttle forward, and the jet engines roared and soon we were rushing over the small chop of the sea at fifty knots. The moon was hidden by clouds, but occasionally threw its white shadow onto the waves, and as I turned my head left I saw the black outline of our sister ship flying just thirty meters to port.

I pulled a waterproof card from my pocket with the call signs, radio frequencies, and checkpoints for our journey. Using a red-lens flashlight, I checked our distance to the next checkpoint and tucked the card away. The cabin was blacked-out dark, but my guys picked up from the tone of my voice that I was wearing a huge grin.

"You havin' fun, Mr. G?"

"Loads."

I was the commander of a Mark V special operations craft detachment, in charge of two boats and twenty-one men, conducting operations in Southeast Asia. We had left Singapore for Zamboanga, Philippines, on a journey of over fourteen hundred nautical miles. If we were successful, this was going to be the longest transit in the history of Naval Special Warfare.

The Mark V (pronounced "Mark Five") is a special operations boat—usually called a "craft"—that was created in 1995 primarily for the clandestine insertion and extraction of Navy SEAL teams.[1] At eighty-two feet long and seventeen and a half feet wide, the craft is large enough to carry a boat crew and sixteen SEALs, yet nimble enough to make hairpin turns at high speed.[2] The boat's shock-absorbing seats offered some relief from the pounding we took as we flew over the waves at fifty knots.

Each boat had four gun mounts, and we often ran with twin .50-caliber machine guns at each mount. On the two boats, we had sixteen .50-caliber machine guns, an incredible amount of firepower. Other times we'd run with a mix of .50-cals and Mark-19s. The Mark-19s are automatic grenade launchers capable of sending a 40mm grenade over twenty-four hundred yards. In the hands of a trained operator, it's possible to launch forty to sixty accurate grenade shots in one minute. In addition to weapons, we carried onboard some of the nation's most advanced signals intelligence equipment.

The Mark V runs on jet propulsion, and its angular shape makes it harder to detect on radar.[3] The back end of the craft is slanted toward the water, and on our back deck we carried Zodiacs—fifteen-and-a-half-foot combat raiding craft—that we could silently slip into the water with Naval Special Warfare commandos onboard.

Running side by side, we were two small fish in a big sea, but we were built to be fast and smart, and—in a pinch—we had big teeth.

The boats were impressive, but it took the right men to bring them to life, and those men in my crew were Special Warfare Combatant-Craft Crewmen (SWCC—pronounced "Swick"). SEALs and SWCC are the two groups of operators that make up Naval Special Warfare, and SWCC—though less well known than their SEAL brothers—are the often-unsung heroes of the force. They make U.S. Naval Special Warfare the best maritime special operations force in the world.

SWCC go through training at Coronado at the same facilities where BUD/S training is conducted. Though different, SWCC training is also intense, and like BUD/S, has a very high dropout rate. During Crewman Qualification Training, aspiring operators undergo a rigorous physical training regimen and learn radio communications, boat handling, navigation, engineering, and maintenance. They learn how to shoot pistol, rifle, and the heavy weapons that are used onboard special warfare craft. In advanced training, some of the teams learn how to navigate winding, shallow inland rivers, while others learn to parachute from a plane with a ten-ton rigid-hulled inflatable boat (RHIB—pronounced "rib") into the open ocean. The men learn to fire their .50-cal guns with accuracy while absorbing incredible g-forces as the hulls of their boats shoot over waves at full speed.

As the commander of the detachment, I was in charge of the mission, but the men ran the boats. Each boat had a captain, and the captain ran his crew. A navigator, chief engineer, radioman, and back-deck chief formed the core of each crew, while intel specialists and corps-men complemented our team.

As we began to run across the open sea—a long night now ahead of us—our chief engineer, Crazy T, said, "Hey, LT"—short for "Lieu-tenant"—"I was thinking about making you one of those fish crackers, you want one?" Doug Traver—Crazy T—was a former police officer with a great sense of humor who came to Naval Special Warfare for his life's next challenge.

"That's all you, T."

Traver was referring to the "treats" that had been prepared for us when we crossed the equator. One of the great traditions in the United States Navy is the "crossing the line" ceremony that takes place when a sailor first crosses the equator and goes from being a lowly "wog" to an esteemed "shellback."

Usually, only large Navy ships made the journey across the middle of the earth, but when we came to Singapore we were only eighty-two nautical miles north of the equator. We looked back at the history of Naval Special Warfare and couldn't find an instance of any small Naval Special Warfare craft crossing the equator on its own hull. As a team we decided to make a run for it. At the time, I was a lowly wog, so our chief, Steve MacIntyre, and a few of the other shellbacks in our crew organized a special operations–style ceremony. It began while still ashore in Singapore.

As wogs we were split into pairs. I was teamed with Crazy T. Standing on a green field near our barracks, we saw a bright yellow Slip 'n Slide laid out on the grass. At the prompt of the shellbacks, we ran hard for the slide, dove, and as we flew down the field headfirst, we realized that the plastic sheet was covered not with water, but with fish oil.

We ran and dove down the slide several more times, until stinking fish oil dripped from our hair and covered our shirts and shorts. Then the shellbacks put two eggs in our oily hands.

"OK wogs, you have to protect those eggs all day. The shellbacks have set up stations around the base. You'll run from station to station, and at each station you'll have to complete tasks. The faster you complete the course, the more points you get. If your eggs break, you lose points, and you'll be punished by the mighty shellbacks. It pays to be a winner!"

Crazy T and I ran around the base stinking of fish oil. With slippery fingers, we programmed radios and assembled parts into weapons. We did pushups and frog hops in the sand and we crab-walked in the dirt.

We came huffing into the final station covered in fish oil and sand and dirt and sweat. Our eggs were unbroken, but when we tried to hand the eggs to the shellbacks, they told us, "Just set 'em down; we don't want to touch you guys."

Soon all of the stinking wogs gathered outside of our barracks, and then Chief MacIntyre said, "OK, wogs, here's the deal. You now have the opportunity to earn back time that you lost on the obstacle course by consuming delicacies from the Seven Seas."

The shellbacks laid out a plate of crackers that were covered in some kind of Marmite, fish, octopus, and mayonnaise concoction. With my fish-oil-and-sand-covered fingers, I pinched a cracker and brought it to my nose. I took one whiff and lost my motivation to "earn" back time.

Crazy T, however, was always very motivated. Each cracker was worth a few minutes, and T calculated that if he could down six or so crackers, we would win.

"T . . ."

"It's OK, LT, I got it."

T held his nose and swallowed one cracker fast, and then a second. He inhaled a third cracker. I think he even got the fourth cracker in, but the rule was that the crackers had to go down and stay down, and somewhere around the fourth cracker, T's stomach started to spasm.

The crew was yelling for him: "Hold it in, T! Hold it in!"

T managed to keep his mouth shut as he threw up. He bent over and held his legs. All twenty guys in the detachment—wogs and shellbacks alike—were yelling for him: "Hold it in, T, hold it in, you can do it!"

T then brought his hands together in front of his face and threw up into his hands. "You OK, T?" The whole crew stood waiting for T's next move. Spit hanging from his mouth, Crazy T said, "Guys, I can get it back in. I can get it back in."

The crew erupted: "Go for it, T. Go for it!" T stood looking at the mess in his hands awhile, and then I put my hand on his shoulder and said, "That's good enough, T. I think we did it," and T let go of the puke.

The next day we drove our boats down eighty-some nautical miles to the equator, with our sister ship flying a giant black Jolly Roger—the black pirate flag marked by a white skull and crossbones. As we approached the equator, the shellbacks hooked up speakers in the Mark V and—reflecting the varied tastes of our crew—blasted a mix of heavy metal, country, and rap as we shot over short blue waves on the ride south.

Traditionally, sailors are driven over the equator aboard ship, but our shellbacks decided that—being special operations—we had to swim across. We wogs jumped into the open ocean about a half mile from the equator. There was nothing but our boats and salt water in every direction. We started to swim but soon it was clear that the current was running north, and after a half hour we were farther away from the equator than when we started. The shellbacks, however, were not going to let us back onboard. They threw thick ropes off the back of the Mark Vs.

"Grab on! We'll drag you over."

The engines revved and we grabbed ahold. As the Mark Vs picked up speed, the ocean grabbed at us and tried to rip us from the ropes, but we all held on as the boats dragged us across the equator.

Once we crossed we swam to the back of the Mark Vs and were pulled dripping from the sea and welcomed aboard as new shellbacks. We replaced the Jolly Roger with the American flag and we then conducted an awards ceremony on our back deck. A few of my men had made extraordinary efforts and I had put them forward for recognition, so medals were pinned on their uniforms and orders were read on the open sea. Then we asked the chaplain—who had joined us for the journey that day—to say a few words.

As we floated on the ocean, an immense blue sea around us, we bowed our heads as the chaplain spoke. "This has been a wonderful day, and we have fulfilled a great Navy tradition in the best possible way. I also believe that crossing the equator like this demonstrates that sometimes you first have to believe in something to make it real."

I hadn't thought about the equator that way before. There was no magic line in the sea. Everywhere we looked there was nothing but open water.

At the beginning now of our longest journey, Crazy T said to me, "You sure, LT? Those were some good crackers."

We flew over the waves for hours that night. Borneo was far enough away that we had to refuel at sea, and so we had arranged to be met by a civilian refueling ship at a specific time and location in the middle of the night. This part of our operation was not secret. It was, in fact, well publicized because we wanted to demonstrate a growing relationship between America and Malaysia. But when our chief, Steve MacIntyre, met with the civilian refueling ship captain, he found that the civilian crew was very excited to be working with a group of American special operations forces. The captain and his men had shown up to the meeting in the belief that *they* were now being called upon to fight the war on terror.

Steve indulged them. He told the crew that we would link up at night using a "secret" code. When we came over the horizon and got within six nautical miles, Steve would come over the radio on a preassigned frequency and say, "Got milk?" The captain of the refueling craft would say, "No, just cookies." And we would then drive in to meet them.

When the time came for Steve to make contact, he came up on the radio: "Got milk?" There was a brief pause, and then we heard the captain, in South-Asian-accented English: "Oh no, no milk. No. No. Just cookies. No milk here, no milk, just cookies, just cookies." The captain was flustered in his excitement, and so Steve said, "What *kind* of cookies?" This was not part of the script that Steve had given the captain, and the captain said, "Oh my, oh my God, I don't remember, I have cookies, cookies."

Steve said, "Do you have Oreos?"

"Oh, yes, yes, we have Oreos, all of the Oreos you want."

"OK, then," Steve said. "I like Oreos."

"Me too," the captain said, and our secret refueling was under way.

After we'd taken on fuel, we made for Borneo, and as we shot through the dark night, the men at work, the waves rolling under us, I was possessed of a deep sense of happiness.

I had twenty-one good men racing two special operations boats across the sea at night destined for a port where no special operations craft had ever been before, and we were at the beginning of a groundbreaking transit the likes of which had never been attempted. My closest boss was nearly three thousand nautical miles away.

I leaned over to talk with my navigator and we checked our actual location against the course we had plotted. We were right on course, right on time. But as we flew I was thinking about more than just our speed, our location, our communications, and our plan. I was also thinking about my team, and most importantly, my guys' state of mind.

We had a great journey ahead of us, but we had also just overcome what was—certainly for me—the most difficult challenge of the deployment. Our first operation had been in Thailand, where we had participated in one of the largest military exercises in Southeast Asia with our Thai counterparts.

Thailand is a gorgeous country with white beaches and mountains overrun by green foliage. In Thailand, I visited humble stone temples paying homage to the Buddha, and intricate temples built by Thailand's royalty that housed giant golden statues. Sitting ringside in a packed Bangkok arena, I watched a Muay Thai fight, and on days off, I encouraged my crew to see as much of the country as they could.

One free Saturday, Kaj Larsen and I planned an elephant trek in the

Thai jungle. Kaj and I had been through BUD/S; Jump School; Survival, Evasion, Resistance, and Escape school; and SEAL Qualification Training together. He was a fellow lieutenant (jg—junior grade), a fellow SEAL, and the commander of a RHIB detachment with eight guys and two eleven-meter boats. Their primary mission was to conduct boarding missions of other craft at sea. Kaj and I had sweated through more than three years of swims, jumps, dives, and all-night operations together, and we were good friends. We boarded a tourist van on our way to the elephant trek, and a few miles in, Kaj turned to me and said, "So, I've got a heavy one for you, brother."

"What is it?"

Kaj explained that two of his guys had woken him that morning and asked to speak with him. "They told me that last night, they're out in town, and they see Calvin."

"Calvin, the SEAL lieutenant?"

"Yeah, Stuart Calvin, and his eyes are wildly dilated, and they say something to him like, 'Dude, your eyes are blown' and Calvin flips out on 'em, tells 'em, 'What the fuck are you, some kind of master-at-arms?' And Calvin tells 'em to 'stay the fuck away.' Later, they're in the bathroom, and they see Calvin come in with two other guys in his SEAL platoon. Calvin has a baggie and Calvin and his guys walk together into one of the stalls. Then Calvin orders this new SEAL in his platoon to hold security on the door."

"What was in the baggie?"

"They don't know. They think it was ecstasy, or some drug, this stuff called Special K."

"What'd you tell your guys?"

"I told 'em that I'd talk with you, and then let 'em know what we're going to do about it."

Kaj's men knew me and trusted me, and as the elephant-trek van bounced over dirt roads, I called them on my cell phone and his men relayed their story to me exactly as Kaj had told it to me.

Kaj said, "What do you think?"

I said, "We should piss test everybody. Do urinalysis on the whole squadron. All of the SEAL platoons, all the boat detachments. Anybody who's doing drugs'll pop positive, and we'll get rid of 'em. Any other way, and this'll just become a bunch of accusations flying back and forth about what some guys saw in a club."

Kaj called his men. "Guys, we're going to ask for a urinalysis of the entire squadron. Mr. G and I'll be back soon and we'll talk more then. You guys are doing the right thing."

As Kaj and I made a plan, his cell phone rang again, and I could see the worry on Kaj's face as he listened. He hung up the phone and said, "I hate to tell you this, brother, but my guys said, 'We just want you to know, that if you do a squadron-wide urinalysis, the Mark V guys might not come out so well.'"

There wasn't just a drug problem somewhere in Naval Special Warfare; there was a drug problem in my detachment. I told Kaj, "Tell 'em that we're going to do a squadron-wide urinalysis, and tell them that I'm going to start an investigation into my detachment."

A few minutes later Kaj's men called back again and they told Kaj that one of his men "thinks that someone might have slipped something into one of his drinks."

"OK," Kaj said, "we'll talk about this when I get back." It just got uglier. Now Kaj knew that he had a drug problem in his detachment as well.

Kaj and I asked the van driver if he could drive us back to the hotel, but the driver had other stops to make. We discussed having our guys drive out to pick us up, but then we would have to explain to all of the men why we'd suddenly bailed on our outing. We wanted to put a plan together first. We climbed aboard the elephant.

As the elephant thudded through the jungle and we ducked overhanging branches, Kaj and I made calls to Bangkok, to Pattaya, to San Diego. Occasionally the elephant curled its trunk over its head and we fed it a banana, both of us on our cell phones.

It remains my most surreal moment in the United States military, this crisis aboard the banana-eating elephant. I thought briefly of the Carthaginian general Hannibal, who marched war elephants through the Alps at the beginning of the Second Punic War. Did Hannibal feel this ridiculous?

It was a liberty day, and when we made it back to the task unit, we found that most of the men were gone. The next morning, we put our crews on lockdown. Kaj, Chief MacIntyre, two other chiefs, my maintenance officer, and I set up a row of chairs in the common room of one of the hotel buildings. We set out paper and pens to take notes.

I said to Kaj, "You ready for this?"

"I fucking hate that we have to do this. But let's go." We called our men in one by one.

One of the young men in my detachment stepped through the common room door with a big smile on his face—he thought he was about to be briefed about an upcoming operation—and when he saw the line of stern-looking chiefs and officers seated before him, he lost his smile. As we asked him questions, his cheeks went white and his hands started to shake such that he set down the pen he was holding and held onto his thighs. We called in men that we loved, one after another, and we questioned them.

Later, back in San Diego, people would ask me if it was hard to do this: was it hard to investigate my own men, hard to take statements about the conduct of fellow SEALs? I said then, and feel now, that whether or not it was hard was not relevant. It was necessary. No matter how many people we might upset, no matter how many supposed friends we might lose, our duty was to protect our men, the men who were doing the right thing. We couldn't have men using drugs and firing live ammunition, using drugs and executing complex operations, using drugs and representing the United States. We couldn't have officers selling drugs to young enlisted men. All of this was as obvious then as it is now. It wasn't hard. But when I had to call in front of me men whom I had worked with—some of them for over a year—and when I had to call in front of me men whom I had traded jokes with, whose families I knew, who had asked me to help them plan their careers and their educations—it was sad. I felt—and I know that others felt—deep disappointment that these men who had sweated with us through hours of lifesaving drills on the sun-beaten back decks of our Mark V on the open ocean, men who had shared food with us as we stayed up on all-night operations, men who fired live ammunition just feet from our bodies—it was with deep disappointment that we found that these men who had passed so many tests with us, had failed this one.

By the end of the investigation, three of my men were kicked out of the Navy, one of Kaj's men was kicked out of the Navy, several SEALs were kicked out of the Navy, and Calvin—the SEAL officer at the center of this fiasco who had been using ecstasy and cocaine and was selling drugs to young enlisted men—went to jail.

Kaj and I had to deal with a few idiots—like the SEAL lieutenant in the Philippines who told Kaj and me that we should have punished our guys who "ratted" about the drug use (that same lieutenant later asked us to lie to our commander about our missions and ended up receiving a letter of reprimand for his conduct). But in general, we received incredible support, and my chain of command had my back.

Every culture will encounter its problems. At the end of the day, the Naval Special Warfare values won out. The Navy SEAL Code says that we must "serve with honor and integrity on and off the battlefield."

Another line of the SEAL Code says, "Take responsibility for your actions and the actions of your teammates."[4] Of the three men in my detachment who left the Navy, two were young men on their first deployment. I don't believe that they would have ever sought drugs in Thailand. They were trying to find their way, trying to be warriors, trying to be men, and when they saw Calvin—a SEAL lieutenant whom they admired—using and selling drugs in Thailand, they both made a bad decision and they followed Calvin's lead.

Before those two men left Thailand, I sat down with them. "You guys have made a serious mistake, and you're going to suffer serious consequences for your decision. That's the bad news. This is going to stay with you for the rest of your lives. The good news is that you can both decide how this is going to affect the rest of your lives. You have two options. One choice is to pretend that this isn't your fault, to act like you're a victim, to pretend that you were misunderstood, to pretend that you didn't make the choices that you did make. If you do that, this decision is going to haunt you for the rest of your life. The other choice, the better choice, is to be honest about what happened here. Be honest with yourself and be honest with everyone else. If you're honest about what happened here, this can be a mistake that you learn from, a mistake that you grow from. It doesn't feel like it right now, but you can make this a source of strength for yourself." At the time they said, "Thank you." They said, "We're sorry that we let everyone down." I shook their hands. As I walked back to my now-diminished crew, I wondered, *Was there something more that I could have done, should have done to prevent this?*

I'm still in touch with both men. They send me pictures of their just-born and smiling-in-the-backyard kids. We talk about their careers, their families, and as they've matured over the years, I've been pleased to recommend both of them for schools and for jobs. They put their bad decision behind them in a positive way and they found a way to move on. They both learned—and we all were reminded—that to be a warrior is as much a question of moral character as it is a question of physical courage.

My detachment and the Naval Special Warfare community also moved forward. My commander in San Diego sent men out from California to bring us back to full strength, and I intensified our physical training to build crew cohesion. I took a page from my Oxford boxing coach Henry Dean's book, and we woke each morning before the sun, ran to a nearby hill, and, still shaking off yawns, sprinted as a pack through the grass to the top of the hill and down again. We attacked the hill again and then again and again and then we ran back to the pool on base and broke into two teams for a game of Bull SEAL, a rough form of water polo that threw the whole pool into a churn.

Riding now for Borneo, I felt like the men had left Thailand behind them and were focused on the immediate mission ahead, which was to conduct reconnaissance and serve as American ambassadors of good-will as we traveled throughout Southeast Asia.

En route to the Philippines, we were tasked to stop at a number of ports in Borneo, many of which had never before been host to an American naval vessel. We were part of a long American tradition of sending the Navy forward to act as one part war machine, one part diplomatic mission. Theodore Roosevelt had once said in a State of the Union address to Congress, "A good Navy is not a provocation to war. It is the surest guaranty of peace."[5]

Malaysia and Indonesia both control parts of Borneo and both countries are important potential strategic partners of the United States. Combined, Malaysia and Indonesia are home to 263 million people.[6] Indonesia is the most populous Muslim country on earth. And in 2001, 11.7 million barrels of oil per day and 40 percent of the world's trade passed through the Strait of Malacca,[7] where there's a serious piracy problem.[8] We went to establish and build relationships. If you think of the complex drama of America's strategic relationships in Southeast Asia as an intricate three-hour movie, our crew had only one line to say, but we wanted to say it well.

Our port stops included visits to crocodile farms and orangutan sanctuaries. We pulled into port to visit the Kingdom of Brunei, and after we met with the American ambassador, we floated down the Brunei River in a wildly painted wooden taxi and saw the Istana Nurul Iman palace, home of the sultan of Brunei. We ate *terong belado* (spicy eggplant) and *mei goreng* (fried noodles) at restaurants and we talked with locals. Growing up, we'd seen Navy commercials that promised us that sailors would get to see the world. As we walked through exotic cities and sampled the indigenous cuisine, I felt that the Navy was keeping its promise. Our ultimate destination, however, was a far less scenic spot.

When we pulled into Zamboanga, Philippines, we arrived at what was—in comparison to Iraq and Afghanistan—a little-known outpost in the Global War on Terror. On a Filipino base, the United States ran a small compound. The entire American footprint was probably no larger than half a football field, the compound hidden behind high walls piled with green sandbags and guarded by Marines. Inside, SEALs, SWCC, Marines, and Army Green Berets lived a spartan life. Four meals—breakfast, lunch, dinner, and midrats—were served every day. Men slept in bunk beds lined next to each other. At the center of the compound, basic benches and bars were set out on a concrete slab to make a gym. The routine was simple: wake to a watch alarm and eat a big breakfast of pancakes, sausage, toast, cereal, fruit. Work out at the weight pile for an hour, then head to the boats and prepare for the upcoming operation. Eat a big lunch of soup, meat, fruit, salad, then work again. Plan an operation, and then eat a big dinner.

As the sun fell, we would either head to the boats to conduct a night operation or spend another hour working out. Filipino families lived on the base outside our compound, and they usually disposed of their trash by burning it, and so the air was often full of smoke. Bits of plastic refuse floated down on us from above. The air was unsuitable for running, and as a result of the lift, eat, sleep routine, guys' shirts started to stretch as we each put on "Zamboanga prison muscle."

Todd Leclair, an Army Special Forces major and accomplished athlete, ran the American compound. Leclair was a graduate of SAMS—the Army's School of Advanced Military Studies—where the Army sent some of it sharpest men and women to become expert war planners. Leclair was in charge of the wider mission in Zamboanga, which was to work with Filipino forces to disrupt and interdict terrorist organizations operating in the southern Philippines, especially those associated with the Abu Sayyaf terrorist group.

In the 1980s the Mujahideen recruited Islamic men from around the world to join the fight against the Soviets. One of the young recruits was Abdurajak Abubakar Janjalani, a university-educated son of a Filipino ulema from the island of Basilan, located ten miles south of the Filipino mainland.[9] After the Soviet withdrawal from Afghanistan in 1989, Janjalani returned to the Philippines to continue his war. He gathered around him a group of young extremists and started the terrorist organization Abu Sayyaf.

Abu Sayyaf launched grenade attacks against nuns, priests, and innocent civilians, among them American missionaries. Terrorists bombed Christian missionary ships and cathedrals. In its first four years, from 1991 to 1995, Abu Sayyaf murdered 136 people and injured hundreds more. After Janjalani died in a firefight with police in 1998,[10] the group focused its energy on thuggish kidnappings and attention-grabbing media stunts. In one highly publicized kidnapping in 2000, they held international travelers for ransom and extracted $20 million from the Libyan government.[11] To spread terror, Abu Sayyaf also engaged in beheadings that were videotaped and later broadcast on Filipino TV.[12]

On May 27, 2001, a group of men from Abu Sayyaf raided Dos Palmas, an expensive resort in the Philippines. They kidnapped three Americans, including Gracia and Martin Burnham, a missionary couple from Rose Hill, Kansas. The leader of the raiding party—Aldam Tilao—had been involved in many of Abu Sayyaf's killings and raids. Tilao was a showy figure who enjoyed taunting the government on the evening news, dressed in his trademark black do-rag and sunglasses. Tilao threatened to kill his hostages unless he was paid a ransom.

On May 28, the Philippine president declared war on Abu Sayyaf and vowed to "finish what you [Abu Sayyaf] have started."[13] Two weeks later, on June 11, Tilao made good on his threat and beheaded one of the hostages, Guillermo Sobero, a Peruvian American tourist. Despite the president's bold claim, there was little that the government or the army could do. The FBI had already tried to pay a ransom of $300,000 for the couple, but the money was lost before it got into the hands of Abu Sayyaf.[14] In the dense jungles of Basilan, the Filipino Marines were having trouble tracking Tilao, and because the population of Basilan viewed Abu Sayyaf favorably and often provided Abu Sayyaf operatives with aid, it was difficult to gain any valuable human intelligence from anyone living on the island.

After September 11, 2001, the United States placed Abu Sayyaf on its list of terrorist organizations because of the group's early connections to Osama bin Laden and al Qaeda. Destroying Abu Sayyaf and rescuing the Burnhams became priority missions for the U.S. Navy and the CIA. With the help of a tracking device provided by the CIA, the Philippine Army was able to identify the general vicinity of Tilao as the location of the hostages, and they launched a mission to rescue the Burnhams. Although Gracia Burnham survived the firefight, Martin Burnham died and Tilao escaped into the jungle.[15]

The Filipino Marines knew, however, that soon Tilao would be making a run back to his home island. With the help of Navy SEALs stationed at Zamboanga, the Marines tagged Tilao's boat with infrared sensors that could be tracked by plane. A raid was readied. The night before, four ships left from Zamboanga base. One was the "lure" boat, sent to pick Tilao up and draw him into the open water. Another boat was manned by Filipino Marines. The last two boats were manned by Navy SEALs and SWCC.[16]

Once Tilao's boat was far enough away that his crew could not swim back to shore, the Filipino Marines gunned their engine, rushed the fishing boat, and crashed right through it. In the ensuing firefight, Tilao was killed. It was a critical blow to Abu Sayyaf. But as terrorist groups often do, Abu Sayyaf recruited new members and kept operating.

Abu Sayyaf was still our main local enemy in the area. The Americans had a good force of advisors at Zamboanga, but the Sulu Archipelago where Abu Sayyaf worked is a string of islands 215 nautical miles long. Without fast, agile boats to move through the islands, the American force was stuck on the mainland. With a range of 550+ nautical miles, the Mark Vs gave us the ability to project force and conduct missions throughout the entire Abu Sayyaf area of operations.

For us to be successful in defeating Abu Sayyaf, however, we needed more than fast boats. We had to build capable Filipino partners who could fight on their home turf for years to come. Our Filipino counterparts were Special Warfare personnel who had been trained by Navy SEALs. We first met their men on a sandy beach, and as the members of their team walked over to meet us, I was struck that the Fils walked with the same carriage as our men. Our counterparts' complexions were different and their camouflage was a different pattern. The Fils were smaller than our guys, and their assault gear, canteens, compasses, and backpacks were all older and more deeply worn than the gear we carried. Yet they had the same "fierce friendly" look and the same "relaxed ready" posture that made my men stand out in a crowd, even when they were sitting in a restaurant in civilian clothes. Some of the Fils had grown up in slums outside of Manila and some of my men had grown up on small farms in the American South, but we sat down together with the universal shared understanding of those who have been toughened in the world's hardest schools.

On our first patrols, we took the Fil commandos with us to familiarize ourselves with the surrounding islands. Aboard the Mark Vs, the engines at a low rumble, we crept past a row of thatched bamboo huts, some patched up with corrugated boards and pastel-colored walls, seemingly tottering on their stilts. The fishermen retired here in the evening after a day of pulling in nets. Dogs ran over the bamboo planks of the pier, stopping occasionally to be petted by the local children. Throughout the Philippines, 43 percent of the population lives on less than two dollars a day.[17] Here in the southern islands, poverty was even more widespread. We took photographs of areas of interest—a squat home, for example, with a bundle of antennas emerging from it—a freshly built pier near a newly built mosque. We tuned our equipment to collect signals intelligence, and we asked our Filipino counterparts to tell us about the habits and life patterns of those who lived in these villages.

The draft of the Mark V was only five feet, but our jet engines pulled water from even deeper, and so as we crept past the villages and the shade of the water shifted to light blue, I kept a close eye on our depth. I was reminded of the coastline of Cambodia. There, too, boys gathered in the shallow sea to collect nets, small clusters of homes made a fishing village near the water's edge, and people still suffered, some of them visibly, from the effects of war.

After a few patrols, it was obvious that the Mark V, while well armed, fast, and with excellent range, was far too conspicuous—even at night—to do some of the close reconnaissance that was required here.

The Fils' boat also had its problems. The Fils had captured from smugglers a fifteen-foot flat-bottomed wooden boat rigged with two huge motors. The boat had a red mouth and sharp white teeth painted on both sides of the bow. The Fils called the boat the Shark, but the only menacing thing about it was its name. The boat had a short range, and if the sea was rough, it became hard to handle.

If we were going to conduct close, quality reconnaissance, we had to find another platform. Even our Zodiacs, black and small as they were, cut an unusual profile in the water. We needed to blend in.

I remembered from my time in Cambodia that local fishermen often used small boats in shallow water to fish off the coast at night. We asked our Fil counterparts about the fishing patterns here, and they confirmed that the Fil fishermen did the same. We purchased a few local bangka boats. They were simple wooden boats built like narrow canoes with an outrigger. They had small motors and were typically used by one Filipino man to fish close to home. The boats were often painted zany yellows and greens and purples and turquoise, and at night, dozens of the boats lingered off the coast as men fished, or—as we often saw through our night-vision goggles—napped.

One of the enduring qualities of Naval Special Warfare warriors is creativity. We are taught tactics, but more than tactics, we are taught how to adapt our tactics and take advantage of opportunities to complete our mission. When the instructors yelled "Drop!" we had to drop. But when they were holding a fire hose and the compound was filled with smoke and the night was dark and they yelled "Drop!" we kept running.

The men went to work. We outfitted a few wildly painted bangka boats with GPS units, radios, weapons, and strobe lights. The SWCC operators jumped in the boats and gunned the motors and they learned how the boats handled in the choppy waters just off the coast. We drove the Mark Vs out to sea and practiced launching and recovering the bangkas from the back deck of the Mark V.

I went on the back deck and talked to Kaj.

"We're all clear, bro. Let's launch your team."

Kaj's men stepped into the bangka boats and made a final radio check.

"*Calisto,* this is *Dolphin,* radio check, over."

"*Dolphin, Calisto,* I read you loud and clear, how about me, over?"

"*Calisto,* I have you same. *Dolphin* out."

A group of us bent and grabbed the wooden gunwales of the bangka boats.

"Ready, one, two," and at "three" we pushed all at once and the bangka boats slipped off the back deck and into the sea. They lit their infrared strobes and we watched on night vision as two Filipino fishermen made their way for the coast. On the deck, the Mark V guns were loaded and men sat ready to push the throttle forward if our guys got in trouble.

The night of our first mission, we launched the Mark Vs from the pier. Our bangka boats launched later from the beach, and we rendezvoused at sea and brought the bangkas onto our back deck and motored calmly through the night, our ships a black mass gliding quietly over a black sea. The back-deck chief scanned the waves using night vision, and our navigator studied the radar. Armed with cameras, our operators were able to conduct close reconnaissance of several areas of interest.

Slowly, like a family sitting down to snap together a thousand-piece jigsaw puzzle, we gained a clearer picture of our area of operations. We shared our intelligence with our Filipino counterparts, and after several patient weeks, the Filipino forces decided to launch an assault on Jolo Island in the hopes of capturing the remaining Abu Sayyaf terrorists.

The morning of the operation, we pulled away from the pier before sunrise and drove south. The Fil Marines were going to assault a suspected terrorist compound of huts and houses on the island. Abu Sayyaf had a history of running from trouble via motorboat, and our role in the operation was to cut off any of the Abu Sayyaf gang that tried to flee while the Marines pressed their attack. We set up off the coast and listened to the progress of the operation over the radio as the Marines made movement to contact. We then had to engage in what is one of the most difficult of military disciplines: wait at the ready.

It was a peaceful day. The sun rose and reflected off the sea. We bobbed in our boats. We listened to the crackle of the radio. The day grew hot and we sweated through our brown T-shirts. We drank from our canteens. We ate MREs. A boat might make a run at any minute, but besides keeping an alert lookout, there was little to do. We checked our weapons again. Checked our radios again. We checked the position of our sister ship. Then we heard more calls come over the radio.

"Nothing here."

"They are gone."

The Marines had spent a day walking through the jungle of Basilan in a state of high tension. And then, when they hit the compound, they found nothing.

We turned our bows north and gunned our engines back for Zamboanga.

That night, the men in my detachment refueled our boats, and we cleaned our weapons. We stowed our charts and checked the batteries in our flashlights. We went to sleep ready to start again the next morning—or—if we were called—in the middle of that very night.

Abu Sayyaf had been on the run for two years, unable to threaten Americans or our allies, and we were going to keep it that way. The men in my detachment would have preferred a standup fight, but if Abu Sayyaf was going to hide, then we would seek—day after day—methodically, creatively. We'd become smarter every day. We'd guard and protect. We'd serve with strength and honor, and when it was time for us to go home, another group of Americans and our Filipino allies would take our place. We'd exercise bravery when called on and perseverance every day. The line would remain unbroken and we would win.

# 14 ☆

# Kenya

I T MAY SEEM OBVIOUS, but it is often forgotten that our greatest victories come when we exercise enough courage, intelligence, and discipline to win battles without ever having to fight. In *The Art of War*, Sun Tzu wrote, "To fight and conquer in all your battles is not supreme excellence; supreme excellence consists in breaking the enemy's resistance without fighting."[1] The best preparation for battle will sometimes mean that we do not have to use force at all. I learned this lesson during a deployment to Kenya.

Upon arrival, we drove in a convoy of sport utility vehicles and flew north on the B8 highway from the Kenyan coastal city of Mombasa to remote Manda Bay. There, we had a small base at an important strategic location in northern Kenya, just south of the border with Somalia. Our drivers were members of the Guam Army National Guard, who drove with sunglasses over their eyes, a rifle at their side, and their foot on the gas; they served as a security taskforce for the base. We drove single file on the dirt road, following in the wide wake of each other's dust. Manda Bay, I learned, was a place remote enough that when I told Kenyans in Nairobi or Mombasa where I was going, they raised their eyebrows. I was curious about what I'd find there.

As we approached a village, the man in the passenger seat turned to me and said, "Hey, LT, the people in this village hate us; check out how they look at us." Kids dressed in ragged shirts and shorts—sticks in their hand—stopped, stood, and stared at our convoy. Goats ran away in a bleating pack. Adults in the village stood from their work, turned, and looked at us with hard eyes.

"LT, remember when those guys bombed the embassy?" He pointed out the window. "Intel said that they stayed in that village on their way through. Kenya's mostly Christian, but there are Muslims all up and down the coast, and in these villages they don't like Americans."

I'd been in Kenya ten years earlier on my way to Rwanda, and it might have been my earlier nonmilitary experience in the country, but when I looked at the villagers looking at us, I didn't see terrorist sympathizers. I saw angry parents. We had our windows rolled up, sunglasses on, rifles in our hands, and we were driving dangerously fast through a village full of goats and children. I was new, though, just arrived. These men had been here for months, and so I kept quiet.

I had arrived as the new commander of Naval Special Warfare Task Unit Manda Bay. I had been sent to relieve the previous commander, who had damaged relations with the local leaders, the Kenyan Navy, and his own men. My mission was to serve as commander of the operational task unit and also as base commander. I would be responsible for U.S. and Kenyan relations on the base, and I would learn a lot about how to be an ally and a friend there.

In 1998 two men drove a truck bomb to the gate of the parking garage under the U.S. embassy in Nairobi. The passenger jumped out of the truck, threw a grenade at the guard, and ran. The guard survived, the gate remained down, and when the terrorist driver saw the guard radio for backup, he realized that he would not be able to drive into the garage. Instead, he drove as close to the U.S. embassy building as he could and pressed the trigger.[2]

Two tons of explosives ripped apart a seven-story building next to the embassy, leaving only a pile of rubble and billowing smoke. All the windows of the Cooperative Bank House—a twenty-two-story structure a block away from the embassy—were shattered, as were the windows of other buildings as far as ten blocks away. Glass littered the streets. The embassy—built and used by the Israelis, who were accustomed to bombing attacks—withstood the blast and no one inside died.[3] In all, 224 people died in the bombing (including 12 Americans) and an estimated 5,000 people were injured.[4]

In 2005 we continued to receive reports of terrorist activity in Kenya, much of it associated with the country's neighbor to the north, Somalia. Ever since the collapse of the Somali dictatorship in 1991, Somalia had existed in what political scientists called the "closest thing to anarchy" in the modern age of nation-states. Warlords fought fiercely over territory, and their clashes caused 350,000 people to die of starvation and disease.[5] When the international community tried to ship food aid to the Somalis, warlords stole 80 percent of the aid and traded it for weapons.[6] The United States provided military and technical support that drastically reduced mass starvation, but when the local warlord Mohamed Farrah Aidid killed twenty-four Pakistani peacekeepers, the U.S. role changed from peacekeeping to hunting down Aidid. It led directly to the "Black Hawk Down" incident in 1993, when local militia shot down a U.S. helicopter, leading to a seventeen-hour firefight during which eighteen soldiers and hundreds of Somalis were killed.

The suffering of Somalis remained severe. The country was still ruled at the local level by warlords who fought over scarce resources and terrorized local populations. Four hundred thousand people were still displaced and living in overcrowded and unsanitary refugee camps.[7] Some foreign aid workers had been killed and many others driven out, and a severe drought created the lowest crop harvest in a decade. To the extent that it was possible to collect any reliable data, it seemed that 43 percent of the population lived below the *extreme* poverty line.[8]

Somalis needed food aid more than ever, but pirates continued to raid these shipments, creating the lowest levels of food aid stocks in five years. The problem of piracy was so severe that in 2005, the World Food Programme, the UN's food aid branch, switched to transporting goods overland instead of by sea, despite the 25 to 30 percent increase in costs.[9]

With the history of terrorism in Kenya, instability to the north in

Somalia, and piracy at sea, Manda Bay was an important outpost in the wider struggle against terrorism. Our American compound stood on the campus of a large Kenyan naval base. Our grounds were probably no larger than two football fields. We would later name the base Camp Simba, after the young hero in the Disney animated film *The Lion King,* because we thought of ourselves as small but ambitious. The chain of command told us, however, that "Camp Simba" wasn't a tough enough name, so after that we just called the base Camp Lion.

As I stepped onto our base, a dozen baboons rushed into the tree line. Our compound was centered around a small house that had once been in shambles—broken roof, smashed walls, trees growing through the floor—but was now, after several deployments of special warfare personnel, structurally sound with a new red roof and a fresh coat of white paint. Inside the house we had a closetful of MREs, a room for treating medical casualties, and a small cramped office loaded with desks and computers and radios.

Surrounding the main house stood five khaki-colored, ten-man tents that hummed with small air-conditioning units used to keep them cool at night. Our camp dog, Basa—short for Mombasa, the port city where we picked up supplies—had been a sick, wounded stray. The guys nursed him back to health, and he was now a vigorous thirty-pound mutt whose self-appointed mission was to deter baboons from stealing our MREs. Basa would bark and run at the baboons when they approached our camp, but the baboons didn't fear Basa; one time I even saw a male baboon pick the dog up and toss him two feet through the air. Hippos cooled in a watering hole down the road.

We were a joint special operations task unit, "joint" because we had Army, Navy, and Marine Corps personnel, and "special operations" because the fighting portion of our unit was mostly Navy SWCC operators, who conducted operations with RHIBs, jet-ski-like vehicles, and indigenous craft, while also running a training school for Kenyan special forces personnel. The mission in Kenya, much like the mission in the Philippines, was to work with, by, and through local Kenyan forces to conduct counterterror training and operations.

In places like the Philippines, and here in Kenya, we aimed to build relationships of goodwill and mutual advantage. We needed to be prepared for a gunfight, but we expected to have few outright battles with terrorists. Our objective was to create positions of strength and to accumulate advantages that would help us defeat terrorists if they surfaced, hunt them if they were hiding, and minimize their ability to recruit others to their cause.

America had declared that we were fighting a "war" on terrorism, and Americans tend to think of war in terms of ultimate victory, like achieving checkmate in chess. But that way of thinking about conflict can be misleading. As others have pointed out, "Chess has only two outcomes: draw and checkmate. The objective of the game is absolute advantage—that is to say, its outcome is total victory or defeat—and the battle is conducted head-on, in the center of the board." But in a conflict with terrorists, the fight is different. If we wanted to make an analogy to a board game, it was better, perhaps, to think in terms of the Asian game of go: "The aim of go is relative advantage; the game is played all over the board, and the objective is to increase one's options and reduce those of the adversary. The goal is less victory than persistent strategic progress."[10]

Our goal in Kenya was persistent strategic progress. Our men launched their boats into Manda Bay alongside their Kenyan counterparts. They taught the Kenyans how to track suspect craft, how to control prisoners, and how to fight as a team. Our men ran sprints with the Kenyans down asphalt roads—fireman-carrying each other on their shoulders—to build character and camaraderie. If we trained Kenyans who could stop al Qaeda associates running explosives and weapons from Somalia, we made strategic progress.

We sent our men with cameras and radios in indigenous craft to conduct special reconnaissance operations in places that had previously not been accessible to us. If we saw more, understood more, and became wiser, we made persistent strategic progress. We visited with mayors from nearby towns and our civil affairs officers sat with them over tea to discuss wells and schools and the health of local children. If we could build allies so that al Qaeda would have fewer friends, then we made persistent strategic progress.

We also experimented by, for example, mounting guns and GPS units and radios on our jet skis for operations. I wasn't sure how practical the jet skis really were as operational craft—they ripped around the bay, motors screaming; they had limited range, couldn't carry a boarding party, and had no room for sensors. But we all loved the idea of using the jet skis to run down terrorists and pirates, and if we could invent new, effective tactics to deter terrorists, we made progress.

Our actual operations were straightforward. Our task unit executed operational preparation of the environment (OPE) missions in towns along the Kenyan coast. The task: provide senior commanders with critical information regarding the logistical infrastructure of Kenyan ports so that we could plan for future operations along the entire Kenyan coast, from Tanzania to Somalia. If we wanted to conduct operations out of Kenyan coastal towns, we had to know where we could harbor boats safely, where we could buy fuel, where we could post guards, and where we could feed and rest our special operations teams. It's fun to think strategy, but logistics are the key to successful operations, and by conducting these assessments, our task unit made it possible to carry out operations along the entire coast of Kenya. Persistent strategic progress.

At the same time, we worked closely with Kenyan Navy authorities to secure permission to use their radar stations along the coast in conjunction with maritime interception operations (MIO). The Kenyans had large radar stations capable of monitoring traffic off the coast, but they'd never used these stations to work with Kenyan special boat units. For the first time, we established radio communications and standard operating procedures to use the radar stations to help us intercept suspect vessels. This new capability greatly improved the ability of the Kenyan Navy to exercise control over their own coastline. Persistent strategic progress.

We established a more aggressive MIO schedule for the RHIB detachment. We doubled their time on the water and interdicted more suspect craft. In practice, this meant that the Kenyan Navy, like a beat cop, was on post more of the time. A space that had been largely ungoverned was now patrolled by Kenyan special operations units. Persistent strategic progress.

For us, the key to every positive step was to build strong allies. As the base commander, part of my job was to oversee the quality of Kenyan-U.S. relations in the area. And here is where I learned the most important lesson of my Kenyan deployment: a single, perhaps inadvertent, slap can undo months of patient work to build good relations. In my case, the slap centered on a marooned forklift.

A few months before I arrived, our jet skis were motoring back to port after a test run in the bay. The driver of the jet ski stepped off his ride into shallow water and waved to an American contractor operating a forklift on the beach. The guy on the forklift thought that the guy with the jet ski was signaling for help, so the forklift driver started to drive the forklift down the beach to tow the jet ski out of the water. The man on the jet ski saw trouble and waved with two hands to tell the man to stop. The forklift driver interpreted this as an "emergency" wave and stepped on the gas. The surface was soft and the forklift became impossibly stuck in the sand at low tide. The water started to rise. By high tide, the ocean covered all but the driver's cage at the very top of the forklift.

The port where the forklift was marooned was, unfortunately, used by both U.S. and Kenyan personnel to put boats in and out of the water. The buried forklift presented a hazard to navigation and the Kenyans wanted to move it.

What should have been a very simple affair (hire local Kenyans with a tow truck to haul the forklift out of the sand during low tide) became unsimple. In my office, previous commanders had a stack of memos filled with advice about "the Forklift." I learned that the United States couldn't legally give the forklift to the Kenyans (they offered to drag it out for free if they could use it for scrap metal) unless it was officially declared unserviceable. And though the forklift had been stuck in salt water for months, officers in Djibouti—one thousand miles away—wanted to debate its functionality. Moreover, to give the forklift away, the U.S. government had to figure out who actually owned it. Whose forklift was this, anyway? No one in the U.S. government seemed to know. For months, the greatest superpower in the world was unable to move a forklift, and we couldn't even grant permission to the Kenyans to take it. It was an absurd situation, and for me it stood as a reminder that there are two U.S. militaries. There is the fighting military, where troops are led and operations are conducted. Then there is the Department of Defense. Many great people and great warriors work in the Department of Defense, but too often, men and women dressed in camouflage sit at computers alongside civilian contractors and send e-mails and reports and briefs in circles around what is the largest and often one of the most risk-averse, uncreative, inefficient bureaucracies in the world.

I was told that the commander of the Kenyan base was unhappy with the American military presence for a number of reasons—forklift included—so I drove with my senior enlisted advisor to pay the base commander a visit.

The captain's office was simple—white walls unadorned but for a single calendar and the black, green, and red flag of Kenya. A low stack of papers sat on his desk. The captain, a thin man about five eight, had cracked a window to let in a breeze, and he was chewing a cheekful of khat—a mild stimulant popular in Kenya. We shook hands, his secretary brought tea, and we sat on a couch just outside his office.

"Sir, thank you for making the time to see us. It's good to meet you. Your men have been a pleasure to work with and I understand that the maritime operations course is going very well."

The captain gave a half-smile. "Yes, we are very proud of this course."

After a cup of tea, we came to discuss the forklift, and he said to me, "This is a troubling and confusing issue. I don't understand why the Americans cannot move it or why *we* cannot move it. We can move it for you."

"I agree," I said. "You and I see the issue the same way."

"Yes, but it has been months, it is sitting there in a port. It's not in a convenient place. I don't understand why it can't move. It's a very funny thing, isn't it?"

We talked for a good half hour about many things that we had in common—the future of the maritime operations course, the need for a boat ramp at the post, the baboon population on base. At the end of the conversation, I invited him to dinner. I said, "You are very gracious hosts for us here on the base, and we'd love to have you come to our compound, to host you and your team for dinner. It would be an honor to have you there."

He said, "Thank you, that would be nice. But you know, I went there some months ago and they asked to search our vehicle. And I was surprised because this is my base. And that was a very funny thing."

"I apologize," I said. "These men, I understand, had orders to search every vehicle that came into our compound. The fact that they failed to recognize you is embarrassing for us because, after all, this is your base, sir, and you are in charge here."

He didn't accept my invitation, but I left impressed by the captain's patience. I imagined how an American base commander would respond if a visiting Kenyan unit marooned a forklift in our port and searched our senior officers on American territory.

I went back to our compound and read through a stack of forklift e-mails. It became clear that no one had actually ordered us to leave the forklift in the bay. Instead, what had happened was that people had started asking for permission to move the forklift, and then a few dozen e-mails bounced from Manda Bay to Nairobi, to Bahrain to D.C. to San Diego to Djibouti, and back to Manda Bay, but everyone was waiting for permission from someone else. I drove back to see the captain again.

"Sir, this forklift has been an issue for you for far too long. So let's get it out of your port."

"So, we can move it?"

"Yes sir, feel free to move it as you see best, and of course my men and I will help you to move it, if you'd like for us to do so. And this, sir, is for you."

I handed him a VIP placard that he could put in his vehicle so that our security task force could identify him and render the proper respect when he came to our compound.

I also paid a visit to the mayor of Lamu, the nearest city. Old Town Lamu, Kenya, is one of the oldest inhabited towns in East Africa. Mentioned in the journals of Ptolemy in the second century, Lamu has always been a bustling merchant town that has attracted traders from Persia, India, Portugal, and other trading posts around the world.[11] As we approached the city in a Kenyan water taxi, I saw white block houses, some thatched with dried palm leaves, others with flat tops and red terracotta roofs. Green palm trees climbed for the sky between the houses, and wooden ships lined the harbor wall, piled with crates of food and boxes of construction supplies. Many of the ships were loaded so heavily that the bay water lapped inches from the gunwales. Sunken ships and drownings, I learned, were not uncommon.

I stepped off our boat and walked up the wet concrete steps onto the wide dirt road that ran along the harbor wall. Here knobby-kneed boys with sticks tapped the backsides of donkeys carrying loads of concrete, wood, and grain. Donkeys were everywhere. Donkeys nosed in the faded yellow-and-green telephone booths and slumbered outside mosques. Other donkeys carried coral stone loaded in woven sacks and dragged long wooden poles cut from mangrove trees. Still other donkeys were ridden by young boys who raced them along the packed dirt roads of the island. I was told that there were over two thousand donkeys on the island.

I sat with the mayor and talked over tea. He was a middle-aged man of obvious energy, dressed in slacks and a button-down shirt. I had heard that he had the privileged use of the town's only motor vehicle besides Lamu's one ambulance. At one point, the mayor pointed out the window, not in any specific direction, but only to indicate "out there," and he told me that American civil affairs officers had promised to help build a school, but that the construction had been halted. I shook my head as I left.

As Americans we often have a tendency to want to build things in an effort to promote goodwill. We'd often be far better off investing in people. Trying to build a school in Kenya is a difficult venture, hampered by corruption and local politics. In any building project there is a strong tendency for local officials to fight over petty advantages. Building projects are capital intensive, and because Americans usually aren't closely involved in the actual building process, once a school is built, the U.S. often receives little credit. The United States will, however, be blamed for every failing roof, broken desk, and cracked sink. More importantly, a building cannot speak, cannot act as an ambassador of goodwill. At best, Americans are present for a ribbon-cutting ceremony, and then we're gone. We'd be far better off paying for the quality training of quality teachers and then even paying some teachers' salaries. A beginning teacher in Kenya makes $1,560 a year.[12] By investing in people, we could build pro-American ambassadors to teach the next generation of schoolchildren, and those teachers would feel personally connected to the United States. They would be in the classroom every day. If we were investing in projects to make friends, why wouldn't we invest in people? It's hard to be friends with a building.

Every morning I went out to run along the straight dirt road that led away from our base. The road, wide enough for a car and a half and flanked by thin-trunked trees on either side, served as a gathering place for baboons. I'd seen baboons in zoos before, and years earlier when I'd come through Kenya on my way to Rwanda, I'd seen a troop of baboons in a game park—but I'd never been this close to them. Baboons are scary. The males standing on the side of the road looked like they weighed seventy to eighty pounds, and when they tilted their heads back to yawn, I saw pairs of two-inch yellow fangs. They lounged on the road like a pack of thugs. One of the guys told me to clap when I saw them, and so I raised my hands in the air and clapped and the baboons turned and saw me and scampered into the tree line.

I picked up my pace. I was training for a marathon at the time, and I hoped that some kind of Kenyan marathon magic would find its way into my legs. About a mile outside the base, I came to a village, and the road was lined with children walking to school in their uniforms: bright white shirts and blue shorts.

"Jambo," I said.

"Jambo," replied a boy.

"How are you?" I smiled at them.

"Good. How are you?" one boy said and started to run with me. The kids got used to seeing me every morning, and as I ran, they would call from house to house, "Mzungu, mzungu"—the white man is coming—and kids streamed out of houses and ran beside me. Often I'd have three or four boys join me for a full quarter mile, smiles on their faces, their backpacks bouncing on their backs as they jogged alongside.

When I returned to the base after a run one day, one of the Kenyan guards stood from his seat to greet me and asked, "Sir, you're a runner? How far do you run?"

"About eleven miles today," I said.

"You should run with me," he said, "so we can see who is faster." A smile turned up the corners of his mouth.

The next morning I met the guard, Daniel, at the guard shack. About six foot two, Daniel started down the road, and his legs seemed to leap from the ground with the most fluid, powerful stride I had ever seen. As I huffed beside him I asked, "Have you run much?"

"No, not lately. The last time I competed internationally was in South Africa several years ago."

I said, "Well, that's OK, the last time I competed internationally was never." As we ran, we talked. I learned that Daniel worked an eight- or twelve-hour shift at the guard shack every day. He lived in a room with dozens of other guards, and he hadn't been paid in two months.

"Do you," he asked, "work with the men on the special operations training course here?"

"Yes, we do," I said.

"Those men," he said, "are very proud. One day I would like to join those men."

Time and again, when we met Kenyans one on one, they gave us friendly smiles, exuded hospitality and warmth. It was only when we drove through town in a nasty dust cloud, or fouled a harbor, that we were resented.

Our relations seemed poor to me, and so I wasn't surprised that the U.S. intelligence picture in the Horn of Africa was weak. Much of what I read consisted of recycled news headlines repackaged as intelligence. Real, valuable intelligence only came from real people, yet we hadn't done much to meet and work with the people of Kenya. I told my senior enlisted advisor that I wanted to take our guys to the "bad" village that we'd driven through on our way to Manda Bay. We'd get out of our trucks, meet people, and buy some fruit.

"You sure you want to do that? Something goes wrong, and that's a career ender."

"I'm sure," I said. "We need to do something to begin to build some good relationships here. And the guys'll be happy about the fruit."

We had no fresh fruit or vegetables at Manda Bay. Our supply officers in Djibouti tried to get us fresh fruit, but it was difficult to transport an orange from Europe to Djibouti, from Djibouti to Mombasa, and from Mombasa up to Lamu. We ate peaches soaked in syrup packaged in MRE bags. Meanwhile, local markets had stalls full of fresh fruit and vegetables. The Department of Defense wouldn't provide us with funds, however, to make purchases from an "unapproved supplier." The guys were fine living on MREs, but I thought that buying at the local market would be an excellent way to build positive relationships with the local villagers.

I grabbed a wallet full of my own money and a holster to conceal a pistol, and we drove a small convoy to the local village. The guys stepped out of their vehicles and—as I'd asked them to—pushed their sunglasses up on their heads so that the villagers could see our eyes. We shook hands with people. As we picked through the fruit stalls, the villagers—who had previously only seen us driving back and forth with our sunglasses on, windows rolled up, rifles in our hands—asked us questions.

"Where are you from?"

"How do you like Kenya?"

"Do you want something to drink?"

In the name of "force protection," the military often rolls up windows, builds walls, and points rifles at the outside world. The best force protection, however, is to be surrounded by friends and allies. If we'd had permission to buy local food, we could have fed ourselves at one-tenth or even one-twentieth of what it costs American taxpayers to provide us with food. We'd have had better food, and we might have built valuable friendships.

Some reports indicated that when the terrorists who bombed the American embassy came to Kenya, they stayed in the village where we were now buying fruit. The whole attack might have been prevented if we'd had a few friends willing to share intelligence with us. I knew that we weren't going to change the world buying a few bags of fruit, but the risk-averse mindset of much of the military bureaucracy can often prevent leaders from taking even small commonsense steps. A leader who walls his men away from the local population in the name of force protection is rarely questioned, while those who take risks to build relationships are sometimes punished in case of failure. As we drove back to base, the guys were chattering like I'd never heard them before.

"Yeah, I started talking with that one guy about fishing . . ."

"I bought ten of those mango things. Dude, these are good."

"That one lady liked you, man. She was all smiley and stuff."

"Did you see that kid's shirt with all the holes in it? We should take him one of our shirts."

Shortly after, the captain of the base invited *us* to join *him* for a dinner to celebrate another joint Kenyan-American course completed.

Later, when I went to Iraq, I'd find that the entire campaign turned on simple actions like these; where we built friends and allies, we won. George C. Marshall, commander of American forces during World

War II, and later secretary of state, secretary of defense, the architect of the Marshall Plan, and the recipient of the Nobel Peace Prize, had three simple rules for going to war: "Never fight unless you have to, never fight alone, never fight for long." What he believed then is still true now: the longer we fight alone, the longer we'll have to fight.

Daniel and I kept up our morning runs, and the night before I was scheduled to leave, Daniel biked to our base. Our guards radioed me from the gate, and I told them to let Daniel in. I walked out to meet him and he pedaled to me and then stopped and stood with the bike between his legs. We shook hands.

"How are you, Daniel?"

"Very good, sir, very good." There was an odd formality in Daniel's voice. I wondered if it was because he was on our compound.

Daniel looked at the ground. "Sir, I was wondering if it would be possible to get some MREs before you leave."

"Of course, Daniel," I said.

Working with foreign military forces, Americans often have to negotiate how much to give. In places like the Philippines, Kenya, and Afghanistan, the gulf in resources between American forces and our counterparts can be so vast that it makes for awkward choices. We can't be seen as a piggy bank to be dipped into and taken advantage of, but if we assist with nothing, we lose face and friends.

We couldn't have every Kenyan on base bicycling in to ask for boxes of MREs, but Daniel had become my friend. "So Daniel, you know if I come back, I'll come back faster."

"Yes, perhaps," he said, "but maybe I'll be faster, too."

I helped Daniel tie the box of MREs onto his bicycle. We shook hands again, and he pedaled away.

# 15 ☆

# Iraq

EACH MAN'S BOOTS left an impression in the dust-covered street as the patrol walked south. We split into two columns, and each column walked a street through the industrial sector of Fallujah. If there was a suicide car bomb operation in the city, there was a reasonable chance that it would be here, and we wanted to find it in time. It was March 2007, and suicide car bombs and suicide truck bombs were exploding around the city and across Iraq. As terrorists detonated themselves in a life-ending fireball, the concussive wave from their bombs ripped through shoppers and storekeepers in open-air markets, worshipers leaving mosques, and lines of children standing in the sun. The explosions rippled through the air like a racing line of mirage, followed by shrapnel that tore through arms and legs and lungs and faces. This was sometimes followed by the poison effects of chlorine packed into the bombs.

I arrived three and a half years after the American invasion and saw the beginning of the surge strategy in Iraq. Every day, American troops walked a difficult path between acting as enemies to al Qaeda and as friends to Iraqis. Unfortunately, the bad guys didn't wear red T-shirts, the good guys didn't wear blue, and on chaotic streets, our warriors had to serve as diplomats.

I patrolled with six Marines and fifteen Iraqi troops that morn-

ing. The Marines were members of a MiTT force, or Military Training Team, whose mission was to train and conduct combined operations with Iraqi forces. The Marines were several months into their
deployment: their body armor rode well, their hand signals were clear,
and most of them knew the names of more streets in the city of Fallujah than in their own hometowns. As the sun rose higher, the building shadows shortened and the temperature climbed and I could feel
beads of sweat running underneath my uniform and fifty pounds of
body armor.

The streets were empty, but they were empty in the way of scenes
from old Westerns, when the sheriff comes to town and the cattle rus-
tler/murderer/train robber is lurking out of sight. All the townspeople
had fled the streets for the shelter of their homes and shuttered busi-
nesses. We felt eyes on our backs.

One of the Marines knelt beside a garage door and pulled at a lock
that held the door in place. The door just clanged at his effort. He lowered his shotgun, held steady, fired a slug, and blasted the lock open.
He cocked his shotgun, threw the remains of the broken lock into the
dusty street, and yanked open the door. The room was full of heavy
machinery and industrial parts covered in rust and sludge. Every inch
of the floor seemed to be stained with oil. We stepped through the garage, pointing our rifle muzzles into dark corners.

"Clear."

"Clear."

"Clear."

We poked through the garage in search of weapons or explosives or
any other evidence of ill intention. Nothing. A bunch of junk.

We started down the street again. I was patrolling with Travis Manion that morning. Travis had a broad smile that brightened when we
talked about his family, but today his chin was set hard underneath the
strap of his helmet.

As a Navy SEAL and commander of an al Qaeda targeting cell, my
objective was—again—to kill or capture high-level al Qaeda targets.
There were, however, too many targets to engage using special opera-

tions forces alone. Our chain of command had asked us to find creative ways to capture al Qaeda operatives, working with conventional forces and the Iraqi Army. We had to find ways to share intelligence, and we had to assess whether the Marine MiTTs and their Iraqi counterparts were tactically proficient enough to conduct these operations. If we were able to join forces, we could greatly increase pressure on the al Qaeda network.

I'd spent the first few months of the deployment in Balad, Iraq, working as an assistant operations officer. The only thing I had been firing were e-mails. In the Joint Operations Center, I did, however, see reports come in from all over Iraq. In October of 2006, we lost 106 men. In November, we lost 70.[1] There were few places in the country that we controlled. The war was not going well. For a long time, soldiers and Marines had been talking about the need to better understand the Iraqis and to bring them in as allies in our work.

When I'd ridden in a Humvee through the streets of Fallujah for the first time, I saw gangs of young Iraqi men smoking, idling in front of shops. At best, American forces drove through the city a few times a day while on rotating seven-month deployments. These Iraqi men and their families had lived on these streets every day of their lives.

We would never be able to control Iraq on our own. We did not speak the language. We did not know the culture. If we were ever going to achieve victory, we had to involve the Iraqis in the business of capturing and killing al Qaeda and protecting their own cities. Americans couldn't guard every home. The Iraqi men I saw smoking on the corner, however, could stand on that corner all night with a rifle, keeping guard over their neighborhood.

Most of the special operations personnel I had worked with were engaged in nighttime capture or kill operations, focused on specific al Qaeda–associated targets. As a group of highly trained operators, those men would step into their Humvees, helos, and Strykers at night alongside other highly trained men. Provided with the best possible intelligence and the best possible equipment, special operations forces snuck up on and attacked their targets. The night gave them the cover of darkness, and generators whirring in the cities often masked the sound of their approach.

The Marines had a different mission. The task of the conventional forces was to control a battle space, to control a neighborhood, by day and by night. Spec ops personnel were hunters, operating in a dangerous foreign forest. Conventional forces were farmers. They had to work the land. They had to do more than just clear it; they had to sow seeds. Conventional forces had to *create* peace, and this meant that they had to create allies.

Iraq has 28 million people. The country is the size of California. Even the briefest of helicopter rides over the countryside or drives through the streets is enough to make clear to an outside observer the painfully obvious fact that America could never have enough troops on the ground to physically control Iraq. We needed to win hearts and minds, as the Vietnam-era phrase once put it.

The Marines I was patrolling with trained Iraqi troops, they met with sheiks, they funded schools: they built allies. It was the least glamorous, possibly the hardest, and certainly the most important job on the battlefield. My task was only a small piece of a much bigger puzzle: figure out if we can we use these Iraqi allies in Fallujah to capture or kill al Qaeda targets.

"We've got two men down."

"IED."

We continued walking south as details came in over the radio. One of the Humvees in our sister column, a block to the west, had been hit by a roadside bomb. Two Iraqi soldiers were dead. I'd later see the seats where they had been sitting, dark bloodstains the color of mud on the floor of the Humvee.

I heard an explosion. "Grenade," came the call over the radio. A grenade had been thrown at our sister column. It had rolled into the street; men ran. No casualties.

AK-47 fire barked to the north. I turned. *Someone firing at us?* One of the Iraqi soldiers started to run in the direction of the shots, and I grabbed his arm as he passed me. He wanted to fight, and I appreciated his instinct, but we weren't taking effective fire and we had no targets. If he ran from cover and into an open intersection, he'd make an easy target. A young kid might have shot into the air to lure us into the open, and a sniper might have his sights fixed on the open intersection.

"We stay," I said to the soldier. Then, "Travis, let's send one of the Humvees north of us to watch our back."

Travis spoke into the radio and twenty seconds later one of our Humvees with a .50-cal gunner turned a corner and ran north in the direction of the AK-47 fire.

The Iraqis were not yet well trained. Out on patrol, we had to keep one eye on the street and one eye on them. Were they watching their field of fire? Were they bunched too close together? It was mentally taxing to be worried about insurgents, doubly so when we were also worried about our allies. We wanted and needed them to be successful. If the Iraqis failed, it meant that they weren't ready, which meant that we hadn't trained them well enough, which meant that we were going to have to stay here longer.

On patrols like this, the conventional forces were often hunting runts in the al Qaeda hierarchy. Some of the targets were men who'd been paid thirty dollars to bury a roadside bomb. I was surprised when I arrived in Iraq to find that we had pictures of many of our targets: Iraqi men dressed in orange tops looking straight at the camera. We had their pictures because we'd captured them before, then let them go.

*Is it worth it to risk my life today?*

Many of these Marines had been on hundreds of patrols in Fallujah, and they were shot at almost every time they left the base. On one patrol, a flash snapped to our right as a rocket-propelled grenade (RPG) was fired at the Humvee in front of us. The rocket bounced a foot in front of the Humvee and exploded when it hit a building on the other side of the street. On another patrol, the distinctive bark of an AK-47 broke through the night as the Marines turned a corner and then ducked behind cover. Today a roadside bomb had been triggered beneath them. Every day, every patrol, they—and we—seemed to take fire.

On base, you always knew that things had gone badly in the field when they shut off the phones and e-mail. A man had died, and the command didn't want word to get back to an unsuspecting wife or father or mother via a phone call or e-mail that might be laced with rumor. When the phones came back up you knew that a chaplain and an officer were visiting with grieving loved ones.

The streets of Fallujah were laden with dog feces. Plastic bags snagged on pieces of trash and flapped in the wind. For some reason, I thought of the Lakota war hero Crazy Horse, reputed to have said, as he rode into battle, "Hoka hey"—Today is a good day to die. The shops we poked through were full of rusted motors, rusted frames; all of the equipment seemed too far gone to be of any use, even for a suicide car bomb. Patrolling on the feces- and trash-covered streets, I thought, *Today is not a good day to die.*

Two Iraqi soldiers started to smoke and chatter behind me and I waved at them, "Hey," and pointed for them to get back in the line of the patrol. The *jundis*—Arabic for "soldiers"—were a mixed bag of often ill-disciplined and frightened men of limited physical ability who had a tendency to group together and talk on patrol. Some jundis "swept" each other, pointing the muzzles of their rifles at their friends. Others tried to learn to become good soldiers: they kept a sharp lookout and patrolled with discipline. Yet for all the tactical frustrations they presented, the Iraqis were extraordinarily valuable.

Venturing out at night with the Army Rangers in Ramadi, I was impressed with their tactics. As soon as we stepped out of the Stryker, the Rangers fell into a perfectly spaced formation. As I looked through my night-vision goggles, I could see that every open window, every open door, was covered by a laser sight. When the Rangers came to an alley, they bumped across one by one, with precision. They approached houses quietly, efficiently blew open doors, and would sweep through a house and clear it in seconds.

Once they were inside, however, the Rangers ran into trouble. They couldn't speak with anyone. The Rangers usually had a translator with them, but that translator was often scared, and sometimes wasn't even

Iraqi. The Rangers would do a valiant job of searching a home for intelligence—they'd grab papers and confiscate computers and sometimes take prisoners—but without the ability to talk with people, they'd often leave a house as ill informed as when they entered. And they made few friends and potentially many new enemies when bursting into house after house like that.

The Iraqis were the opposite. They swept each other on patrol. They bunched together at alleyways and ran across three at a time. I saw one Iraqi come to the wall of a house that he was about to raid, hand off his weapon, climb up the wall, jump into the courtyard, and then shout to his friend, who tossed his rifle over the wall to him. The Iraqis were tactically weak. Yet inside a house, they had great advantages. The Iraqis would search the occupants of a house for weapons, and then they'd stand with the man of the house and smoke together and talk. Often they'd learn something. They could apologize for the intrusion if they had to, and they stood a chance that their apology would be accepted. The Iraqi soldiers were not always loved, and sometimes they were even hated, but they all at least had the ability to communicate.

Americans were often blind to the cultural intelligence of the Iraqis. Most Americans can walk through an American house and, without asking any questions, know a little girl's room from a teenage boy's room. We can be pretty sure just by walking through a house whether or not a man lives there. The Iraqis, likewise, could look at a pile of mats and blankets on the floor of a house and tell if there were men living there. They could look at a tea set, clothing, and decorations, and be able to make a pretty good guess about where a family was from. In short, they were culturally sharp, and they did a better job than Americans could ever hope to do of talking with Iraqis to gain the kind of human intelligence that was necessary to defeat an insurgency, control a battle space, and create peace.

We walked up to a bright blue gate locked against the trash-covered street. One of the Iraqi troops fiddled with a bar, then pushed open a door. The Iraqis stepped in, and as I stepped through the door I saw a large gray brick warehouse-like building to the north, a small white shack to the west, and next to the shack, the remains of a broken-down car. And there—in the middle of the concrete compound—sat what looked like a large metal dog cage with a wire running from it to the house.

"Kef," I said to the Iraqi soldier in front of me—*stop*. When he turned around, I pointed at the cage. The wire bothered me. *IED?* I thought. The wire seemed to be wrapped around a brick under the cage.

It ran across the open courtyard and into the shack, which looked to be a night watchman's house at the far end of the compound. The car, without wheels, rested on blocks of concrete just a few yards from the house. *Car bomb?*

*Why would they have an IED set in the middle of their courtyard? Could the brick be fake?* An Iraqi soldier shouted, and a frail old man in a blue dishdasha tentatively stepped out of the shack, setting one foot down, and then another. Two heavyset women wrapped in abayas leaned their heads into the open doorway, watching us.

The Iraqi soldier shouted again, and when the old man started to step toward the dog cage in his ragged brown sandals, I knew, somehow, *Not an IED.*

As I walked forward, I saw bird poop in the cage. The cage rested on the brick that the wire was wrapped around.

The Iraqis began to question the old man. I couldn't understand his answers, but I noticed that his speech was slurred and his pupils seemed dilated, and he had sweat on his neck.

"What do they use the cage for?" I asked the translator.

"They catch birds," an Iraqi said.

Another Iraqi made a motion with his hands to indicate that they were eating the birds they caught: *What birds,* I thought, *the pigeons here?* Then again, I knew that the industrial sector in Fallujah was almost completely shut down. Unemployment was rampant. *People living on pigeons?*

The old man stopped on wobbly legs, then sat down on a crate outside his shack. He let out a moan, "Ohhhh," and he reached his right arm for the ground, his left hand clutching his chest. He fell and lay crumpled on the ground.

The women began screaming. One of the Iraqis told me they were yelling, "He needs his medicine!" "He's got bad heart!"

Our doc bent to one knee to check the man's vitals. The women kept screaming.

An Iraqi soldier walked with the women into the shack and they grabbed the old man's medicine. Two other Iraqi soldiers walked over to the commotion, and I said, "Doc's got it. Stay spread out. Keep moving." We were in an open courtyard, overlooked by two two-story buildings across the street. A sniper in one of those buildings would have an easy shot. I walked away from the old man lying on the ground, and one of the Marines said, "I hope that fucker doesn't die. Huge fuckin' headache."

The compound was secure, and by the time I'd walked back, the old man was sitting again on his crate, drinking water.

"He seems fine," the doc said.

A Marine glanced to the side and spit. "Fine as a motherfucker can be living in this shithole, eating pigeons. Goddamn."

Travis turned to me. "Any suggestions on what we should do here?"

"We've been here awhile," I said. "We need to be thinking that a sniper might have set up to take a shot as we leave through the door. That door's the only exit, but let's pull the whole gate wide open so we're not squeezing through that little hole—harder for them to take a shot as we run out. And let's get down the street. They've watched us hit shop after shop. Let's bump past the next shop in case they're expecting us there."

Snipers had become a major threat in Fallujah. Whenever we were on the streets, we moved constantly. Talking with an Iraqi in the street, men stepped forward and backward and swayed side to side. *Always assume somebody's trying to line your head up in his crosshairs. Every second you're still is another second a sniper has to put a bullet through you.* When we were outside of our Humvees, the drivers would pull a few feet forward before we got back in, in case a sniper had lined up a shot on a Humvee door.

We heard the bark of an AK-47 a block to the west and the radio crackled with reports of small-arms fire. One block away, a war was on and men were trying to kill each other. Our street was quiet.

We cleared another two shops and that ended our sweep. The patrol took up defensive positions and I bent to one knee behind a concrete barrier that gave me a well-protected view of the street while we waited for the Humvees to pick us up. Apache gunships appeared overhead, their metal bodies angled under their rotors like birds of prey ready to strike.

The Humvees brought us back to the Marine base at the center of the city. As I walked inside to drop my body armor, I heard yelling from down the hallway, and as I jogged down the hall I saw elbows flying and legs kicking in what looked like a schoolyard fight. A circle of Iraqi soldiers were kicking at a man on the ground who kept shifting and moaning and crying out. A lone, hooded figure, his hands were bound behind his back. Marines stepped between the angry soldiers and the hooded captive. I stepped in front of a jundi, his eyes red with a wild crying anger, and he leaned his head back and let out a moan, his mouth open and teeth bared as he brought his fists down and punched his thighs. One man with tears running down his face kept trying to kick at the captive, and the shouting grew louder, jundis yelling at Marines in high-pitched Arabic. Fingers pointed and the tension rose as men shoved, all of us sweating, hungry, exhausted, and armed.

The captive was brought to his feet by a Marine. An enraged Iraqi swung his arm and squarely punched the captive, causing him to fall back to the floor. I heard yelling in an adjacent room, and I realized that a similar fight was taking place there. Joel Poudrier ran into the room then, and he stood beside me as we both motioned to the Iraqis: "Calm down. Calm down." More Marines came running down the hallway, rifles in their hands. I tried to stay aware of the whole room—the Iraqis, their wild eyes, their weapons. *If just one man does one really stupid thing, this is going to get very bad, very fast.* I had my pistol strapped to my thigh.

At six foot two, Colonel Ali dwarfed every other Iraqi in the unit as he walked in. He had tightly cropped black hair and a black mustache. Rumor had it that under Saddam Hussein, Colonel Ali was part of the Iraqi Special Operations unit that invaded Kuwait in the first Gulf War. Once our enemy, now—we hoped—our friend.

He held an AK-47 in his left hand and yelled loudly in Arabic, and then he yelled again, and the room quieted but for the Iraqi with tears on his face who'd punched the prisoner. Then we learned the reason. The crying soldier's friend had just been blown up and killed in the bomb blast that morning. The two captives had been responsible for setting off the explosion. The crying soldier shouted again at the captives. As Colonel Ali walked up to him, he stumbled back several steps and Ali backed him into the wall. Colonel Ali shouted at the soldier. The man yelled back at Colonel Ali and with a powerful twist of his shoulders, Ali turned and hit the soldier in the sternum with the barrel of his Kalashnikov. Finally, the room was quiet.

Two of our medics seated the prisoners and examined them for injuries, and I learned what happened. The other patrol had traced the trail of the detonation cord from the IED to a shack near the road. Seeing soldiers approach, two men ran out of the shack. The Iraqi soldiers gave chase and grabbed them. The men pleaded that they hadn't done anything. The Iraqi soldiers felt otherwise. Even if these men hadn't triggered the IED, they had watched the Iraqi patrol walk up to the bomb and they had given no warning.

The Marines had impressed me with their discipline, their calm, their willingness to put themselves between angry soldiers and captured insurgents. The system for dealing with prisoners, however, caused anger among both Americans and Iraqis. The way that we dealt with detainees was possibly the least impressive aspect of the U.S. engagement in Iraq.

No single U.S. government department seemed to have jurisdiction over the issue of creating a functional judicial system in Iraq. The military captured, the Justice Department advised, the State Department liaised, the Iraqis floundered, and the chaos was splayed out on the ground for all to see in a rotating system of in-and-out detention for Iraqi insurgents that seemed almost comically designed to help them become radicalized in prison without doing very much to thwart the insurgency.

No matter how firm our suspicions were, we could only hold captives for a few weeks. The most hardened al Qaeda veterans knew this and could usually outlast all the tactics of our junior interrogators. If the al Qaeda captives could stay quiet long enough, they knew they would be released soon enough. As a result, men with little intelligence value—those who placed roadside bombs for cash—would confess, while senior al Qaeda leaders would say nothing and be released. Many times we were forced to release men who we strongly suspected were al Qaeda insurgents, only to be told months later, as we were handed a picture of an insurgent in the orange jumpsuit he wore after the last time we detained him, "We need to capture this guy."

The problem was compounded by a shortage of prison space and interrogators. If Marine teams captured seven suspected insurgents on any given day, we might be able to hold and interrogate five. If we captured thirty, we still might only be able to hold five.

The situation was made worse by the lack of honor and failure of discipline that had been on display at Abu Ghraib. After Abu Ghraib, the military made a strict effort to avoid another incident, and decision-making power was taken away from on-the-ground commanders. If, for example, a commander thought that it would be best to hold a particular captive for an extra week past his normal stay, the commander needed approval from Washington. It was hard to obtain. I wasn't an expert, but it seemed to me that the process for asking for extensions had become so difficult that commanders rarely asked.

The most knowledgeable person I met in Iraq on the issue of Iraqi prisoners was a Marine lance corporal who worked with the Iraqi police in Fallujah. We talked for half a day as he described to me the personalities of the Fallujah police officials, their methods of operation, their flaws, failures, frustrations. He explained that the Iraqi police had their own prison system, separate from the American military system, and when I asked him where the police in Fallujah kept their prisoners, he said, "Want to see?"

"Sure."

We walked across the compound with a skittish, overweight translator—"We should run, maybe mortars coming"—and we stepped through a door that led down a flight of steps. I caught the heavy scent of body odor, sweat, urine, fear. Humans in captivity.

At the bottom of the narrow, concrete stairs, an Iraqi guard leaned back in a chair, his forehead pressed with greasy hair, his police cap pushed back on his head. An AK-47 rested across his thighs. We turned right into a narrow hallway where two more Iraqi police sat on guard.

The lance corporal asked—via his interpreter—if we could have a look in the holding cell, and one of the Iraqis stood and walked to the iron door. He grabbed a knob attached to a slot that was set at eye level and he pulled it open.

I stepped forward and felt a wash of hot, heavy air escaping from the cell, and I caught the stench of captive human beings in my nostrils. I looked through the slit and dozens of pairs of swaying, staring eyes looked back at me.

The men all seemed to be standing. *Were they too packed in to sit?* Their eyes caught mine. They were captive. I was free. They might be standing there all night and all the next day, and the next night after that.

The guard pulled the slot shut. I turned around.

Those dozens of men were packed in a holding cell like animals—*Where do they piss? How much water are they given?* The Iraqi police operated completely outside U.S. jurisdiction or influence. *Were the prisoners tortured? Left to rot?*

Our chain of command knew about the prison, but the Iraqi police were independent of us. I knew how many innocent people we picked up on our patrols, and I imagined that it had to be the same for the Iraqis.

We often think of wartime "collateral damage" as innocents who end up dead or wounded. Some of the men in those cells were terrorists, yet I knew that at least a few of those eyes staring back at me were bound to be those of innocent men.

Americans could argue that we were "independent" of the Iraqi police, but we were fighting right alongside them. We were there. I was there. "What can we possibly do?" was the same response that every human being has given as they shrugged and turned their backs on suffering.

The world, I believe, is not constructed so that it presents us with perfect choices. I'd joined the military, in part, because I saw that to protect the innocent, we have to be willing to fight. It is also true, however, that for all the warrior's discipline, when we pick up the sword, innocents will suffer.

Suffering is a theme in Greek literature and philosophy, and in the Western world's first war story, *The Iliad*, Homer portrays the injuries that war does to the innocent. After Andromache—the wife of Hector, prince of Troy—loses her entire family, she begs her husband to withdraw from battle, saying, "You, Hector—you are my father now, my noble mother, a brother too, and you are my husband, young and warm and strong!"[2] Yet Hector returns to battle. He dies, and when Troy falls Andromache is made a slave and her infant son thrown from the walls of the city. Throughout my life, I turned back to the Greeks, because their ideas, even when presented in a dramatic play or formal verse, seemed to be grounded in reality.

The Greeks often talked about *phronesis,* practical wisdom. It's a concept that has no direct equivalent in English. We sometimes talk of "knowledge" or "common sense," but *phronesis* implies something more. *Phronesis* is the ability to figure out what to do, while at the same time knowing what is worth doing.

*Phronesis* allows soldiers to fight well and leaders to rule well, and, as Aristotle argued, it can only be obtained through experience. My own experiences in Rwanda, in Iraq, and elsewhere had not made me a militarist or a pacifist, or any kind of "ist." I knew that the world would continue to require us to make hard decisions about when we draw the sword and I'd seen that the use of force was both necessary and imperfect. There is no school of thought that can save us from the simple fact that hard decisions are best made by good people, and that the best people can only be shaped by hard experience.

After the patrol, men washed their faces, cleaned their rifles, and threw frozen pizza pockets in the microwave. We debriefed and then joined our Iraqi counterparts sitting at a long table for a late lunch of cucumbers, tomatoes, salt, beans, and lamb soup.

The language barrier and utter exhaustion led to stilted conversation. But there is still something deeply human about breaking bread together, and as we stood from lunch any damage from the afternoon's fight seemed to have been repaired.

As the night wound down, we gathered around a small TV to watch what was then the newest James Bond film. Exhausted, we gradually morphed into silliness, joking about all of the high-speed "secret agent" gear we needed to win the war in Fallujah. The jokes—"Hey, Joel, I thought you were supposed to get those devices for your Humvee?"—weren't funny, but still we laughed.

When the film ended, we stood in a post-movie stupor and walked to our bunks. I lay down with some comfort, knowing that this was going to be my last night in the city of Fallujah. I had no idea that at that moment an Iraqi man was planning his own suicide, and that he'd be coming to find us before we woke.

# Epilogue: The Mission Continues

I COULD HEAR the whomp of the Chinook helicopter's blades before I saw its gray outline against the black sky. I stood thirty yards from the airstrip with my bags at my feet, and despite the plugs in my ears, the high-pitched whine of the twin engines was deafening as the helo set down and kicked up a swirling storm of dust. I shook my buddy's hand, picked up my two stuffed duffel bags, and jogged toward the bird.

For me, the whomp and dust of a helicopter always suggested the promise of something about to happen, and I felt a familiar buzz of adrenaline as I stepped up the ramp and into the helo. I carabineered my bags to the deck of the aircraft and stepped past Iraqi prisoners sitting blindfolded, their hands zip-tied behind their backs. I wondered what was going through their minds. They had been captured, yanked from their homes, only a few hours before, and now they were on a helicopter for the first time in their lives surrounded by unfamiliar smells and sounds, with no idea where they were headed.

This helicopter was devoted exclusively to our task force, and along the sides of the aircraft sat special operations personnel wearing beards and nontraditional uniforms, their weapons resting lightly in their hands. Beside them sat civilian contractors, one of them wearing new, ill-fitting body armor that rode high on his heavy stomach.

The bird made a number of stops in the black of night, and at each stop the crew chief held up a sign that said RAMADI or BAGHDAD or the name of some other base, to let everyone know where we had touched down. Commandos walked off, others stepped on, the helo's blades still spinning. As we took off from Baghdad and headed for Balad, I thought, *This is the last leg of my last trip of my last day in Iraq.* In Balad I was scheduled to board a plane for home. I sat on the port side of the helo, and as we flew I looked past the gunner out the window onto a black night. I let my mind drift. I was going to be met in Virginia by a beautiful girl, devilishly smart, warm, with an eyes-over-the-shoulder smile that always made my world brighter. I was thinking about walking with her down the beach.

Bright red tracer rounds flew past us into the sky. I expected some reaction from the crew—a hard banking maneuver, some return fire from the door gunner, but we flew straight ahead, tracers still ripping into the sky. *Why aren't we evading?* Over the past few months, six helicopters had been shot down over Iraq. My mind worked to come up with some explanation. *Maybe those are our tracers? But they're too close.* The tracers kept whizzing by, our pilot flying the same line.

I thought, *Not now, on the last leg of my last ride on my last day of this deployment.* Then the helicopter banked hard to port. A few more tracers flew past and then finally the door gunner racked his weapon and pulled the trigger and bullets barked out at the ground below.

When we landed safely in Balad I knew that, barring anything bizarre—being hit by a wild mortar round, choking to death on a turkey leg in the chow hall—I'd get home safely, and when I made it to my rack on base I dropped my duffel bags and took off my body armor. I unbuttoned the left chest pocket of my desert camouflage top and took out a St. Christopher medal given to me by a Catholic friend, a Buddhist prayer scroll from a Buddhist friend, an angel coin from a Protestant friend, a hamsa from a Jewish friend, and a coin imprinted with a Hindu deity from a Hindu friend. Before the deployment I had figured that it would be a bad move to turn down any prayers that were offered. I'm not sure which one did the trick, so I said simply, "Thank you, God," as I stepped out of my uniform.

When I made it home I called Joel Poudrier, whose head injury in Fallujah had led to his evacuation all the way to Virginia. I hadn't seen him since the morning of the truck bomb. When I got him on the phone, Joel said, "They put a ridiculous number of staples in my head, and the Marines are making me go to a psychologist to see if I'm crazy. Problem is, I was nuts before the explosion, so he's got no way to tell if I've changed." Joel told me that his golf game was coming back and that his family was happy to have him home. We made a plan to get together.

Three weeks later, still getting used to the routine of home, I was stepping out of my truck when my cell phone rang.

"Hey Eric, it's Joel."

"Hey man, how's it going?"

"I got some bad news."

"Yeah?"

"Travis Manion was killed yesterday in Fallujah."

I stood on the street. A red-and-white taxi slowed at a stop sign and then accelerated away.

Joel said, "I heard this morning . . ."

I thought of the last time I'd seen Travis. The day of the suicide truck bomb, Travis had run straight across the compound—rifle in hand and Marines behind him—to aid us. He was the first man to join me on the roof.

When the casevac convoy arrived to take the injured to Fallujah Surgical, I said to Travis, "You got it?"

"Yeah, I got your back, sir."

"Take care of your people" is one of the principal lessons of military leadership, and my people were not just SEALs, or SWCC, or the men in my targeting cell. Serving overseas, everyone in uniform is part of the same team. Everyone is away from their family. Everyone is exposed to danger. Everyone endures the same long, hot days, hears the same bad jokes, reads the same old magazines. Everyone loses friends. If we take care of our people on deployment, why should that change when we come home?

After Joel and I met with the Manion family, I made arrangements to visit the wounded at Bethesda Naval Hospital. As I pulled into the hospital, I thought, *There is only one reason I'm not a patient here: luck.* If one RPG had been better aimed at our Humvee, if the suicide truck bomb had detonated two feet closer, if the shots at the helo had hit their mark, I could have been lying in one of those beds.

As I pushed open the heavy brown door to one of the hospital rooms, a young soldier lying in bed caught me with his eyes and followed me as I walked into the room. Gauze bandages were wrapped around his neck. He'd taken a bullet through the throat.

"How you doin'?" I asked, and he wrote on a yellow legal pad, "Fine, was actually having fun over there before this."

His young wife sat next to him with red-ringed eyes, her hand on his shoulder. Most of the Army's wounded were at Walter Reed, but this soldier—for some reason having to do with his care—had been brought to Bethesda. I joked that he was in enemy territory at a Navy hospital, and he wrote, "Navy actually OK, some of them," and he smiled. We communicated a bit more, and as I walked out of his room, I was thinking, *What's this guy going to do next?*

I walked into another room where a Marine had lost part of his right lung and the use of his right hand. With his good hand, he took mine and shook firmly. His mother sat hunched at his side, and it seemed to me that she'd been there for a very long time, trapped in worry and confusion and heartache. I guessed that the Marine was nineteen, maybe twenty years old. He reminded me of many of the men I had served with. I could picture him cleaning his weapon on a sweltering morning in Southeast Asia, turning a knob to check his radio frequency before a mission in Kenya, or strapping on his body armor before a night patrol in Iraq.

We talked for a while about where he'd served, how he'd been hit, and where he was from. I asked him, "What do you want to do when you recover?"

"I want to go back to my unit, sir."

I nodded. "I know that your guys'll be glad to know that."

In Survival, Evasion, Resistance, and Escape school we were taught the "Stockdale paradox," named after Admiral James Stockdale, a POW in Vietnam for seven and a half years who received the Congressional Medal of Honor for his leadership while in captivity. Stockdale taught that as a leader, you must embrace reality and be brutally honest about the harsh facts of your situation. At the same time, you must maintain hope.

The reality and the brutal fact was that this Marine was not going to be back on the battlefield with his unit any time soon. So how could he maintain hope? In Croatia, Rwanda, Bolivia, India, and a dozen other places overseas, I'd seen people rebuild their lives by renewing their sense of purpose.

I said to the Marine, "If you can't go back to your unit right away, what would you like to do?"

He said, "I thought about that a little bit. You know, I had a rough childhood growing up. The Marines was the best thing that happened to me. Those men steered me in the right direction. I've thought that maybe I'd like to go home and maybe be a coach. Maybe I could go home and be some kind of coach or mentor for young kids."

In another room, I talked with a Marine who had lost both his legs. His head was shaved in the Marine Corps high and tight, and his upper body was still powerful.

I asked him, "What do you want to do when you recover?"

"Go back to my Marines, sir."

After we talked a bit longer, I asked him, "And if you can't go back right away, what would you like to do?"

"I think that maybe I'd like to stay here at Bethesda. I want to find a way to help these other Marines to recover, let them know there's hope for them. I was pretty down when I first learned that I lost my legs, but I've had a lot of wonderful people that helped me, and so I'd like to help out other guys that come in."

Later, I talked with a Marine who had been hit by a roadside bomb.

"How's your hearing?" I asked.

"In one of my ears it's bad. In the other it's getting better. The doctors say they think it'll come back. I hope it'll all come back soon."

The Marine's father stood leaning against the wall. When I asked him what he would like to do if he couldn't go back to his unit, he said that he might want to become a teacher. His dad added, "We've been talking about him going back to college to get a teaching degree."

As I left the hospital that day, I knew that these men and women had a long stream of visitors who were coming to the hospital to tell them, "Thank you." The visitors—other service members, government officials, celebrities, friends, Boy Scouts and Girl Scouts—were all telling these men and women, "Thank you for your service. Thank you for your sacrifice." And it was clear that our men and women appreciated that. It meant a lot to them when they heard, "Thank you."

I also realized that these men and women had to hear something else. In addition to "Thank you," they also had to hear, "We still need you." They had to know that we viewed them not as problems, but as assets; that we saw them not as weak, but as strong. They had to know that we were glad they were home, that we needed their strength here at home, that we needed them to continue to serve here at home.

I knew from my experience working with Bosnian refugees and Rwandan survivors that those who found a way to serve others were able to rebuild their own sense of purpose, despite all they had lost. I knew from my time in refugee camps and my time working with children of the street that to build a new life in the face of great challenge, what mattered was not what we gave them, but what they did.

Our wounded and disabled veterans had lost a lot. Some had lost their eyesight. Some their hearing. Some had lost limbs. All of that they could recover from. If they lost their sense of purpose, however, that would be deadly. I also knew that no one was going to be able to give them hope; they were going to have to *create* hope through action.

I did some research when I left the hospital and found over one hundred organizations that served wounded warriors. There were groups that paid for the education of the children of fallen soldiers, groups that assisted wounded veterans to build adaptive housing so that they could live independently with disabilities, and groups that served as advocates for veterans.

I found plenty of organizations ready to give to veterans or to advocate for them, but no organizations that were ready to ask *of* wounded veterans that they continue their service.

I wanted to welcome returning wounded and disabled veterans not just with charity, but with a challenge.

So I donated my combat pay to begin a different kind of veterans' organization, and two friends contributed money from their disability checks. My plan with The Mission Continues was to offer fellowships for wounded and disabled veterans to serve at nonprofit, charitable, and public benefit organizations. We would provide wounded and disabled veterans with a stipend to offset cost-of-living expenses and with mentors to help them build plans for their post-fellowship life. Most importantly, we would provide them with the challenge and the opportunity to rebuild a meaningful life by serving again in communities here at home.

When I committed to work as a volunteer CEO, a good friend asked me to rethink my plans. "How are you going to make money? How are you going to support yourself?"

I thought of Jason and Caroline, who had left everything to work with the street children of Bolivia. I thought of the nuns I had seen in the home for the destitute and dying in Varanasi, India, of the aid workers who had flown to Rwanda. I thought of Earl Blair, who dedicated his life to teaching young men to box. I had learned that there came a point in their lives when they simply had to listen to their hearts and trust that if they did the right thing, all would work out in the end.

If we were going to build a culture of service, I would set the example. I knew that there were a number of fellowships that existed to support leaders of innovative organizations. If I led well, I might obtain a fellowship to support myself. It would be a challenge, but if I was going to challenge others, I had to challenge myself.

Tom and Janet Manion inspired me. They had set up the Travis Manion Foundation, its motto being the famous saying, "If not me, then who?" I thought about that for myself. I had been in some of the world's worst situations, and I had learned from people who had turned pain into wisdom and suffering into strength. I had studied public service organizations for years, and because of my military service I understood these men and women; we had worn the same boots, carried the same rifles. *If not me, then who?*

I also thought about the guys in the hospital at Bethesda. I thought about the challenge that they faced. They had served overseas, been wounded, and now I was going to ask them to build new lives here at home. If I was going to ask that of them, then certainly I could ask it of myself.

My most difficult moment in Hell Week had come in the tent—when I let myself focus on my own pain and fear. Then I became weaker. The same thing was happening here. When I asked, "How am I going to support myself? What if I fail? What if this is an embarrassment?" then I grew weaker. When I thought about Joel, when I thought about Travis, when I thought about all of the wounded and disabled veterans fighting to rebuild their lives, then I grew stronger.

I focused on changing one life at a time.

Chris Marvin was driving home from a physical therapy session when a radio commentary by my friend Ken caught his ear. Ken was talking about the war stories his grandfather had told him as a child. When Chris pulled into his driveway, he cut off his engine, but kept the radio on: "Bullets today aren't any friendlier than they were back then. I've seen what they do. And now there are IEDs and suicide truck bombs and all manner of horrors my grandfather never faced. War stories will never sound the same to me as they did when I was little. I see past the punch lines now. Yeah, I still laugh along with the double amputee who jokes about losing $300 worth of tattoos. But I know how real the pain is when he tells me his only regret is that he didn't stop enough shrapnel with his own body to save his squad mate from getting hit."[1]

A tear rolled down Chris's cheek. Three years before, Chris's Black Hawk helicopter had crashed during operations over Afghanistan. He broke his legs, his foot, and his right arm; shattered the bones in the right side of his face; and severely damaged both knees, his hips, and both shoulders. He was barely conscious when a man ran up to the wreck.

"Is the aircraft on fire?" Chris gasped.

"No," said the man.

"Am I the worst one?" Chris asked, thinking, *If I'm the worst injured, everybody else will be OK.*

What Ken described—a man who failed because he couldn't save the life of his fellow soldier—was what Chris felt after the helicopter crash. Before hearing the commentary, no one had put into words that feeling of sacrifice and camaraderie forged through service.

After the radio piece finished, the host announced: "Commentator Ken Harbaugh is a former Navy pilot," and explained that he worked with a nonprofit that aimed to help wounded and disabled veterans volunteer in their communities.

Chris thought, *I'm a wounded veteran. I should contact that guy.* Chris Marvin became our first fellow.

As a fellow, Chris served with other wounded warriors. He led service projects, counseled his wounded friends, and worked with us to create a model for helping wounded veterans begin to serve again here at home. Dozens of wounded veterans owe their first steps in service to Chris. Today, Chris is an MBA student at Wharton and still an active member of our team.

Even with the success of Chris's fellowship, our work remained a struggle. I lived on an air mattress in an empty apartment, and after we'd made a commitment to fund our second fellowship, I was planning to fund it using my credit card.

A few dozen people came to our opening in St. Louis on February 28, 2008. Among them was Mathew Trotter, our second fellow.

Mathew was an eleven-year veteran of the United States Navy. In late 2004, in a shipboard accident, he tore the Achilles tendons in both his legs. In addition to the torn Achilles, small bits of bone splintered and planted themselves in the muscles along the bottom of his feet. Every time Mathew moved, bone splinters cut his tendons. He underwent reconstructive surgeries to repair the damage, but with both legs in casts during his recovery, he could not stretch, and scar tissue damaged the nerves in his legs.

When the doctors cut his casts, Mathew tried to walk, and "every step felt like I was walking on nails." Excruciating pain shot from his heels, up his legs, and into the small of his back. No longer able to do physical training, he gained 150 pounds. He fought to rejoin his men on the ship, but after his fourth surgery, the Navy handed him his transfer papers. At the bottom of the first page, in the box labeled "Reason for Discharge" it said, "Service member is unserviceable for shipboard use, therefore unable to proceed in the Navy." Mathew had served ten years in Navy aviation, and he had sometimes filled out paperwork that designated certain equipment as "unserviceable." Now he felt like he'd been stamped "unserviceable."

When he returned home to Texas, he moved into a trailer and lived off his disability pay. No one would hire him. "It was the hardest time of my life. I used to be in charge of 160 people. Now here I was, absolute bottom of the barrel. My wife left me then and I sunk even further." In late 2007 Mathew heard about The Mission Continues. When we talked with Mathew we asked him the same question we've asked every wounded and disabled veteran since then: we need you; how are you going to continue to serve?

Mathew told us that he wasn't sure, but that he'd always liked working with horses, had always liked working with kids. So we contacted a Texas nonprofit called Horses Helping the Handicapped, which spe-

cializes in horse riding as a form of therapy to help children with physical and mental disabilities.

For six months, we paid for Mathew to serve as a mentor and role
model for children with physical disabilities. Mathew did incredible
work with children, and then on his own initiative he visited the burn
unit at Brooke Army Medical Center in San Antonio. Standing in the
physical therapy room in front of some of the country's most severely
wounded veterans, he talked about his experience.

"Equitherapy is physical therapy, except with a horse. Any physical
therapy done on the ground can be done on a horse. When I started
physical therapy, I was only able to walk a hundred yards. With equitherapy, I could ride a horse for six miles. You work your upper and lower
body, strengthen your core, legs, and arms. Before therapy, I had to use
a cane to walk. After therapy, I haven't touched my cane in months."

At the end of his presentation Mathew asked the veterans, "Now,
how many of you want to do some of your therapy with horses at the
Equitherapy Center?"

Everyone in the room raised his hand.

"Well," Mathew said, "I'm not going to take any of you."

The veterans traded confused looks.

"I'm not going to take any of you," he paused, "unless after your
therapy is done, you come back to the Triple H Ranch and volunteer
to be mentors to the kids who come to the ranch for their therapy."
Mathew explained that his life had changed when we challenged him
to begin to serve again. Now he was going to challenge these wounded
veterans to begin to serve again.

When Mathew's six-month fellowship finished, he was hired full-
time at the Triple H Equitherapy Center. He continues to serve as a
role model and mentor for children with physical disabilities, and he
continues to oversee a group of veterans who do therapy and then return to mentor children. Today, Mathew is going back to school part-
time to become a licensed physical therapist while continuing his em-
ployment at Horses Helping the Handicapped.

When Mathew became a fellow, I named his fellowship in honor of

Travis Manion and invited Janet Manion to come to our launch in St. Louis. There she met Mathew, who told her, "This fellowship changed my life. I am trying to live Travis's values every day, so that what he stood for will live on."

He continued, "I measure my goals in 'This guy's able to walk' and 'This guy's able to move his hands.' And it's just so much more rewarding. It allows me to help other guys who are in the same situation or worse than I am. I bring the veterans in, so that once they go through the therapy, they get back out there helping the community by helping the kids in the program. We use the military guys as role models for the kids, and they inspire the kids to get better."

Later, when I spoke, I saw my mom sitting next to Janet Manion, both of them crying, and I knew that it well could have been Travis here talking and my mom showing a video. Since that day, I've talked hundreds of times about our work. That speech was my hardest, but as I watched my mom and Janet side by side, I knew that I had made the right decision.

From our very humble beginnings, The Mission Continues has awarded over one hundred fellowships to wounded and disabled veterans like Chris and Mathew, and in October 2008 the President of the United States stopped in St. Louis to recognize our work. In our Tribute Service Projects, men and women come together to "continue the mission" of fallen service members by serving in their communities. We believe that the greatest way to honor those who have fallen is to live their values. With our wounded veterans as examples of courage, we have built a movement of service, and we have had over twelve thousand volunteers who have performed over seventy-five thousand hours of service in communities across the country.

Viktor Frankl, a Holocaust survivor and author of *Man's Search for Meaning*, wrote that human beings create meaning in three ways: through their work, through their relationships, and by how they choose to meet unavoidable suffering. Every life brings hardship and trial, and every life also offers deep possibilities for meaningful work and love.

I've learned that courage and compassion are two sides of the same coin, and that every warrior, every humanitarian, every citizen is built to live with both. In fact, to win a war, to create peace, to save a life, or just to live a good life requires of us—of every one of us—that we be both good *and* strong.

Recently I was at Special Operations Command in Tampa, Florida, to do my reserve duty. Toward the end of a long run, another SEAL and I caught sight of a statue of a lone armed soldier looking out—eyes forward. Was he resting a moment? Midstride? Standing guard? Behind him the names of fallen warriors were engraved in a wall. We walked to the wall and searched for the names of our friends. I looked at name after name, but . . .

"Here they are."

I walked over. We both touched the names of our classmates, our fallen friends. We stood awhile.

"You ready?"

"Yeah. Let's go."

We ran in quiet for a while, both of us humbled by our good fortune to have known worthy people and to have loved them. Both of us humbled by the incredible gift of continued life.

I write these lines sitting at peace in a cabin in mid-Missouri, where a single quotation hangs on the wall: "I shall pass through this world but once. Any good, therefore, that I can do, or any kindness that I can show to any human being, let me do it now. Let me not defer or neglect it, for I shall not pass this way again."[2]

Life is short. Life is uncertain. But we know that we have today. And we have each other. I believe that for each of us, there is a place on the frontlines.

# Author's Note
# and Acknowledgments

This book relates my experiences on the frontlines of humanitarian service overseas, military training and war, and public leadership in the United States. It is not a full account of my service or, more importantly, the incredible service of those I have worked with. I have included here only a few critical moments from a few key endeavors; other parts of the journey—Albania, Chiapas, a White House Fellowship—I have left out completely.

In sharing this manuscript with friends, the most frequent comment I heard was some version of, How could you leave out the time we . . .

> were almost attacked by hippos?
> lost twenty pounds and looked like walking ghosts?
> were compromised on that reconnaissance mission?
> fed that starving girl?

To those not finding their stories here, I am sorry. They may not be on these pages, but I still carry them with me.

This book is not the story of my life. If it were, my family and others close to me would feature more prominently. I have worked with some incredible people—Mother Teresa's Missionaries of Charity, who wake every day to work among the poorest of the poor, and members of America's most elite commando units, who have given their lives defending their friends and our country. They are real heroes, and I hope that this account has shone some light on their incredible lives.

I hope that this book will be of use to those seeking to find their own place on the frontlines, as well as those concerned about loved ones who are serving or thinking of serving there. On a regular basis, I am asked things like, "I want to be a Navy SEAL, what should I do?"; "Who makes it through SEAL training?"; "My daughter wants to serve in an orphanage overseas; should I let her go?"; "Is there any way I can be of service here at home?"; or "What can I do to help veterans?" Most people, I have found, are trying to figure out how to live their lives well. I hope that this account of my experience—complete with low points and high points, mistakes and successes—will prove valuable to those who are finding their own way.

It's always tough to piece together the past, but I've been fortunate to have a number of good friends who accompanied me on this journey and have been able to shore up my memory and correct the record where necessary. I've also been fortunate to have access to the thousands of photographs I took during my travels, and the notebooks in which I recorded my observations. In addition to letters, I also have e-mails, memos, papers, and reports to look back on. My colleague Tim Ly further helped me by conducting interviews and researching key events. Still, errors undoubtedly remain. There was a boy who died when I was working in a home for children of the street in Bolivia. His story is recounted here. I was confident enough in my memory that in my earlier book, *Strength and Compassion,* I wrote that a broken leg had led to his admission to the hospital. After digging through bins in my basement, however, I found a notebook from my time in Bolivia where I'd written that the initial injury had been a broken collarbone. It's a minor detail, perhaps, but details matter, and I've tried to get them as right as possible. I take full responsibility for any errors of fact that remain.

It might go without saying that some of the conversations included here are not verbatim. I'm thinking specifically of the scene in Chapter 4 in which my grandfather lectures me on the virtues of Chicago pizza. I remember this lecture well, and my aunt and brother both agree that the speech sounds like him. But the incident took place twenty years ago. I've tried my best to present conversations accurately, but for some of the casual conversations recounted here, the best I could do was capture the spirit of the dialogue.

I've used pseudonyms for all living Navy SEALs and Special Warfare personnel mentioned in the book, except for those who are public figures. I have used the real names of those who died in combat. There are also two names that I assigned: "Karen" was a woman I worked with in Rwanda, and "Denis" was a Bosnian boy I knew in the refugee camps. Though I remember these individuals vividly, I was unable to confirm their names, and it was awkward to keep referring to them as "the blond volunteer from Texas" and "the pensive Bosnian boy."

I did not use composite characters or scenes in the book, and the sequence of events is largely chronological, except where indicated otherwise in the text.

I owe a huge debt of gratitude to the many people who helped with this project. My literary agent, E. J. McCarthy, encouraged me in this endeavor and has offered counsel and friendship every step of the way. Bruce Nichols, publisher at Houghton Mifflin Harcourt, believed in this project from the beginning, and his insightful editing strengthened the final product. Tim Ly did excellent research and conducted hours of quality interviews. He is a wise and hardworking friend, and his sense of humor made him a valued assistant on this project.

My best editors are people who know me well, and my thanks go out to Audrey L. Jacobs, Rob Greitens, Marc Greitens, Barb Osburg, Sheena Chestnut, Silvette Bullard, and Jimmy Soni. Melissa Dobson served as an exceptional copyeditor. At Houghton Mifflin Harcourt I had a great set of friends and allies. Thank you to Lori Glazer, Larry Cooper, Megan Wilson, and Carla Gray. Jacques Chazaud created excellent maps, and Richard Schoenberg graciously allowed me to use his exceptional photographs from BUD/S training. My thanks also to Bob Holden, who loaned me his cabin for several days of focused writing.

I served with hundreds of incredible people—too many to thank by name, for fear that I might leave someone out. Thank you. My final acknowledgments go to the children, their families and communities, and the many relief workers and volunteers who welcomed me into their lives. Many of them told their stories to someone who could do little for them. This work is too weak a gesture to serve as a thank-you, but I hope, at least, that it reflects some of their strength.

# Notes

### 1. IRAQ

1. "Hall of Valor: Travis L. Manion," *Military Times,* http://militarytimes.com/citations-medals-awards/recipient.php?recipientid=3739 (last accessed May 26, 2010).

### 2. CHINA

1. Nova Online, "Shackleton's Voyage of Endurance: Meet Shackleton's Team," www.pbs.org/wgbh/nova/shackleton/1914/team.html (last accessed May 26, 2010).

### 4. BOSNIA

1. John Kifner, "In North Bosnia, a Rising Tide of Serbian Violence," *New York Times,* March 27, 1994, www.nytimes.com/1994/03/27/world/in-north-bosnia-a-rising-tide-of-serbian-violence.html (last accessed March 30, 2010).
2. Brett Dakin, "The Islamic Community in Bosnia and Herzegovina v. The Republika Srpska: Human Rights in a Multi-Ethnic Bosnia," *Harvard Human Rights Journal* 15 (Spring 2002), www.law.harvard.edu/students/orgs/hrj/iss15/dakin.shtml (last accessed March 30, 2010).
3. Roy Gutman, "Death Camp Lists: In Town After Town, Bosnia's 'Elite' Disappeared," *Newsday,* November 8, 1992.
4. Samantha Power, *A Problem from Hell: America and the Age of Genocide* (New York: Harper Perennial, 2003), 256.
5. Roy Gutman, "Unholy War: Serbs Target Culture, Heritage of Bosnia's Muslims," *Newsday,* September 2, 1992.
6. Eric Greitens, *Strength and Compassion: Photographs and Essays* (Washington, D.C.: Leading Authorities Press, 2008), 132.

7. United Nations, International Criminal Tribunal for the Former Yugoslavia, *Prosecutor v. Radislav Krstic,* case no. IT-98-33-T, August 2, 2001, p. 72, available at http://icr.icty.org.

5. RWANDA

1. "Rwanda: A Historical Timeline," *Frontline,* www.pbs.org/wgbh/pages/frontline/shows/rwanda/etc/cron.html (last accessed March 30, 2010).
2. United Nations Children's Fund, "State of the World's Children 1996: Children in War," www.unicef.org/sowc96/1cinwar.htm (last accessed March 30, 2010).
3. Stefan Lovgren, "'Hotel Rwanda' Portrays Hero Who Fought Genocide," *National Geographic,* December 9, 2004, http://news.nationalgeographic.com/news/2004/12/1209_041209_hotel_rwanda_2.html (last accessed March 10, 2010).
4. Akagera National Park, www.expertafrica.com/area/Akagera_National_Park.htm (last accessed March 10, 2010).
5. Rwanda Safaris Guide, "Rwanda Primate Safari Monkeys: Nyungwe's Monkeys," www.rwandasafarisguide.com/rwanda-national-parks/nyungwe-forest/rwanda-primate-safari-monkeys.php (last accessed May 28, 2010).
6. Eric Greitens, *Strength and Compassion: Photographs and Essays* (Washington, D.C.: Leading Authorities Press, 2008), 6.
7. Ibid., 11.
8. Samantha Power, "Bystanders to Genocide," *Atlantic Monthly,* September 2001, www.theatlantic.com/magazine/archive/2001/09/bystanders-to-genocide/4571/6/ (last accessed March 30, 2010).
9. Philip Gourevitch, *We Wish to Inform You That We Will Be Killed Tomorrow* (New York: Picador, 1998), 150–51.
10. Online NewsHour, "Search for Stability: Promoting Peace," March 25, 1998, www.pbs.org/newshour/bb/africa/jan-june98/rwanda_3-25a.html (last accessed May 28, 2010).
11. Greitens, *Strength and Compassion,* 13.
12. Ibid., 12.

6. BOLIVIA

1. Edith Hamilton, *The Greek Way* (New York: Norton, 1964), 9.
2. William Jennings Bryan, ed., *The World's Famous Orations* (New York: Funk & Wagnalls, 1906), available at www.bartleby.com/268/8/33.html (last accessed August 26, 2010).

7. OXFORD

1. Albert Camus, *The Plague,* trans. Stuart Gilbert (New York: Modern Library), 231.
2. Eric Greitens, "The Treatment of Children During Conflict," in *War and Underdevelopment,* vol. 1, edited by Frances Stewart and Valpy FitzGerald (Oxford: Oxford University Press, 2001), 149–67.

3. Caroline Moorehead, *Dunant's Dream: War, Switzerland, and the History of the Red Cross* (London: HarperCollins, 1998), 3–4.
4. Population Research Institute, "Israel's Demographic Geopolitics," November 29, 1999, www.pop.org/00000000190/israels-demographic-geopolitics (last accessed August 24, 2010).
5. ReliefWeb, "The Gaza Blockade: Children and Education Fact Sheet," July 28, 2009, www.reliefweb.int/rw/rwb.nsf/db900sid/LSGZ-7UDDVG?OpenDocument (last accessed May 26, 2010).
6. Moorehead, *Dunant's Dream*, 6.
7. Eric R. Greitens, "Children First: Ideas and the Dynamics of Aid in Western Voluntary Assistance Programs for War-Affected Children Abroad" (DPhil diss., Oxford University, 2000).
8. John Stuart Mill, "The Contest in America," reprinted by the Penn State Electronic Classic Series, www2.hn.psu.edu/faculty/jmanis/jsmill/Contest-america.pdf (last accessed May 29, 2010).

## 8. OFFICER CANDIDATE SCHOOL

1. United States Navy Officer Candidate School, "Officer Candidate Regulations," www.ocs.navy.mil/pdfs/Updated.Gouge.Pack.OCS2.pdf (last accessed April 7, 2010).

## 9. SEAL TRAINING

1. NFL Players Association, "NFL Collective Bargaining Agreement 2006–2012," March 8, 2006, 179, http://images.nflplayers.com/mediaResources/files/PDFs/General/NFL%20COLLECTIVE%20BARGAINING%20AGREEMENT%202006%20-%202012.pdf (last accessed April 7, 2010).
2. Navy Cyberspace, "Military Pay Chart 2010," www.navycs.com/2010-military-pay-chart.html (last accessed May 28, 2010).

## 10. HELL WEEK

1. Department of Defense, *The Armed Forces Officer*, 1.
2. Fred J. Pushies, *Weapons of the Navy SEALs* (St. Paul, MN: MBI Publishing Company, 2004), 18.
3. Derrick Wright, *Tarawa 1943: The Turning of the Tide* (Oxford: Osprey Press, 2000), 93.
4. Abraham Lincoln Online, "First Political Announcement," March 9, 1832, http://showcase.netins.net/web/creative/lincoln/speeches/1832.htm (last accessed August 13, 2010).
5. This translation of the epitaph, which is attributed to Simonides, is in the historical note preceding Steven Pressfield's *Gates of Fire* (New York: Bantam, 1999).
6. Mir Banhmanyar, *U.S. Navy SEALs* (Oxford: Osprey Publishing, 2005), 3.

## 11. ADVANCED COMBAT TRAINING

1. Dick Couch, *Finishing School: Earning the Navy SEAL Trident* (New York: Crown, 2004), 135–36. Actual phrasing is slightly different (original passage is "The ocean is the hardest element for any soldier to operate in—but we must be masters of the sea").

## 12. AFGHANISTAN

1. Stephen Tanner's *Afghanistan: A Military History from Alexander the Great to the Fall of the Taliban* (New York: Da Capo Press, 2002) is the source for historical information on Afghanistan in this chapter unless noted otherwise.
2. Steve Lohr, "Moscow's Millions of Deadly Seeds: Afghan Mines," *New York Times*, March 2, 1989, www.nytimes.com/1989/03/02/world/moscow-s-millions-of-deadly-seeds-afghan-mines.html (last accessed May 28, 2010).
3. Ahmed Rashid, *Taliban: Militant Islam, Oil, and Fundamentalism in Central Asia* (New Haven, CT: Yale University Press, 2000), 25.
4. Michael Evans, "Warlords Set to Reap Profits of Poppy Harvest," *Times*, November 26, 2001, www.opioids.com/afghanistan/warlords.html (last accessed March 10, 2010).
5. Doug Stanton, *Horse Soldiers: Extraordinary Story of a Band of U.S. Soldiers Who Rode to Victory in Afghanistan* (New York: Scribner, 2009), 96–97.
6. Barbara Crossette, "Taliban Seem to Be Making Good on Opium Ban, U.N. Says," *New York Times*, February 7, 2001, www.nytimes.com/2001/02/07/world/taliban-seem-to-be-making-good-on-opium-ban-un-says.html?scp=10&sq=taliban%20opium&st=cse (last accessed May 26, 2010).
7. Stanton, *Horse Soldiers*, 98–99.
8. Military Force Authorization Resolution, Public Law 107-40, 107th Cong., 1st sess., September 18, 2001, http://frwebgate.access.gpo.gov/cgi-bin/getdoc.cgi?dbname=107_cong_public_laws&docid=f:publ040.107 (last accessed May 26, 2010).
9. Stanton, *Horse Soldiers*, 58–60.
10. Ibid., 345. For casualty count up to the fall of Kandahar on December 7, 2001, see www.icasualties.org/OEF/Fatalities.aspx.
11. Chairman of the Joint Chiefs of Staff Instruction, "Standing Rules of Engagement for US Forces," January 15, 2000, www.fas.org/man/dod-101/dod/docs/cjcs_sroe.pdf, A-5 (last accessed May 26, 2010).
12. United Nations Development Programme, "Human Development Report 2007/2008: Fighting Climate Change: Human Solidarity in a Divided World," 261, http://hdr.undp.org/en/media/HDR_20072008_EN_Complete.pdf (last accessed May 28, 2010).
13. United Nations Development Programme, Human Development Reports, "Composite Indicies—HDI and Beyond," http://hdr.undp.org/en/statistics/indices/ (last accessed May 29, 2010).

14. Carnegie Council for Ethics in International Affairs, "Afghanistan Briefing Transcript," www.cceia.org/resources/transcripts/0235.html (last accessed May 27, 2010).

15. See David R. Moran, "About Sherwood Ford Moran: 1885–1983," http://home.comcast.net/~drmoran/home.htm (last accessed March 31, 2010), and Stephen Budiansky, "Truth Extraction," *Atlantic Monthly*, June 2005, www.theatlantic.com/doc/200506/budiansky (last accessed May 27, 2010).

16. Jack Cloonan, "No Torture, No Exception," *Washington Monthly*, January 2008, www.washingtonmonthly.com/features/2008/0801.cloonan.html (last accessed May 26, 2010).

17. Carnegie Council for Ethics in International Affairs, "Afghanistan Briefing Transcript."

18. U.S. Department of Transportation Federal Highway Administration, "Census 2000 Population Statistics," February 9, 2004, www.fhwa.dot.gov/planning/census/cps2k.htm (last accessed May 26, 2010).

13. SOUTHEAST ASIA

1. "Mark V Special Operations Craft," www.globalsecurity.org/military/systems/ship/mark_v.htm (last accessed March 31, 2010).

2. "Patrol Boat Mark V Special Operations Craft (SOC)," www.militaryfactory.com/ships/detail.asp?ship_id=Patrol-Boat-Mark-V-SOC (last accessed May 26, 2010).

3. "Mark V Special Operations Craft (MK V SOC)," www.americanspecialops.com/boats/mark-v-special-operations-craft/ (last accessed March 31, 2010).

4. Sea, Air, Land Online, "SEAL Code: A Warrior Creed," www.navyseals.com/?q=seal-code-warrior-creed (last accessed August 26, 2010).

5. Theodore Roosevelt, "1902 State of the Union Address," www.presidentialelection.com/students/wiki/index.php/Students_1902_State_of_the_Union_Address (last accessed May 29, 2010).

6. "Country Comparison: Population," CIA World Fact Book, www.cia.gov/library/publications/the-world-factbook/rankorder/2119rank.html (last accessed March 31, 2010).

7. Dennis Blair and Kenneth Lieberthal, "Smooth Sailing: The World's Shipping Lanes Are Safe," *Foreign Affairs* 86, no. 3 (May–June 2007), 7.

8. Michael Shuman, "How to Defeat Pirates: Success in the Strait," *Time*, April 22, 2009, www.time.com/time/world/article/0,8599,1893032,00.html#ixzz0p5UEDZms (last accessed May 26, 2010).

9. Zachary Abuza, "Balik-Terrorism: The Return of the Abu Sayyaf," Strategic Studies Institute at the Army War College, September 2005, 2, www.strategicstudiesinstitute.army.mil/pdffiles/pub625.pdf (last accessed May 28, 2010).

10. BBC News, "Guide to the Philippines Conflict," http://news.bbc.co.uk/2/hi/asia-pacific/1695576.stm.

11. Online NewsHour, "Profile: Abu Sayaaf," January 2002, www.pbs.org/newshour/terrorism/international/abu_sayyaf.html (last accessed May 27, 2010).

12. BBC News, "Philippine TV Shows Beheading Video," February 19, 2002, http://news
.bbc.co.uk/2/hi/asia-pacific/1829211.stm (last accessed March 31, 2010).

13. Gracia Burnham, *In the Presence of My Enemies* (Carol Stream, IL: Tyndale House, 2003), 20.

14. Mark Bowden, "Jihadists in Paradise," *Atlantic Monthly,* March 2007, www.theatlantic
.com/magazine/archive/2007/03/jihadists-in-paradise/5613/2/ (last accessed May 27, 2010).

15. John W. Fountain, "A Phone Call Brings Sad News but Fails to Dent Faith," *New York Times,* June 8, 2002, www.nytimes.com/2002/06/08/world/a-phone-call-brings-sad-news-but-fails-to-dent-faith.html?scp=7&sq=gracia%20burnham&st=cse (last accessed May 27, 2010).

16. Bowden, "Jihadists in Paradise."

17. United Nations Development Programme, "Human Development Report 2007/2008: Fighting Climate Change: Human Solidarity in a Divided World," 238, http://hdr
.undp.org/en/media/HDR_20072008_EN_Complete.pdf (last accessed May 28, 2010).

## 14. KENYA

1. Sun Tzu, *The Art of War,* ed. James Clavell (New York: Dell, 1983), 15.

2. Jason Burke, *Al Qaeda: The True Story of Radical Islam* (New York: I. B. Tauris, 2003), 158–59.

3. Karl Vick and T. R. Reid, "It Was an Ordinary Day, Then Horror," *Washington Post,* August 10, 1998, www.washingtonpost.com/wp-srv/inatl/longterm/eafricabombing/stories/explode081098.htm (last accessed May 27, 2010).

4. Samuel M. Katz, *Relentless Pursuit: The DSS and the Manhunt for the Al-Qaeda Terrorists* (New York: Forge Books, 2002), 243–44.

5. "3 Killed as U.S. Chopper Is Shot Down in Somalia," *New York Times,* September 25, 1993, www.nytimes.com/1993/09/25/world/3-killed-as-us-chopper-is-shot-down-in-somalia.html?pagewanted=1 (last accessed May 27, 2010).

6. Jane Perlez, "Somalia Aid Workers Split on Troops," *New York Times,* November 27, 1992, www.nytimes.com/1992/11/27/world/somalia-aid-workers-split-on-troops
.html?pagewanted=1 (last accessed May 27, 2010).

7. United Nations Security Council, "Report of the Secretary-General on the Situation in Somalia," October 11, 2005, http://daccess-dds-ny.un.org/doc/UNDOC/GEN/N05/544/15/PDF/N0554415.pdf?OpenElement (last accessed April 7, 2010).

8. United Nations Development Programme, "Crisis Prevention and Recovery: Fast Facts—Somalia," www.undp.org/cpr/whats_new/Regions/somalia.shtml (last accessed May 27, 2010).

9. Famine Early Warning System Network, "The Impact of Piracy on Livelihoods and Food Security in Somalia," www.fews.net/docs/Publications/1000872.pdf (last accessed April 7, 2010)

10. Henry A. Kissinger, "America's Assignment: What Will We Face in the Next Four Years?" *Newsweek,* November 8, 2004, www.henryakissinger.com/articles/nw110404 .html (last accessed March 23, 2010).

11. P. Mangelus, *Lamu: Preservation and Presentation of Its Cultural Heritage* (Paris: United Nations Educational, Scientific, and Cultural Organization, 1983), 1, http:// unesdoc.unesco.org/images/0005/000582/058202eo.pdf (last accessed May 29, 2010).

12. Education International, "Kenya: Teachers Demand Immediate Salary Increases and Respect for Union Rights," www.ei-ie.org/en/news/show.php?id=953&theme=rights &country=kenya (last accessed May 26, 2010).

### 15. IRAQ

1. Iraq Coalition Casualty Count, "Iraq Coalition Casualties: Fatalities by Year and Month," www.icasualties.org/Iraq/ByMonth.aspx (last accessed May 27, 2010).

2. Homer, *The Iliad,* trans. Robert Fagles (New York: Penguin Classics, 1991), 210.

### EPILOGUE: THE MISSION CONTINUES

1. National Public Radio, "A Grandfather's War Stories," October 9, 2007, www.npr .org/templates/transcript/transcript.php?storyId=15127337 (last accessed August 26, 2010).

2. This quotation has been attributed to many people, including Mahatma Gandhi, Henry Drummond and William Penn.

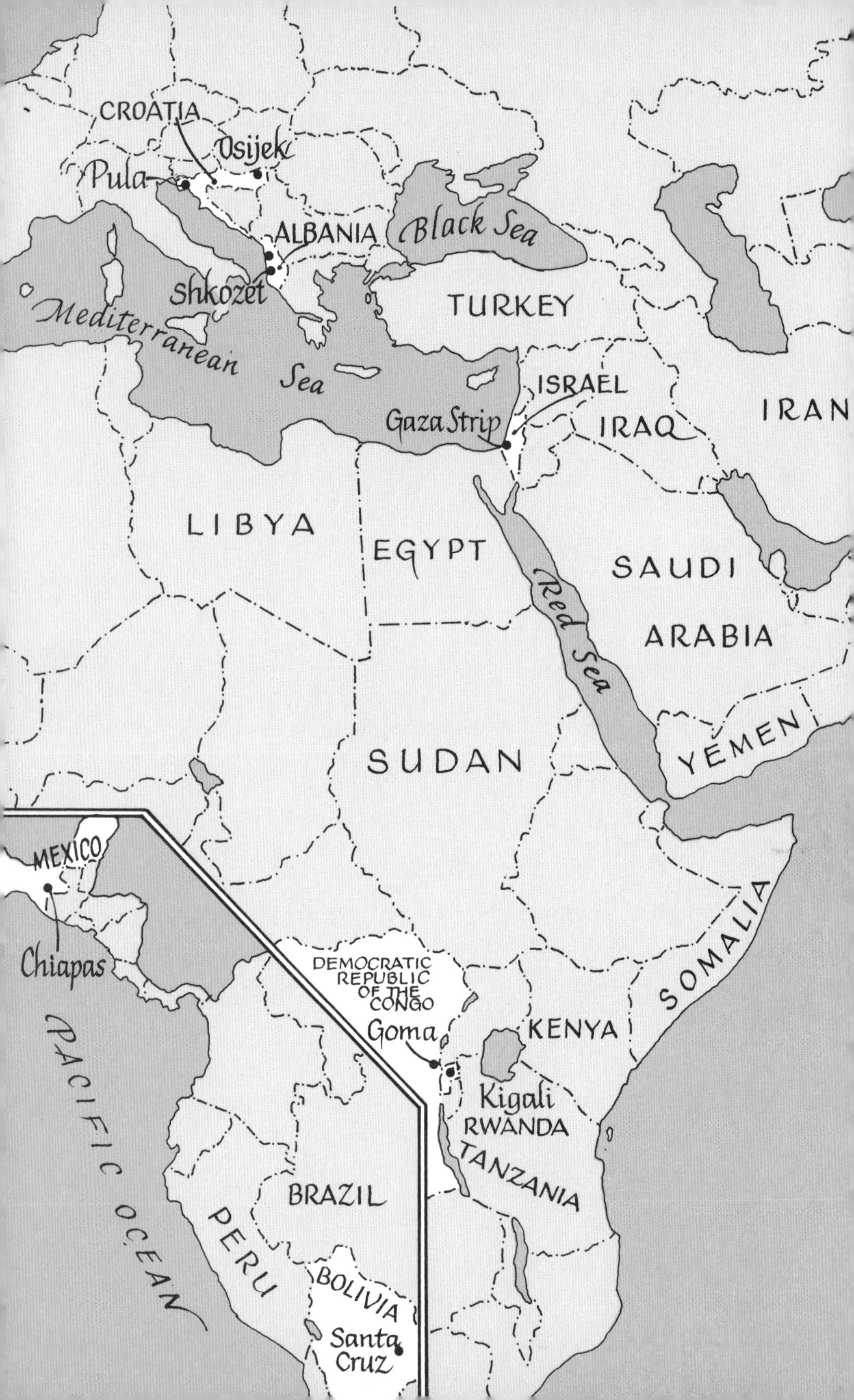
CROATIA
Osijek
Pula
ALBANIA
Black Sea
Shkozet
TURKEY
Mediterranean Sea
ISRAEL
IRAN
Gaza Strip
IRAQ
LIBYA
EGYPT
SAUDI ARABIA
Red Sea
YEMEN
SUDAN
MEXICO
Chiapas
SOMALIA
DEMOCRATIC REPUBLIC OF THE CONGO
PACIFIC OCEAN
Goma
KENYA
Kigali
RWANDA
TANZANIA
BRAZIL
PERU
BOLIVIA
Santa Cruz